Faye

Manic by Midnight

AmErica House
Baltimore

Copyright © 2000 by Faye Joy Shannon

All rights reserved. No part of this book may be reproduced in any form without written permission from the publishers, except by a reviewer who may quote brief passages in a review to be printed in a newspaper or magazine.

First printing

Edited by Mary Jo Elsasser

ISBN: 1-58851-838-8
PUBLISHED BY AMERICA HOUSE BOOK PUBLISHERS
www.ericahouse.com
Baltimore

Printed in the United States of America

Acknowledgments

I have received wonderful medical care and would like to thank the two physicians who provided the care. Dr. James Phillips was my initial physician and his expert guidance helped me recover from the episode described in this book. His encouragement helped me to accept this illness and salvage the important relationships in my life. Dr. Gary Bawtinhimer assisted in my adjustment to a new home and helps keep my moodswings in balance with medication and by carefully listening to my concerns.

My inlaws, Dr. George and Frances Shannon, have been my second set of parents. They have supported me through all kinds of difficulties and shared my joy as well. My mother-in-law encouraged me to write a book after Benjamin died and went so far as to hand me a tablet and pen. I love and appreciate them both.

Without the help of my sisters, Ruth, Donna, and Teresa, this story could not be told. Their willingness to share a glimpse of our lives in order to help others is greatly appreciated. My life is so much fuller with their love. It is a comfort to know they were there to share the good and bad times.

My husband George lived through the nightmare with me. He worked hard to understand this illness and to resolve the problems that surfaced at that time. He encouraged me to write this book and gave his time and effort to see it through. I am fortunate to have him as my husband and as the father of our children. George, I love you more than I can say.

I thank everyone who helped me, but most significantly my parents. I love you, miss you and think of you everyday. They worked hard to provide for me and my family. They told me they loved me and that I could always come home, no matter what mistake I made. Even with their own troubles they showed up everyday to be my parents. Mom and Dad taught me about honor, respect and having a good sense of humor. However, I most admire them for teaching me to keep facing life and never give up.

Dedication

To Benjamin who waits for us in heaven
and to my husband George
and our sons George and Hunter
You are my sunshine!

June 1995

"Surely you don't think you will be left in charge again when the boss is off? I don't think you understand how strangely you behaved. No doctor will want you working with their patients. I would be surprised if you are allowed back to work in the hospital at all. As a matter of fact people are asking why you keep coming here when you are on medical leave. Security would have taken you from the building if you had not left the last time. You were one of the best social workers we had, but now your career is over," my coworker said.

I responded, "I know things were really bad, but I am taking lithium now. I'm not sick if I take my medicine."

"Oh, you are taking medicine. I didn't know that. Then you need to get back to work right away. That is the only way you might save your job. People are sick of doing your work for you," said the coworker.

"I have overcome obstacles my whole life and this is just one more. I am going back to work as soon as the doctor lets me. I am okay now," I said.

As I drove home, I could not help but cry. I wished I felt as confident as I tried to sound. It was unclear to me if the opinion given was from one person or everybody. Actually I didn't know if I could cut it either. Besides the troubles at work, my personal life had been devastated as well. Despite almost thirteen years of a stable, loving marriage, I had filed for divorce, moved out, and was in a custody battle for our children. Most of my personal possessions were given to others. I wasted money on frivolous items and signed a lease for an apartment that was not realistic for one income. My father had died, my mother was an invalid, and my sisters lived across the country and were not in a position to financially assist me. I was broke, grieving, lonely and afraid. My manic behavior had worn out friends and colleagues, now I understood how some people become homeless and believe they are worthless.

Chapter One

When did my nervous breakdown begin? There are so many possibilities. The words "nervous breakdown" have always left me with a bad feeling, beginning with my mother talking about friends and acquaintances who suffered through them and up through my years as a therapist offering assistance to clients who tried to rebuild their lives after one. There are more correct phrases such as bipolar illness, major depression, psychosis, post traumatic stress and panic attacks to describe the misery inflicted by mental illness. Professionally and in regard to anyone else, I would insist on correct terminology of these medical illnesses. Yet, when these frightening words became a part of my life and I could reflect on my illness in the aftermath, I decided the words were a good description of what had occurred.

I was diagnosed with bipolar illness, more commonly known as manic depression, which is a brain disorder, at age 38. The diagnosis and treatment came after a two and a half month campaign of psychosis ruling my mind, which led to damaging my career, my friendships, my finances and, more importantly, throwing a grenade at my marriage and my role as mother. When my battle for sanity was waged and sanity returned, I hoped the effect would last. Facing the remnants of life as I knew it was bitter, having exhausted and insulted those who dared help me. After my spree of insanity, I was left alone, humiliated, penniless and very lucky to be alive.

I inherited the possibility of having this brain disease, yet it lay dormant and did not emerge until the level of stress in my life had become unbearable.

In retrospect, signs of the illness had been apparent for much of my life, but they were not significant enough for me to see the whole picture. I developed an overly talkative conversation style with frequent changes in the topic. Only with great restraint could I not interrupt, talk over or finish another's sentence. A yes or no question could become a documentary. Whether it be laughing at a joke, changing seats, or not eating the snack on a plane, I kept a running commentary. I felt it necessary to explain myself at all times. With money or resources I was generous to a fault. The social worker in me cheered on charities and I always contributed to the going-away party and gift of a coworker. Often I coordinated the party and if necessary, playfully intimidated my peers to contribute. I liked to show my affection or appreciation with little gifts. Often I gave too extravagant a gift, but derived pleasure to see the happiness it created. It puzzled me that others were not as generous. Much of my life I lived one step ahead. I walked, talked, ate and thought faster than others. It seemed my life was spent in a different gear than my peers. At an elementary school picnic one of my classmates commented on how fast I ate. I was embarrassed. She then whispered, "Watch, she'll eat real slow now." She would be the first of many to say this. Years later, I would still look up from a meal and realized I had done it again, my food was gone and my companions would still have three quarters of a plate left.

Walking fast was commonplace. As a field supervisor my students could barely keep up with me as I walked around the hospital. The same was true if I were shopping, visiting a museum or out for a stroll. When I took my exam to be board-certified, I looked up after reviewing my answers to see I was the only one finished in a room of over a hundred people. After waiting another twenty minutes and trying to determine if I had missed a section, I got up and left. Everyone else was still working. When I returned to the site an hour later, more than half the exam-takers were still working on the test. I passed easily. This was a common occurrence in school as well. My confidence could go through the roof or lay shriveled on the floor, depending on my mood. Most people found me amusing when I was on the upswing. Friends would say I could be a stand-up comedian at those times. Sometimes I could not express to others why I found some comment especially amusing. On those occasions I felt eccentric. I was not intimidated by much. Life was fun and manageable.

Unfortunately, just as the evening follows the day, my moods would change from joy to gloom. Bouts of depression left me feeling worthless and miserably trying to forgive myself for my many failures in life. If another made the same error, I would see the error as a simple mistake. I would wake in the early morning hours to wrestle with seemingly insurmountable problems, but with the light of day were manageable. My taste buds seemed to stop working and my appetite diminished when I was very sad. Reading an article or book could trigger a depression if within the pages were mention of a loss or sad event. The mention of a color or type of food could be matched with an unpleasant event of the past and I was on my way to despair. Dark thoughts within me were signaled to surface. Anniversaries of sad events hit me like a ton of bricks. At other times the bad feelings seem to come from nowhere. Concentration was difficult if I was either extremely depressed or frantic with emotion and irritability. Shopping or music sometimes lifted my dark moods. Comfort food helped. At times I was revved up and unable to relax or sleep. Not sleeping well would turn out to be quite significant in the onset of a manic episode or depressive episode. When I was manic, I would awake at three a.m. with no interest in returning to sleep. When I was depressed, I would wake around four-thirty or five a.m. and worry. If I was extremely depressed I could sleep all day. Management of sleep would be my key to staying healthy.

In addition to my moods and personality style there had been plenty of events which stressed and troubled me. My childhood had probably been more difficult than most. Living in poverty with a mentally ill father and severely depressed mother made me grow up faster than others. Watching my sister battle with schizophrenia over the years left me feeling frustrated and helpless. Being stalked by a family friend shattered my feelings of security when my life had began to blossom. My career as a social worker involved years of hearing the saddest of events befall my clients. I had let their pain become mine. The sadness in their hearts and mind were absorbed by my sensitive nature. On a daily basis I relived traumas with my clients as they worked to free themselves. I carried their troubles home with me and had difficulty shaking off thoughts of the abuse, crimes, and horrifying accidents which traumatized my clients. I had aspects of post traumatic stress from my career. The world ceased to be a happy and safe place. Changes made me anxious. Tough times, financially and emotionally, had troubled my life. A struggle with infertility had worn me out. Yet it was not until life showed me some things just can't be fixed, that my ability to cope wavered and part of me died inside. You can't wish a trauma away, or go back to instant replay and change the outcome, it just keeps coming. Only a love so pure and a wound so deep could jar my existence so completely. I believe my insanity began with the disappointment and sorrow of a broken heart.

It began with having to accept the unacceptable and live on through the darkness with the faint hope light might again come to my life. Spiritually I prayed for strength and patience. In addition I created a set of rituals to get me through. Daily walks, planting trees and writing in my journal put structure in my life, but visitation was my primary ritual. I always felt like I was in a movie when I made the drive. My stoic expression hinted of quiet despair and even amidst abject misery I had a flare for drama. A sad movie would have been tolerable. It would have ended soon enough. But it was reality leading the way as the blue Plymouth glided down the two-lane highway. On either side of the highway, cotton and soybean fields carpeted the land. Classical music was the only sound inside the car. After driving through the decorative iron gate, where elegant flower beds greeted me, I drove toward the babyland section of the cemetery. What was now a cemetery had once been a pecan grove and the remaining trees, still fruitful, added a sense of serenity. Our infant son, Benjamin, was buried there.

Reaching for the flowers I had brought with me, I paused to see if any more babies had been buried. I had come to think of them as Benjamin's eternal friends. The other parents were special to me as we had a common bond. We had all suffered immeasurably; our children were taken from us for reasons we would probably not understand in this lifetime. Benjamin's gravestone was lovely. A great deal of thought was given to it. On a previous visit I had been traumatized because the cemetery crew was digging up his gravestone. The mother of another child complained that his headstone was a few inches higher than her child's and she had not been allowed to have her child's the height she preferred. It amazed me someone could carry on so about a headstone. Then I considered the injustice of losing a baby. It was not too much for the grave to be the way you wanted it. The height of the stone was not a problem to me. Needing to buy one was the problem. While walking through the cemetery my mind rapidly filled with images of the pregnancy and, once again, I relived the shock and disappointment.

George and I were blissful after years of infertility to finally say the words, "We're having a baby." The most logical reason for the infertility was that I had been exposed *in utero* to a drug named Diethylstilbestrol or DES which had been prescribed to my mother to prevent a miscarriage. It was later determined that children whose mothers took this drug while pregnant may experience infertility and premature births. I was quite upset when the letter informing me I had been exposed arrived from my mother's obstetrician. My doctor suggested I find out if I had been exposed when he noticed some abnormal cells on my cervix during an infertility work-up. I disliked my new label as a DES daughter and worried about it. However, I was delighted when I became pregnant and pushed the worry from my mind. I was doing well. My fears decreased and I felt confident about the pregnancy. We were thrilled to share our happy news.

My mother-in-law was the first to send us a gift and share in our happiness. She mailed a baby blue maternity top for me and a tiny white christening gown for the baby. The gown was beautiful in its simplicity and if I closed my eyes I could picture the baptism. Almost every day I would take it out of the closet and hold it on my lap and smooth the fabric and imagine when my baby would get to wear this.

It was all so wonderful and it was happening to us. We would be fine parents if sheer determination counted for anything. Watching my belly grow and surveying baby products in the stores were our sources of entertainment. It was a magical time and the happiest we had ever been. Our lives were complete. I walked daily and ate nutritiously. Any book I could get my hands on relating to pregnancy and birth was read cover to cover. I had numerous questions from my reading and eagerly presented them to the doctor. My checkups went along quite well. We had a perfect blend of anxiety and joy.

Our blissful feelings changed quickly when my water broke around four-thirty a.m. when I was 25 weeks pregnant. As we frantically drove to the hospital, I knew it was not going to be okay. Being a clinical social worker gave me just enough information to know a true medical crisis when I saw one. As I closed my eyes on the journey to the hospital, the baptism scene in my mind's eye had vanished. Instead I saw flowers and I knew they were for a funeral.

Upon arrival at the emergency room my husband ran ahead to get a wheelchair. He yelled to the staff that I was in labor. They teased him until they asked how many weeks into the pregnancy I was. There was no eye contact as I was wheeled past the ER staff, nor was there a sound. If we had not already known we were in sad shape we knew it then. The wheelchair had a missing foot rest. The orderly who wheeled me to delivery accidentally ran over my bare foot with the wheel of the wheelchair. It did not matter.

Nothing mattered if our baby was not well. It would take hours before our son emerged. Long before the actual birth we had been told there was not an infant heartbeat. A sweet young nurse tried to cheer us up as we awaited the birth. She said there were some very little babies in the preemie nursery. It took all that remained of my courage to tell her the doctor believed our baby was dead. Time was suspended as we sat waiting. A nurse quietly charted. I expressed the need to urinate. She asked if I would be more comfortable if my husband left. I could not find a way to tell her she was the one I wanted to leave.

George kissed me and told me he loved me. I wondered why others could have babies and I could not. Yet nothing in the universe was significant now except for our child. Just when I thought I might survive in the quiet world of shock and disbelief, reality returned with the intensity of labor pains. It was a relief after the last push for the physical pain to stop. The obstetrician had to catch our baby as he was so small he came out quite rapidly.

Quite unlike my fantasies of giving birth, the first words we heard were, "I am sorry." After a few moments, I asked if I had a boy or girl. I was shocked to learn he was a boy. I had been so certain our baby was a girl. The nurse took a couple of pictures of the baby for us to have. We were left alone for a while with our baby. From the trauma of premature delivery his body was blue and purple. We held his tiny form and he felt warm as he had just come from inside me. The warmth made it harder to accept that he was dead. However, as time went on his body cooled, along with any hope I had remaining.

Our minister from the First Presbyterian Church came to be with us when the nurse's call to him shared our sad news. We had not been in town long so we were still getting acquainted. He walked in, wearing a Kelly green sports coat and an expression of absolute sincerity. I was holding the baby. No doubt it was a difficult visit to make. We had no family in town so his presence was of particular comfort. Seeing tears in his eyes and sadness on his face, I could tell he was a very kind and sensitive man. At one point he paused to compose himself. He ended his visit with a lovely prayer.

I was incredibly calm. Certainly I was in shock or denial. I felt numb. Surely I had aged 10 years in the last few hours. We began the difficult task of sharing our sad news with our families and friends. There were heart-wrenching phone calls to make. Saying it out loud made it real and made it harder to slip into feelings of denial. Talking about it brought back the tears. George made calls and began the plans for a funeral. We were most fortunate because a business woman who was on George's museum board kindly offered to pay for the funeral She owned funeral homes and set us up with the deluxe package. If ever a gift was heaven sent it was that one. The burden of funeral expenses had been lifted from us. We had used up our savings moving for George's new job. Even in the midst of blinding grief, we were so grateful.

A menu was handed to me later in the day. Food was not a priority for me under the circumstances. As I looked it over, I cringed when I came to the menu item, baby carrots. It would be the first of many reminders in the environment to come. I felt so tangled up inside with feelings of anger, hurt, and disappointment I thought I might die or explode. It was too much. I ached to hold my baby. It was not a good time for a tragedy. But there never is. Things were not supposed to turn out this way. It all had to be a mistake. I kept hoping to wake up and for it to have all been a nightmare. But it just kept on happening, and I wasn't asleep. In fact I was beginning a pattern of not sleeping well.

Song lyrics came into my mind as they always did in moments of deep feeling. One song was "Somewhere Out There, " as performed by Linda Ronstadt and Peebo Bryson. George and I sat looking out the window of my hospital room that evening as the words to the song filled my mind. There was something beautiful about the moment despite the hurt.

It was nice leaving the hospital. It felt like I had been away from home for months. When we got home, I walked over to the new almond-color refrigerator, where I had planned to keep baby bottles. I leaned against the refrigerator and screamed, "NOOOOOO!" I slumped to the floor shaking and sobbing, not caring if people several blocks away could hear me. I wanted them to hear me. I wanted it noted that the world kept on turning while my heart was breaking.

Except for the moments I was crying, I felt like I was made of wood. It was difficult to get my body to follow commands. My arms and legs felt heavy and my movements were awkward. My concentration was impaired and I generally felt tired. My facial muscles felt tight with my mouth feeling frozen in a frown. If another person did not want to stay with the topic of my misery, I shut them out. My grief was very intense and I entered into a depression. I would wake in the early morning hours and burst into tears. I felt hollow inside and it seemed like the essence of my personality had drained away with my tears.

I began a journal with a tablet and pen Mrs. Shannon gave me. My entries helped me feel connected to Benjamin. It was comforting to feel like I could talk to our son. It gave me some relief in a way other conversations could not. Besides it was always available and never criticized me.

The morning after we went home from the hospital, George was reading the newspaper. He saw the section which related to birth announcements and for a second looked excited that we might see Benjamin's name. We had been through labor and we had a baby. His face fell when he realized our son was stillborn so there was no birth announcement. There was a notice of his funeral, however. For George to face yet another disappointment caused my heart to break a little more. I had not realized there was another piece of my heart left to break.

The minister phoned me as he was preparing the funeral service. He asked if there was any particular sentiment I wanted expressed. I told him I wanted people to know Benjamin was not a stranger. He lived inside of me, I felt his movements and kicks. We awaited his birth with an intensity I never thought possible. We talked about him, dreamed about him, shopped, decorated and made up songs for him. This little boy was a person and he did matter. Benjamin Shannon had existed.

We buried him in the tiny white christening gown. He was entitled to a beautiful gown as this was the only ceremony I could ever give him. There would be no birthday parties, graduations or weddings for Benjamin. No children or grandchildren from him to pamper. No puppies or Christmas mornings. His time on earth was gone. I knelt before his grave and read it yet again. Benjamin Shannon - Beloved son of George and Faye - Budded on Earth to bloom in Heaven - Forever in our hearts - November 7, 1989. A little butterfly was on the stone as there had been one at his funeral, along with a rosebud like the beautiful Sonia roses at the funeral.

When it felt right to leave, I walked around to visit the other babies, straightening up tipped-over flowers or toys. A pecan was procured as a keepsake from the ground near the grave, and would be kept in my jewelry box. With a final look over my shoulder and a whispered goodbye, I headed back home with Benjamin in my heart as well as my mind. Life had been so hard these past weeks. It was true that you do not really understand something unless you experience it firsthand. I had counseled women who lost babies. I tried to console them and imagined they were very sad. I did not have a clue of what it was really like. The range of my imagination for pain did not reach to that extent.

Chapter Two

"Believe me, you don't want to see the baby!" the undertaker told us. We had called because my in-laws had arrived in town. My mother-in-law had asked to see Benjamin, and I wanted to see him again too. It had been a couple of days. The funeral was scheduled for the next day. George hung up the phone and repeated what the man from the funeral home had said. As we tried to overrule the undertaker's decision, George was adamant we let things be. Apparently the man told George the baby would look horrible to us and he had not been prepared for showing. The funeral would be closed coffin. The best thing would be to leave things alone. Since there had not been an autopsy, I could not see the harm in looking. I wanted to show he had existed. I let it drop because maybe the undertaker knew best. We did go and see the floral arrangements for the funeral.

Even though we had only been in town for a few months, there was a tremendous outpouring of sympathy. We received dozens of pastel sympathy cards with pictures of flowers and sweet words of encouragement from family, church members and coworkers. I read each one many times, even memorizing the quotes on some of them. Each day I looked forward to the postman to see if there were any more cards. While I had sent sympathy cards to people, I never realized what a comfort they were. It was like getting a hug. My sister Ruth and I talked on the phone frequently and she sent me the words to the song "Bridge Over Troubled Water" by Simon and Garfunkle. She felt the song best described the comfort she wanted to give to me.

My little sister Teresa and niece Jessica came to comfort us. It meant so much to me for them to be there. I felt stronger for their presence. When Teresa looked at me, she could tell every tear I had cried, how I blamed myself and how desperately I needed her to be there. We went for a drive and talked soul to soul about everything that had been and what could be. It was a beautiful conversation with each of us sharing our deepest feelings. The words spoken would long be forgotten but the spirit would not.

Teresa had come to represent the family and pack up my baby clothing and supplies. I decided I wanted to pack them myself. Some would be given to Goodwill. Not sleeping well I would wake at odd hours and start putting clothing or household items in a give-away box. I had started a box for Teresa and put it in her bedroom. At five a.m. I started filling it up. She asked me after my fifth trip to the box to add linen to please take the box out of her room to work with it. I had not realized I was interrupting her sleep. I had been so caught up in the activity. If I had needed her I know she would have woken up and sat with me, but the activity was getting me through the day. I continued my mission, although more quietly.

Everything that reminded me of the event must go. So any maternity clothes, linen, magazines, shampoo, brand names I cooked with, and so forth were unpleasant reminders. If I spotted something connected to the painful experience, disposing of it made me feel less anxious. The bad feelings would temporarily cease. While it may be irrational, it helped. If nothing else, it kept me busy. I was trying to cope in any way I could.

Later that day, my sister, niece and I sat at the table with our beverages. Jessica, my niece, turned my bottle of prenatal vitamins which was resting on the table. My doctor told me to finish out the bottle. I looked at her with curiosity and she explained she did not want me to be sad. She thought it would hurt me to see the picture of a baby on the bottle, so she turned the bottle. I appreciated her sensitivity, but the picture did not bother me for some reason. I expected to see a baby on the bottle. It was all the other places that caught me off guard. She was such a sweet little girl, it made me happy to be with her. I decided she could be my little girl too. I could send some of my maternal aspirations towards her. Only a few weeks later, she would hang in the balance between life and death, at risk of having a leg amputated, due to a bite from a brown recluse spider. It would be years before I would be told of her hospitalization, because my family wanted to spare me the agony.

I sent home a plant with Teresa and Jessica. It would be a good thing for them to have a plant in Benjamin's memory. He could live on that way. Besides, I wanted to show my appreciation for the comfort they had given me. All of the plants and flower arrangements could serve as a tribute to our son.

Beautiful flowers were everywhere. Like the cards, each plant had been such a thrill to receive. My parents sent a funeral wreath and it was the first piece to arrive. It was very elaborate despite their quite limited income. With their poor health they could not attend, but the wreath was very special to me. I know it reflected their loss of a grandchild and their concerns for one of their little girls who was in pain.

George's parents stayed with us a couple of weeks. Each of George's parents spent time with me and shared heartbreaking experiences that had befallen them. I felt closer to them after hearing of the difficult parts of their lives. Perhaps it was what they said or maybe just that they took the time to say it. I was lost and they helped me get back on track. Mrs. Shannon bought me a plush, light blue blanket to use when I took a nap. It was her belief that it helped to have something soft around you when you did not feel well. She tried to find me things to eat. The only craving I had was for Coca-Cola. I had abstained from it during my pregnancy. Mrs. Shannon tried to convince me to eat and would try to tempt me with pizza, a submarine sandwich, or her first class spaghetti and meatballs. She pampered me in a way no one ever had.

No doubt it had been stressful for my in-laws, not only to lose a grandchild but to see George and me so devastated. I would awake in the middle of the night and sob when the realization hit me, waking everyone in the house. My feet shuffled along behind Mrs. Shannon as we shopped. My swollen eyes would stare off into space or blankly at whoever spoke to me. Concentration was quite limited.

We made numerous trips to the graveyard to bring flowers. On one of our visits to the graveyard Mrs. Shannon and I picked up pecans. It had been a great year for them. I joked to Benjamin it was time he understood how eccentric his family was, because they picked up pecans where he was buried. The visits to his grave consoled me. Thinking up things to bring to his grave gave me something to think about besides how sad I was.

George and I had to learn to be independent again. His parents could not stay forever. Yet I wanted them to stay. Any departure reminded me of the one who should have stayed. I was so grateful to them for being with us during those days. I don't know when I needed someone more. George's mom told him she did not want me left alone in our dark house every day.

We celebrated Thanksgiving one day early and his parents left on Thanksgiving day to take their trip back home. I am sure they needed to get back to their lives. As much as I wanted them to stay because I did not like people leaving me, I knew life had to go on. We saw them off and I clung to George. Initially it bothered me if he wanted to go off by himself. But I knew he needed to. It was difficult not to worry about him. I did not like being alone with my pain, yet I had been so withdrawn I might as well have been alone anyway. One night I went into the front yard and lay on the grass, spread my arms out and sobbed. It made me feel closer to my son and less alone.

Each evening I would get on the phone and reach out to someone. Talking comforted me and I was compelled to go over every detail of the events surrounding the stillbirth. Unfortunately almost all my family members and close friends were long distance. Our phone bills were astronomical, but the calls helped me so much. I could fall asleep after one of these long phone calls. No one ever put me off. My family and friends demonstrated absolute patience with me.

While shopping with George, I came upon a newborn doll and held it up to study. It was so sweet I brought it to George and asked what he thought about buying a doll for me. He looked at me with concern and fear. He squinted his eyes, shook his head and said it would not be healthy for me to bring a doll home. Though he did not say it, I knew he wondered about my mental stability. I learned to keep any other unusual impulses to myself or in my journal. I obsessed about the baby and what might have been. I still tried to solve my despair as though it were a Rubik's cube. If I could find the right combination then it would all work out okay. It would have all been a mistake.

On Christmas day, nothing helped our sad mood. A guy I had worked with said we might as well write off Christmas that year. The only thing I enjoyed was taking an ornament collection, setting it on the lid of a trash can and taking my husband's pellet pistol and shooting the ornaments one by one. I had saved Campbell's Soup ornaments for a few years because they were so adorable. Now I never wanted to see them again. They were supposed to be for the baby we would have someday. I bordered on hysteria a few times. Yet when I tired of target practice I felt calmer. A friend had written on a Christmas card, "There will be other Christmas days." As I struggled to fall asleep, her words of hope inspired me and I wished so much they would be true.

In the days to come poems and songs played in my mind endlessly. They comforted me and encouraged me to go on with life. The poem "Michael" by Merrit Malloy from *My Song For Him Who Never Sang To Me* was so dear to me I posted a copy at my desk at work and placed a waterproof copy on his grave.

Eventually I came to realize there was a silver lining to my cloud of grief. Benjamin was safe and life would not hurt him. I did not have to worry about accidents, criminals, or disease touching my child. He was in heaven. Now it was time for me to save myself.

Chapter Three

I felt nauseated as I sat in the support group named SHARE (Source of Help in Airing and Resolving Experiences). The group was for infant loss either before, during or after birth. My body was so tense and nervous. It was December and a couple of weeks before Christmas. I did not want to be eligible to be there. I made eye contact with a woman across from me. At that moment I realized someone knew exactly how I felt. Listening to her describe her ordeal was so helpful and so healing. She had expressed ideas I had not let surface as well as some I thought about at length. She and the other group members and group leaders helped more than anything. At group there were no wrong feelings. Sometimes we would talk half the meeting about how sad we were and the rest of the time how very much we wanted to try again.

We were a tight-knit group. We often talked on the phone or stood talking in the parking lot after the meeting. It was safe to express my worst fears and wishes for another baby. I attended the group for about a year and a half. During that time, I researched the likelihood of carrying another child to term. George had been supportive and assured me we could be happy without children. We did have other interests and we could find ways to fill the time. It was important to me that he be a father. As the only male child he wanted to carry on the family name. He deserved to be one. I wanted to be the one who could give him a child. The baby had died inside of me. I felt like a failure in the most feminine way. I still hoped for that blessing. It felt like a part of me had died also. It seemed as if I were only going through the motions of living.

Meanwhile it seemed like every time we went out to dinner we would be seated next to someone with a baby. George and I would look across the table at each other with a knowing look of 'Not again'. We tried to distract ourselves from their baby, pretty blankets and squeaky toys. It wasn't that we could not be happy for the others, it was just that we wanted to be happy too. Almost every time the infant would fuss or cry and we would be disturbed.

Not because it was offensive or interrupted our conversation, but rather because it was like a slap in the face. It was the sound we ached to hear in our lives. I would be misty eyed by the time we were handed the bill. It finally occurred to me to channel my feelings of loss into concrete tasks such as sponsoring a hymnal at church or planting a tree in his memory. When I arrived at that point, I knew I was going to make it. I decided good could come from his life, however brief it was. Happiness could return to our lives. Maybe someday there could be another baby who needed a mommy and daddy. My wish to be a mother was balanced by a pervasive fear of trying, failing and reliving the pain. I did not want to disappoint my husband and I had dark periods when I entertained thoughts of divorcing him or killing myself so he could meet someone who could bear a child. I felt certain he would not divorce me. However, there had been so much pain and sadness. After praying about it, I realized I would hurt a lot of people if I did something so drastic. The last thing I wanted was to hurt anyone else. Somewhere I would find a healthy alternative. I continued to pray for courage and peace of mind. The dark spots became less frequent and hope had returned to my heart.

One day I put on a cassette and instinctively started to dance. I stopped myself and said to myself, "I can't dance because I am a grieving parent." Then I realized I was not helping the baby by punishing myself. Dancing around the house had always been a fun way to relax. I doubted our son would want to be remembered as the reason Mom stopped dancing around the house. I continued with the group and was given some of the national newsletters for SHARE One of the gang from the group was working on a local newsletter. As I looked over the newsletters with stories from all over the country, I became absorbed with the stories. When I came home from group, I ran to George and showed him the column about the couples who had a loss but went on to have success stories. I felt so hopeful as I shared with him how those people must have been afraid like we were and we might have a success story someday too.

When the anniversary of Benjamin's birth and death came, George was out of town at a seminar. Alone, I went to the grave and kneeled and lit one candle and ate a chocolate cupcake and whispered prayers and poems to myself and Benjamin. It was a cool November day and the pecans were not as fruitful as the year before. I still wondered how things could have turned out as they did. I had tried to be a good person. That should have exempted me. Certainly I had made mistakes but I agonized over them and attempted to be the best person I could be. My hope was to get pregnant again so I tried to increase my good deeds for mankind.

Since my next pregnancy needed to turn out differently, a new doctor might bring me luck. Pursuing a physician who was comfortable with high-risk pregnancy was proving to be a difficult task. I met a doctor who was unenthusiastic about following a high-risk pregnancy. He listened to my history and said he could put me on a monitor to test for symptoms of preterm labor. He doubted he could get me past thirty weeks. He did not appear interested in taking my case. I left feeling horrified. The idea of a monitor was new to me and was encouraging. I shared with my friends the visit with the latest physician candidate. I was quick to point out he did not say, "You can't have a baby."

One of my friends said, "I would not want to be the doctor who said you cannot have a baby!"

In the midst of all the thinking about a new family, I became involved in lobbying for an allotment from the state to improve the museum where my husband worked. A lot of my energy was focused on George's museum. For once, having a baby or not was not the only thing on my mind. My life was in balance again. I would make it through the storm.

"I'm pregnant," I announced while happily waving my test result. George looked pleased. We were not ready to share the news and wanted the pregnancy to progress before we had to endure a public pregnancy. We told our parents anyway. They were positive and encouraging. We tried to stay in good spirits. Sometimes we were calm and enjoyed our secret. Not surprisingly we worried the rest of the time. The question that loomed before us was, would we make it? We had overcome the hurdle of my getting pregnant. That was a start. But the finish line was months away. With apprehension I attended my last meeting of the support group with my secret. I was not ready to tell. The group had been a stabilizing force in my life but it was time to let go. I would eventually share our news with the group members. I knew if anyone would understand our decision to be cautious in sharing, they would.

As I continued to choreograph the pregnancy, it seemed right to have a new doctor. I chose the female physician I had heard so many positive comments about. I could not wait to see her. I hoped she would have the missing ingredient to a successful pregnancy. It was not long into our conversation before I understood the trust so many people had in her. She was very bright and had an easygoing nature. She instilled confidence and hope. If she felt intimidated by my case I could not tell. Earlier in her practice she had worked with high-risk pregnancies related to DES exposure and had seen happy outcomes. One of the features I especially liked was how she made a plan to check a multitude of problems along the way. She was everything I had heard and more.

She kindly wrote out a prescription for a different brand of prenatal vitamins when I asked. She seemed to understand how every detail was important to me. The more little concerns I had control of, the less fearful I felt. My magical thinking about doing everything differently gave me a minor amount of comfort. She was the perfect physician for a terrified and traumatized mother-to-be. Whatever the outcome of the pregnancy, I knew this woman would give it her all. As I would. I prayed it would be enough. I went home determined to get through the days until my next appointment. Inside me a baby was growing and so was a tiny seed of hope.

One night after work I drove up to our home and through a lighted window I noticed George had set up the baby crib. I closed my eyes and silently prayed, "God, please don't let me disappoint him." It made me feel pressured, though. I mentioned it might be too soon to set up the crib because I was only six weeks pregnant. He told me quite emphatically, "We are having this baby! Besides we did not set up the crib last time. Maybe it would be good luck if we did this time." We were both ready to cling to any beacon of hope. "George, I just don't need more pressure. I can hardly stand it now. I already feel like such a failure and I am just scared to death. I don't know what I'll do if this baby dies too." We hugged and there were no more words to say.

The crib stayed up. George and I stayed optimistic most of the time. Being busy helped me more than anything. I used the crib to store the baby stuff we began to accumulate. Day by day we faced the pregnancy. Every night I was grateful for another day of a healthy pregnancy. When I felt afraid, I would either walk or call one of my sisters. Little by little we made progress. I thought of the "Take it one day at a time" slogan. When I thought of it that way, the journey did not seem so long. My efforts were focused on getting through the day. The next day I started over. Day by day we kept going. Sometimes we faced it one baby step at a time.

So many people were rooting for us. George's mom had friends who were making us a gift. When Mrs. Shannon told me what the gift was, I held my breath for a moment. It was a very elaborate christening gown.

My first impulse was not to accept the gift. It brought back memories I did not want to have. Then she told me it was not white, as the other had been; it was an ivory color. Somehow the difference helped me to accept it. Mrs. Shannon said she would not mail this one, but would bring it in person when she came to visit later in the pregnancy. When Benjamin died, Mrs. Shannon promised me she would stay with me and help me if I became pregnant again. She planned to come in the fall.

Around twelve weeks into the pregnancy my doctor discovered I was a gestational diabetic. In my efforts to eat all the right things I was eating too much. The lethargic feeling I had attributed to being pregnant was in part due to the gestational diabetes. Between the stress I was under in this pregnancy and "eating for two" I had gained too much weight too quickly. My physician picked up on the condition around twelve weeks into the pregnancy. She was on top of the situation. I monitored my blood sugars and met with a dietitian for counseling.

The dietitian I saw was a friend of mine from church. She was a delight to work with. I also had a nurse who specialized in diabetic teaching who showed me how to test my blood sugars. I kept a record and showed them to my doctor on my visits. Since I wanted a healthy baby, I was very compliant. To have a specific problem and management of it set out in clear directives was a relief. If I had been asked to walk on my hands balancing a ball on my nose I would have.

Following the diet made me feel better and it felt good to know I could help the baby and myself. I learned how to check my blood sugar and make appropriate meal choices. I measured food servings and exercised. The pregnancy was going well. Focusing on the day-by-day strategy I was handling the pregnancy well.

In addition to monitoring my blood sugar, at around twenty weeks into the pregnancy I began monitoring twice daily with an instrument belted around me and connected to a recording device. It measured the amount of contractions I was having. After fifty to sixty minutes on the monitor, I could transmit the result to a nurse through the phone lines. If one of the readings was not in an acceptable range, I had to drink water and re-monitor. The monitor system allowed time to talk with a nurse. If the nurse perceived a problem she would talk with my doctor. The symptoms of pre-term labor were given to me in writing and discussed in conversations with the nurse. They included: menstrual-like cramps, low dull backache, pelvic pressure, abdominal cramping either with or without diarrhea, increase or change in mucous vaginal discharge, and uterine contractions every 10 minutes or more.

One of my doctor's suggestions was to screen for infections intermittently throughout the pregnancy. At around twenty weeks it was discovered I had a urinary tract infection. Even after it was treated it caused me spasms. I had to take one capsule each day to prevent an infection. She commented that my bladder was the biggest problem I had at that point.

As we neared the point in the pregnancy when Benjamin had died, I was on needles and pins emotionally. Fortunately I was using a uterine monitor for premature contractions. Each morning I awoke an hour early and hooked up the monitor to record the number of contractions. It had become a familiar routine. Just to know the monitor was there relieved much of my anxiety.

One morning before work I had done my hour-long recording and transmitted it by phone to the monitor company. As I waited for the all-clear signal from the nurse, I felt fine and a little impatient. Leaning against the dresser wearing a crisp white blouse and red jumper, my only thoughts were about a presentation I was scheduled to give that day. When the nurse told me I had more than the acceptable number of contractions and was in premature labor, I was shocked. The nurse phoned my doctor and I lay on the bed trying to relax and rest. Fighting back tears I tried to be calm and rational. I would not and could not let myself think about failing. After all this time, everything could fall apart. I calmed myself enough to call George and notify my workplace I would not be coming in that day. After drinking a glass of water, I lay back on the bed and re-monitored. Since the contractions had slowed, I stayed in bed all day.

George came home to be with me. He had been very involved in a project but came as soon as possible. He looked at me with worry etched on his face. He asked if it was going to be okay. My mouth was clenched shut and I was a bundle of nerves. I managed to choke out, "I don't know if it will be okay, but I will do everything I can!"

I received flowers from friends and family. My sister Ruth sent me an arrangement done all in pink. I convinced myself this baby would be okay because it would be a girl. Maybe I could carry a girl baby. My mom only had girls so maybe I had some unusual condition. This thought helped me feel safe, and while magical thinking was not medically correct, it helped.

George's parents had been coming anyway but would leave a couple days earlier. The waiting was sheer terror, but I managed to find a calm feeling for the sake of the baby. I prayed for our unborn child and how George deserved to be a daddy. I was not sure I deserved anything so I pledged to be the best mother I could be and assured God I would love our baby with all my heart. Inside I prayed, "God please let us have a live baby this time, a baby we can take home with us!"

Chapter Four

Seeing the doctor was a big relief. She examined me and told me my cervix had not begun to dilate and my contractions were in a normal range. She was calm, rational and had clearly been down this road before. My mind was eased. I did not return to work at the hospital and would not until the baby situation was resolved. It was for the best. She reassured me could get our baby here safely. I felt her confidence becoming mine. George's parents had arrived to help us through the rest of the pregnancy. It was great to have them. I enjoyed just chatting with them about anything. George's mom brought the christening gown. While the other gown had been quietly beautiful, this was a two-piece, ivory-colored ensemble. It had lots of ruffles on the underslip and gown. There was nothing understated about it. Royalty should have such a christening gown. To know these two women toiled to produce this fabulous gift for us was so flattering. A handmade gift is truly a show of kindness. Knowing they made it specifically for our baby touched my heart. Having my in-laws stay with us was a comfort. The day after they arrived I woke up with strong contractions. I was asked to re-monitor. While I monitored I was crying to myself and could hardly speak. I wanted to get my mother-in-law's attention after hearing the official news from the monitor nurse. She was sleeping in the remote bedroom and I was afraid to get out of bed or scream for fear of straining myself. Not long after I wanted to call to her she got out of bed and came to the living room and I did call for her then. Mrs. Shannon heard my cry for help. She was there in a second and trying to comfort me.

My mother-in-law had thought out her strategy ahead of time. She would distract me from worrying to help me relax. She wheeled a TV and VCR into my room and plopped in *Gone With the Wind*. I was quite scared. I waged my own battle as the Civil War occurred on screen. After a while, I asked her to turn down the volume and eventually I asked for it to be turned off. It was too much stimulation. This did not cause her dismay. She fluffed my pillow and adjusted the blinds. She reassured me everything would be okay.

My mother-in-law stood by like a nurse on duty. She should have been a nurse; she was born for it. Her ability to bring comfort was extraordinary. She was aware of all the latest over-the-counter medicine and had her own version of a little black bag. I cried and smiled at her. Whatever might happen I would not be alone.

We would replay the scene with premature labor several more times. I was put on medication after a particularly stressful night. My doctor finally told me to quit monitoring and sleep. Once I took a pill I was told I would be taking the medicine for the duration. It meant setting an alarm to take it correctly. No request was too unreasonable. My father-in-law took my pulse each evening to be sure the medication was not disturbing my heart rate.

George's parents kept me company while George worked. There was a compelling real-life drama on TV which we followed every day. Anita Hill was testifying at the Clarence Thomas Supreme Court proceedings. We discussed it at length, as well as other current affairs. My in-laws did the housework and had a hot meal waiting when George came home in the evening. Each day I took a two-hour nap after lunch. Pregnancy helped me sleep like nothing else ever had. Of all the things I did to get through the pregnancy I believe my daily nap was at the top of the list.

My recreation time was spent shopping through catalogs. My favorite was the JC Penney sale catalog. I probably bought more clothing than ever during those months. It helped me feel competent to arrange for clothing to be brought to our home. I learned the innuendoes of catalog shopping as I had time to read the fine print. I had all the time in the world to place orders and chat with the catalog employees. Before long I was up to speed on back orders or the options for monogramming shirts.

Despite all the attention, there were plenty of times I worried and agonized. Our minister came to visit with me on a day I was particularly depressed. He prayed with me and encouraged me. Although I never expressed any fear, he seemed to understand me. He told me that everyone wanted me to have a healthy baby and there was not anyone who did not. It helped me a great deal to hear this as my depression would have me focus on unpleasant times and enemies I had made, fearing they might have the power to send bad vibrations my way. He helped me to realize the Lord was in charge and to pray to quiet my fears. He also sent the church visitation group to visit me. They brought me muffins.

My mother-in-law tried to teach me to crochet. As she demonstrated it, it looked so easy. She looked peaceful while she quietly turned a ball of yarn into a creation. My mom used to love to crochet also. Even her arthritic fingers could work the yarn. She made it look quite simple too. As with many things that look easy, it was not. I tried but it did not relax me. Whenever I had made a little progress, I would proudly look back at my work, only to be dismayed. The blanket I was working on had many dropped stitches or stitches so tight it threw off the pattern. It was a disaster. Needless to say I had no plans to enter it in a craft fair. I moved on to other interests, safe in the knowledge that the baby had plenty of blankets already.

There was a lot of time to read. George's mom had brought me a book about Pocahontas. During the most crucial month of the pregnancy, I would read a chapter a day and there were close to thirty chapters. My goal was to complete the book at the rate I had been reading, and when the book was through I would be at a much safer place in my pregnancy. There were plenty of other good books too.

Sometimes when I felt afraid I would squirt a little Johnson's baby lotion on my wrist and smell it. It gave me encouragement to keep trying for a healthy baby. I would look at the crib already full of baby items and for just a moment or two imagine a little baby lying in the crib just waiting to be loved. I would rub my tummy and tell the baby to please wait just a while more.

Mrs. Shannon would drive me to my appointments in her deluxe Buick station wagon. If she saw anything resembling a bump she would slow down so she would not jar me. As the days and weeks passed, the rides were more relaxed. It was great to get out of the house. Stopping by the pharmacy was a major thrill. When I set foot in one on the way home from the doctor, it was exciting to see the people bustling and all the shelves of merchandise. I felt as amazed after my weeks of isolation as a visitor from a previous century might have felt.

As the pregnancy progressed, I felt relaxed enough to say to George, "We are coming home with a baby this time. I can feel it." The rest of the pregnancy went well. The time I was able to spend with George's parents was quite valuable to me. We got to know each other well. My own parents were in Michigan with no funds to travel on and in poor health. They called each week to check on me and I could hear concern in their voices. I longed for someone in my family to be with me but it was not to be.

My parents had not made it to Benjamin's funeral for the same reasons they would not come for the new pregnancy. I know they loved me though, despite the occasional doubt. My mother-in-law helped me accept the reality of the situation. I hated that I felt angry and disappointed. I wanted my parents, especially my mother. She helped my older sisters with their babies. Of course she was younger then and in better health. Also, it did not require the expense and travel it would involve to see me. The truth was, if Mom visited me at this point in her life, I would end up caring for her. It was best she not come.

George's parents were in a different financial situation and in much better health. My mother-in-law pointed out how my parents called me each week to ask about the baby and me. At one point I made an excuse to not talk with them. It hurt to talk. I wanted them there in person to care for me. I wanted them to give me something for the baby. The nursery was so lovely and I wanted them to see it. When the baby came, I wanted them to hold our brand new baby and I wanted to hear whatever their thoughts were on who the baby resembled. I mostly wanted them to hug me and tell me it would be all right this time, there would be a bundle of joy for us. I would not have to leave the delivery room with my dead infant being wheeled past me.

Sometimes I wished I could be a little girl again. I would have my sisters to play with and time with my mom and dad. With my sisters I had instant companionship and acceptance. We were quite close. The presence of my parents comforted me. Mom's hands usually smelled like onions as she chopped them in her work. Daddy smelled like fish from his favorite activity, like the foundry where he worked or I could discern the smell of leather and shoe polish from his shoe repair business. Of course my favorite scent was of Mom baking cinnamon rolls from scratch, while my sisters and I anticipated the treat to come. They were comforting scents to me, the scents of my parents and family. I missed them and the security they represented. I wanted to retreat to a more simple time when babies did not die and people lived happily ever after.

Chapter Five

With so many prayers and good wishes it should have come as no surprise that instead of premature labor, I would have to be induced to start labor at 38 weeks. Ultimately I had a C-section. George and I watched as our new son was lifted out of me and handed to the pediatrician for examination. He was crying but needed to be suctioned and his cry slightly resembled a goat's bleat. To us it was the most beautiful sound in the universe. A baby crying, our baby crying. A sound we had waited a long time to hear. The pediatrician brought baby George to me so I could view him before he was whisked away to the nursery. He had low blood sugar. With happy tears in my eyes I reached over and touched his hand. He was beautiful with lots of blonde hair. He was a big baby, 8 pounds 9 ounces, and looked just like his daddy. It finally registered with me that we had an infant to care for and instead of worrying about the pregnancy, we had to be the best parents we could be. George and I looked at each other, both of us joyous. In unity we smiled and words were not needed.

Later in the evening, after I had fallen asleep, I woke up when the nurse handed George to me. My husband was sleeping on a pullout bed nearby. The newest addition to our family was wearing a T-shirt and diaper. He had a little blanket with pink and blue pictures on a snowy white background. I held him for the first time. I kissed his forehead. I tearfully and cheerfully welcomed him. "Hi baby, I'm your mother. I already love you. I have waited such a long time for you and I am so glad you have arrived." George told me later how he enjoyed hearing me talk to the baby. I returned the compliment when I saw him rocking the baby and singing to him. It was wonderful to see my husband so happy. Every so often he would stop and kiss the baby's cheek. Our baby looked so little in George's arms, but he looked so right being there.

Everyone seemed to share in our bliss. My obstetrician and her partner seemed jubilant. Our room was filled with flowers and gifts. It resembled a gift shop. When my sister Teresa called to congratulate us, she mentioned she would send us flowers and I told her to save her money as we had more than we knew what to do with. Our families shared our joy, we all celebrated. When I called my father the following morning to tell him, he was thrilled and said, "I knew he would be born on my birthday." I hated to tell him I had had the baby the previous evening, just a few hours shy of his birthday. Joy was in his voice as well as Mom's. Life was good again.

We discussed the birth weight and how the baby looked like the spitting image of his daddy. While I wished they could see him in person it still felt good to share our happy news. It was a relief for them to know they could stop worrying about the pregnancy. George bought a gift for the baby and me. For the new guy he bought a white musical giraffe with a pastel mane that played "Around the World in Eighty Days." He also bought him a Peter Rabbit ceramic cup and bowl. As for me, I was delighted to be given a gift set of my favorite perfume, White Linen. He wrote a sweet note thanking me for giving him a child. It made me so happy to see George hold our son and rock him while singing, "You get a line and I'll get a pole and we'll go fishing in the crawdad hole." My prayers had been answered. Despite the heartache along the way it was so sweet to have a newborn. We were so thankful.

At home a lovely nursery awaited the new arrival. The crib that had been assembled with such hopes all those months ago was resplendent. The comforter, sheet and dust ruffle had a lamb motif and were done in pastels with the mint green color most dominant in the print. The curtains were solid mint green. A polished rocking chair and footstool sat prepared for the first lullaby. A team of stuffed bears and monkeys, some with diapers on themselves, kept watch over the nursery. A disinfected changing table was decorated in a variety of baby staples, such as Johnson's baby powder, Desitin and A&D lotion, Q-tips, cotton balls and a stack of Pampers. The walk-in closet was filled with a variety of baby outfits smelling of their recent wash with Dreft. In our room was a bassinet dressed to the hilt with a white ruffled cover, freshly laundered sheet and blanket. Everything was lovingly arranged to welcome our son.

Chapter Six

It was a pleasure to care for baby George. To rock my baby was such a peaceful feeling. Feeding him, burping him, washing his clothes and bathing him were tasks I was happy to complete. However, in the wee hours of the morning I was glad to see him fall back asleep. His musical swing helped to soothe him. He also loved to be sung to by either of us. Singing off key did not seem to annoy him. My favorite song to sing was, "A Mountain of Love." Some lines I knew, some I recreated. I mainly just sang the title over and over and hummed.

We were told little George would need to have phototherapy because his bilirubin level was too high and he was looking jaundiced. This required he sleep in an incubator with a light on him around the clock. He had little sunglasses to put on. It was not long before the situation was resolved. It was painful to see him have his heel stuck for blood so the status of his situation could be determined. It was a minor problem, yet we stood ready to tackle any task.

I shared with my doctor how absolutely happy I was. She said having a baby is like falling in love. I sure had the giddy feelings. George was smitten too, I could tell. We took pictures at every opportunity and for once, we took our baby with us to a restaurant. Now we could be like the other worn-out parents who were constantly picking up toys their babies tossed and shushing them so as not to disturb the other diners. The pride I had regarding our son was immense. He was a beautiful baby.

I would fight any battle, sacrifice finances and rest, leave no stone unturned on his behalf, just to have the extreme privilege of rocking him to sleep. Instinctively I knew my parents had felt the same way about me. I learned to recognize his cry for hunger or for diaper duty. Sometimes I would think of parents in other parts of the world or throughout history who had no food for their children. It must have been unbearable. I was so grateful to give our son the food, shelter and the medical care he needed. Our child was a gift.

His baptism, in the beautiful ivory gown, was scheduled for Mother's Day. We held George in front of the church and our minister performed the ceremony with his wonderful southern accent. He referred to our son as he did every infant, "Little child." For this very special Mother's Day, my husband had given me a corsage. It was beautiful but not practical with a baby in my arms. People at the church knew of our circumstances and I could feel the jubilance in the sanctuary. One of my friends from church, who had been my dietitian, told me she did not know which of us were crying more tears of joy. It was such a moving experience. The dream I had held for so long had finally come true.

Chapter Seven

The line at the pharmacy checkout was taking forever. The young lady in line next to me was sharing her experience about a recent visit to the medical school. She was proud to tell how the nurse gave her diapers for a boy, even though she had a girl. Apparently she got almost a whole pack of diapers for free and considered it a victory. She also shared how she had Medicaid so she did not have to pay for the prescriptions. We discussed baby products as the line slowly moved forward.

We finally got around to our plans for the week coming up. I told her I was going back to work tomorrow and was nervous about my child being cared for by someone else. I said, "I really am having a hard time letting him out of my sight." It felt good to express what had been on my mind all week.

She looked at me with distaste and said, "I could never leave my baby with a sitter. I'm too good of a mother to do that."

Salt in a wound would have felt better. I hated going back to work but it was financially necessary. It was an emotional dilemma for me. I had hoped all the way up to returning to work that a magical reprieve would come through. I hurried out of the store once my purchase was rung up. I was already criticizing myself. A comment like that would resonate in my mind the rest of the day.

We had a lovely lady care for him. Mam Maw Dare knew everything about babies and was a legend in our town. A list was provided with the appropriate brands of products to purchase. She preferred Desitin ointment and A and D lotion, Chubs wipes, Pampers or Huggies. The baby food could not have additives which might have ill effects on George. Our son never had diaper rash and was always neat and clean when I picked him up at the end of the day. He was cheerful and pleasantly plump.

Mrs. Dare knew more about babies than anyone I had met. She had the answer for any malady, from gas pain to teething. I never worried when he was with her. She was firm and loving. Her rules were very clear and consistent. She liked to give the children a good foundation. Every work day

I looked forward to getting home each night. My favorite time was when we were in pajamas and George and I sat on both sides of the baby on our bed and watched TV. All was well and all things seemed possible. There were times when I would awake in the early morning hours because I felt there was so much to do. I would clean my house and do laundry at three a.m. I would get caught up on the housework. But I would have been better off sleeping. My body had a schedule of its own. I made jokes about waking up in the middle of the night ready to accomplish tasks. It would be a few years before I would piece that behavior into a lifelong pattern of behavior indicative of a psychiatric disorder.

I read articles and books on parenting whenever possible. With a contented feeling I would select his clothes for the coming week. Little outfits of pastel blue or a bright primary colors would be carefully arranged. George teased me how I liked having a baby because I could pick out outfits as people do for a Barbie doll. At such an early age I read him nursery rhymes. I wanted to give him the world. I breastfed because it was supposed to be the healthiest way and would improve his immunity to illness.

We felt like the wealthiest people in the world. Having a child was our wealth. A child was a gift from God. We were blessed. Parenting was more wonderful than I had imagined. My son clasping my finger or holding his head up for the first time and giving me a sunny smile was the stuff dreams are made of. My father had often remarked that your life does not really begin until you have children. He was so right. When George was eight months old, we flew home to Michigan to introduce our son to my parents and sisters. It was so great to see my dad hold him and say about ten times, "You're not hard to love." Mom bounced him on her knee and made little clicking noises with her tongue. They bought him an outfit with airplanes on it and it fit perfectly. My sisters held him and Ruth bought baby vanilla pudding and teething biscuits. My best friend Jackie visited with us and brought him a sweatshirt. It was such a nice trip. We even stopped in the Grand Rapids area on our way home to visit my Aunt Eleanor and Uncle Gerald. They showed our little boy around their farm. The visit was a celebration.

We took many rolls of film and bought a camcorder to take pictures of our tike. He had enchanting blue eyes and a sweet heart-shaped face like his daddy's. If that did not provide enough photo opportunities I brought him to a photographer to be sure. He was a much loved baby.

George was extremely bright as a child. He recognized the letters of the alphabet at age two. When he stacked blocks, he wanted it done correctly and would become frustrated until he accomplished his goal. My life revolved around what our son's next milestone would be. Much thought was given to adding up the vitamin amounts listed on the baby food jars to determine if he was getting all the nutrients he needed. Perhaps before it was logical, I read stories and prayers to him. I played the Sesame Street or Barney program on public TV while he initially crawled, then walked, around the den. We began to discuss the possibility of another baby yet wondered if we should quit while we were ahead.

Chapter Eight

We decided after George was about a year old to try for another child. We were ready to make a commitment to the pregnancy in case it was another difficult one. After about 3 months, we succeeded in our mission; I was pregnant again. The pregnancy was a breeze in comparison to the previous one. I felt some fear but not nearly as much as before. I did use the monitor again, but I never had a problem.

The gestational diabetes appeared much later in this third pregnancy and was managed well. Throughout the pregnancy I felt well. I worked until just a few days before the birth. The pregnancy had been quite uneventful, unlike the other two. I felt great. Pregnancy agreed with me this time.

This time I had a baby shower, something I never had before. With Benjamin it was too soon and with George everyone wanted to be sure he would make it okay. It was fun to be the center of attention, open lots of pretty packages, have a luncheon and cake. I think it irritated people that I stopped to examine how each gift was wrapped. To me the wrapping paper was like art. The teddy bears, ducks and pictures of trains charmed me. It was wonderful. After all the years of going to baby showers, there was now one for me. At the end of the work day I drove home with a car full of blankets, toys, gowns, and some lovely memories.

At almost two years to the date of George's birth we had a new son, Hunter. He was a very relaxed and easygoing baby who slept through the night at 6 weeks. He was another blessing to our lives. We used most of the same nursery items but bought a new crib. Everything was going our way at the time he was born. George and I were more relaxed since we had been parenting George and surviving. We were pleased to have two children to love. Daddy bought Hunter his own Beatrix Potter set and Babar, a stuffed elephant. He bought me a Hunter green bathrobe and more perfume.

Hunter loved to cuddle and enjoyed my serenade to the tune of the Publishers Clearing House commercial. It was actually just a line of the jingle, "The house where dreams come true." It was that time of year and I could not get the tune out of my mind. Hunter was not a particular guy and it seemed enough for him to know I was trying. He had the most wonderful belly laugh. To hear him laugh gave me such joy. Dad told me his grandmother said when babies cooed it was the angels talking.

Our son George did not appreciate the competition. We had tried to explain he would have a brother. The first time he heard Hunter cry he looked bewildered. He had not seen Hunter yet. Once he realized Hunter was here to stay he did as so many children do and displayed his reluctance to have a new family member. Competition was not welcome. He tried to push the bassinet over with Hunter inside it.

George threw toys at Hunter and tried to poke at him in his crib. We knew it had gone too far when George tried to bite the nose off Mickey Mouse as he dangled innocently from the Disney mobile. George and I took turns to be on guard to protect Hunter. We could not leave them alone in a room. It seemed like it would never end. My son then started taking it out on me.

At one point my eldest son threw a die cast metal Barney car at me and gave me a black eye. I was scheduled to have pictures taken with Hunter. The photographer was able to erase the black eye from the picture. Gradually they reached the point where they could be in the same room together. Eventually the torment subsided and they played together reasonably well.

Mrs. Dare kept Hunter as she had George. George had been nicknamed by Mrs. Dare's husband, who had a gift for summarizing the essence of one's personality. Our children were dubbed King George and Prince Hunter. After a while, George was more welcoming and Hunter became his playmate. We had a nice-sized group. My doctor said we could try for another one as I did not have scar tissue. In the back of our minds we thought about one more try. But there was lots of time, it seemed.

We needed a larger home so we looked until we found a lovely home in a nice subdivision with good schools. It was a brand new home with four bedrooms, three baths and a three car garage. A walk-in pantry, spacious utility room and a whirlpool bath made it comfortable. There was a place for everything, a luxury we had not had until that point in our marriage.

A premium landscape package further persuaded us, including a gorgeous plush lawn and all the azaleas, boxwood and holly one could hope for. The brick had come from a load of bricks purchased by a local developer to use for a lavish home he was building for his family. The brick had originally come from a schoolhouse in Oklahoma that was being destroyed. Our builder bought the leftover brick and used it on our house. It was a charming story, lovely home, and held the promise of an upper middle-class lifestyle.

The home was much more expensive than our previous home, but if everything went right, it should prove to be an investment. We had been caught up in the fantasy of giving our children the nicest environment possible. They would have the home I never had and could be proud to bring friends home.

I wanted them to have a home to be proud of. I had grown up in poverty. My parents both worked, my dad worked two jobs at times, yet they were examples of the working poor. They scraped by from check to check and hoped life would not throw them a curve ball. Having been teased about our home as a child had made me extra sensitive. I knew people had value despite a background of poverty or wealth. My children were wonderful no matter what. However, I wanted them to have the confidence which comes from a nice home and well manicured neighborhood. At the same time it should be understood having material possessions did not make you a better person.

In sixth grade, my favorite teacher of all time asked me where I lived. Before I could respond, a mean boy in my class said, "She lives in a tar paper shack." I was speechless. He was so rude. It was his chance to have a one-up feeling, as I was an A student and he was not even a C student. For an instant, he was the superior one, for I had been humiliated. A jealous student, with little of his own to be proud of, tried to dethrone the teacher's pet. While our house was not a tar paper shack, it was not as far from that as I would have liked.

My teacher thought none the less of me She would later tell me, "Faye, you are a very smart and hard-working girl. You can be anything you want. Don't let anyone ever convince you otherwise."

When I got home from school, I threw myself on my parents' bed and sobbed. With all the passion of Scarlet O'Hara in *Gone With the Wind* clutching a turnip and vowing to never go hungry again, I promised myself that I would have a beautiful home someday. My home would be one my children and I were not ashamed to come home to. Certainly a loving family was the most important, but I also wanted nice things for us. I felt my life had been a Cinderella story in the sense I came from behind and won. I believed working hard and trying to be a good person paid off.

George wanted a nice home also. He had lived in an upper middle-class area growing up and his family had a beach home near the ocean as well. He had aspirations to provide our family with some of the minor luxuries available. We felt we deserved it for our many years of hard work. We scraped together the down payment and became determined we might make some sacrifices but in no time the payments would be comfortable.

With the bliss of a busy family of four and a new home to live in, our prayers had been answered. Surely our lives would be the American dream. As I worked in our yard, I imagined the happy times to come. A camellia bush was planted just outside the kitchen window where I could watch it grow as our children did. A sweet olive bush was planted on a corner of the garage. I had always wanted one after smelling one's aroma in a friend's yard. There was plenty of space to plant to our heart's content. There were many projects in the planning. It was time for coasting a while. We believed the bad times were behind us. In reality they had just begun.

Chapter Nine

My husband greeted me at the door upon my return from a routine trip to the grocery store. I had been marveling over a sale on baby food. He told me my father had had a stroke and, while he was expected to live, there was no promise for a high quality of life. It was important to me to be there for him. So often living across the country caused me to miss heartfelt moments with my family. I did not sleep well. Feeling tired and worried I flew home the next day. It troubled me to imagine what the stroke had done to him. He was such an active man; I feared he might become an invalid.

On the plane I reminisced about the last time I talked with my father. He and my mother found a chipmunk living in the back shed of their home. They were delighted by it. Nature was energizing to my dad. After a few moments of describing the chipmunk's antics, the conversation shifted to me. We of course covered the usual topic of how well George, the boys and I were doing. Then I dredged up the courage and emotional strength to resolve the promise I made to myself just days before. Sharing deep feelings did not come easy to any of us.

I told him something I never said before. There had been a TV special about the battles of World War II. Seeing the conditions the troops lived under affected me deeply. The soldiers marched hundreds of miles, slept in wet trenches, and saw active combat with all its horrors. I told him I was proud he had served in the military and he had helped save so many people. I told him he was a hero to me. He was a machine gunner and an expert marksman. His skill continued throughout his life. He hunted and practiced target shooting. If you were held hostage and needed one shot to save you, your wish would be for someone as skilled as my dad to make it.

I hoped he would be pleased I finally saw his courage and tenacity. However, he seemed sad and it aroused bad memories in him. He sounded choked up. Too many tragedies had occurred. War was a nightmare in retrospect. The topic depressed him and brought to mind battlefields littered with the dead and dying. He would have preferred to have missed the ordeal.

He soon got off the phone and I fretted because it had taken me so long to tell him my feelings and it had occurred too late. He could not feel good about shooting people no matter what ultimate good might arise.

I had realized years earlier Dad had displayed signs of post traumatic stress. He had a difficult time relaxing. There was a look he would get when he talked about the war. It was a mixture of guilt and misery. He had nightmares about the war. He would reflect on it and never seemed to find peace. In his dreams soldiers were walking through battlefields and kicking dead German soldiers in the mouth to get fillings from their teeth. When they were through harvesting fillings, fingers would be cut off to get at rings. He remembered the stench of rotting flesh suffocating him and the bitter cold, rain and snow with which he had to contend.

Memories of him eating his rations while civilians were starving troubled him. He would call them "those poor bastards." They were desperate circumstances, the horrors of war. He saw buddies wounded and killed in action. During an explosion, a piece of shrapnel lodged in Dad's chin and his face was covered with blood. His buddy cried and thought Dad was mortally wounded because of all the blood. Dad asked him what was wrong; he did not feel the shell fragment. At least there was one happy ending in a bleak situation. Dad no doubt feared the battles and prayed to survive. Then there was guilt about surviving when others did not. He never forget the atrocities of war. If he watched the news or a movie about war he was haunted for days sometimes. The exception was the show *"Combat."* He felt that show reasonably depicted the war he remembered. The show comforted him because it would show us what he lived. We loyally watched it with him.

He insisted my sisters and I learn to defend ourselves. He showed us how to shoot a rifle. "After you shoot someone, you need to stick them with a bayonet to be certain they are dead," he would instruct us. We were well versed in marching songs. In addition to hopscotch we learned jujitsu holds. While our neighbors read Dr. Seuss, we learned about battlefield first aid. "If your guts get blown out on your stomach, don't put them back inside. Cover them with a clean wet cloth and wait for the medic."

One must always be prepared. Our basement was stocked with canned goods, some from the store and some we canned. Camouflage was necessary for concealment from the enemy; there were seasonal variations. We learned ways to hide. Dad put his heart into trying to protect us through his instruction. He feared war would come to our country. He had seen things a civilian couldn't imagine. It was a duty to him to prepare us to survive, even if the subject was painful to him. Despite his obvious distress, there was value in his teaching. The four girls were taught to survive conflicts and always be prepared. As it would turn out, most of our battles would not be physical, but psychological in nature. My dad's most difficult battle was the one he spent trying to forget the misery war had brought to his life. His condition was eventually diagnosed by a VA physician as post traumatic stress. The war was only part of his life, albeit a significant part.

My father quit school in eighth grade so he could attend trade school during the Great Depression. He worked as a machinist for Lake Shore engineering. He also had a shoe repair business he ran in his off hours. His passion was fishing, hunting, gardening or any other activity out of doors. He never smoked, seldom drank alcohol and was faithful to my mother. His children were told despite any trouble they got involved in, they could always come home. He was known to be an honest and hardworking man. His talkative and friendly manner allowed him to engage easily in conversation with anyone. Dad had a strong sense of humor as did all the members of my family. When he entered a room, he had presence. If he flashed you one of his charming smiles you just had to smile back.

Dad also had a mental illness. I did not realize this until after graduate school and I had begun my career working in mental health. On a visit for the holidays, Dad and I chatted about my sister who is diagnosed with schizophrenia. I expressed how frightening it must be to hear voices. He responded, "Everyone hears voices."

I said, "I don't. I mean when you're alone." He just averted his eyes and said nothing. The truth felt like a blow. Yet there had been so many clues. His temper, excessive talking, grandiose schemes, eccentricity and rigidity. I never bothered to label the behavior as it was just his way. A neurologist following Dad for his stroke told me Dad was diagnosed as schizoaffective. This is a disorder where the mood swings of manic depression are present along with symptoms of schizophrenia such as auditory hallucinations (hearing voices) at least part of the time. Dad always felt he should have a pension from the Veteran's Administration for his heart problems. He probably could have had 100% disability for psychiatric reasons. His mental illness affected our family in various ways. My ability to stand still in the face of my father's anger was learned in part during first grade. I had brought my report card home with all A's. My teacher had written I was very bright and should go to college someday. Mom had told Dad about it. I never knew exactly why, perhaps the price and unknown nature of college worried him or it might be something completely unrelated. When I asked him to sign it, he became furious and wrinkled up my report card onto a tight ball. A report card was a very important thing to destroy. Inside my heart was beating fast and my muscles tightened but I stood there without comment. There was the outside world, then there was life with Dad. I had to find a way to fuse the two. When he left, I started to panic. I placed the wrinkled report card under a speaker to my sister's record player to smooth it out. I needed time to make up an excuse to my teacher.

It was hard to focus in class because of the crime I was concealing. It might even be against the law to treat a report card in that manner. There were rules to follow. I was afraid. As I sat reading about a cat named Puff, I looked up to see my father walk in the room with the wrinkled report card. He looked sheepish, as he would become after these episodes. I put my head down on my arms and cried with shame. Now everyone would know about my father's temper. The girls in the class came around me and patted me. Someone told me I was tender hearted. They had no idea as to why my father was there. They could recognize upset when they saw it. Dad told the teacher the truth about what happened. A new report card was made and my teacher forgave my lie. I remained an A student and made Daddy proud. He gave me a dime for an A and a nickel for a B. From then on it was decided I would go to college and when the time came, I did.

Prior to college and during high school, my father became extremely uplifted. He bragged to Mom, Teresa and me about an invention he devised. He told us we did not have to worry about money anymore. We would be the richest people in town. His smile was broad and his face lit up and we believed him. Marketing his project was the only obstacle. His plan was to make a change in the water distribution of the local water supply. I could not follow his description as to exactly what would be replaced. He made a drawing of his plan but it did not mean anything to me. He said he had to keep part of it a secret so no one could steal his idea. Since I was not prone to thinking like a civil engineer, I did not feel discouraged initially. I had never seen my father more confident. The fact it was taking my father a long time to pitch his idea to the right person did not waiver my faith in his ability. His brother was a civil engineer and it was plausible Dad was every bit as bright. When my mom called me into her bedroom one night while Dad was on the phone, I knew something was wrong. She said Dad was so excited about his invention he was telling everyone. Since he would not express his idea completely, people were beginning to make fun of him. He had gone to a public meeting and informed the speakers of his plan. Being a bit eccentric was acceptable, but he had gone beyond the edge.

Feeling embarrassed and sad for Dad was not enough. I felt guilty because he had been trying to do good for our family. There was a desperate quality to his efforts. His efforts could have given him a chance to provide for his family the way he would like. He wanted us to adore him. It was a grandiose gesture but it touched my heart just the same. Even with all his quirks I loved my dad. He would have given his life in a minute for any of us. I was disappointed my fantasies would not come true. Dad overheard Mom telling Ruth about his behavior. He began to discuss it less then. Mom was incredibly patient with Dad's odd behavior. Life went on as unusual as it had always been.

Fortunately, Dad received psychiatric medication in his later years. I marveled how he did so well with his limitations. He remained married to one woman and reared four daughters. He worked two jobs and fed his family with food for which he hunted, fished or grew in his garden. I knew people without a psychiatric illness who did not fare as well. To add to his schizoaffective illness the anxiety of post traumatic stress made him even more of a hero to me. He kept going all those years, faced life day after day, despite unpleasant thoughts and feelings. At times he struggled lost in a rage much like an ocean wave, forceful, smashing, then quietly dissipating. I wonder what my childhood would have been like if Dad had had appropriate medication. Despite any shortcomings, I was truly proud of my dad. I wish I had figured it out sooner.

Chapter Ten

I was greeted by my eldest sister Ruth and her youngest son at the airport. She was still the "pretty one," with her sparkling blue eyes, ivory skin and dark brown hair. Ruth was to be envied. Mom used to stand in front of the mirror and tilt her head at different angles and ask, "Do you think I look like Ruth?" I used to think she could be Miss America. Besides wishing I could carry a note and sing in front of others, I wished I could be pretty like Ruth. On a good day I hit cute or attractive, but never beautiful or pretty.

Ruth was also one of the most persuasive people I had ever known. As my big sister she could talk me into letting her watch her favorite TV show. The flip side was I could talk to her about anything and no matter what my anxieties she could quiet them. Her voice had a soothing quality. She had a kindness that was rare. My parents had depended on her a great deal. She thanked me for coming and she sounded as if she were already fit to be tied.

Ruth filled me in about my father's condition on the way to my parents' home. It was not good news. Dad was going to need assistance and it was doubtful having a home health nurse would be enough. He was not a physical rehabilitation candidate as he was confused. He would most likely require a nursing home placement. Their financial matters were in disarray. It was a troubling situation. Dad was always organized with his bill paying. It was about honor. Dad would have kept the paperwork organized. He would starve before missing a payment on anything. The papers in his strongbox needed to be sorted and straightened out. Everything had been paid, but their budget was strained by a recent purchase of a new car with all the extras. Dad allegedly was trying to impress the female salesclerk with all the money he could afford to pay. Since we suspected Dad was not completely himself since a prior stroke, we understood the disorderly personal affairs. Dad had been the one to pay the bills.

It was nice to be home for a little while. I could see Mom was pleased I had come. She sat in her wheelchair looking flushed and worried. Her wheelchair was broken so she had not gone to see my dad. While none of us would have ever suggested it, Mom said she could not take care of Dad. Mom could barely care for herself. Dad had been caring for her. She also had home health services. Meals on Wheels delivered the noon meal, of which they saved half for their evening meal. They had managed to stay independent many years in the modest home where I grew up. My father had sacrificed over the years so he could pay the taxes on the land where their house was built. It meant so much to him that his daughters would have an inheritance. Now the situation was left for his children to solve.

We discussed the money needed for household repairs and personal items for Mom. I initially doled out money left and right. Then I noticed I was the only one doing so and their needs were a bottomless pit. Besides, Dad was not coming home and mother would not be able to live alone as she was legally blind, had several types of arthritis, diabetes, high blood pressure and needed hip replacement surgery. For her to walk to the bathroom was painful. Her fingers were bent and locked. Her grip was weak. Her back had been fractured during the many falls she had been having. She was relatively quiet as ideas were considered for Dad's care. She had emotionally excused herself from the problem solving. My sisters and I had been Mom's buffer to the world for many years. I did not expect her to participate.

My nine year old nephew was also quiet during the discussion, which was unusual for him, because he was being treated for Attention Deficit Hyperactivity Disorder. He and my dad had argued the day before and he allegedly hit Dad in the head with something. He had heard my mother say Dad might have thrown a clot because of the fight with my nephew. He had been understandably troubled since then and unknown to us, believed his grandfather had died and we were lying to him. He was an intelligent child, but at times had trouble understanding the process of everyday life. He had been close to his grandfather and was troubled by the events.

Ruth and I prepared to go to the hospital to see our father. Besides Mom's broken wheelchair she was too worn out to go anyway. We were waiting for a quiet moment to steal away. It was not to be. As we prepared to leave, Ruth's son insisted he go too. Ruth told him that she and I had to talk with the staff to make plans for Grandpa. She told him children could not go to the floor Dad was on. He became more agitated and declared he was going or no one was going. We all argued. Thinking my sister did not know how to be firm with her son, I proceeded to firmly state he could not go at his time. Perhaps we could work something out for later. He became enraged, took the keys from my sister and threw them into my dad's garden. I was speechless. We searched the garden, and miracle of miracles, Ruth found the keys.

We prepared to leave and again my nephew objected. I repeated in a calm, firm manner that he could not come with us. He said he would slash the tires on the car and I only half believed him. Sure enough he ran outside wielding a knife and headed for the car. Ruth pulled him off the car. As she was pulling him away, he stopped squirming just long enough to throw the knife at me. It missed me and he told Ruth later he had only intended to scare me. Once the knife had been thrown, things seemed to calm down. Again I headed for the car.

It looked like we might leave. My nephew then grabbed a broom with the handle being held as a weapon and came towards me. I grabbed a long-handled shovel and fought him off with it. Our haphazard weapons crossed and blocked repeatedly. It was like a movie battle scene about knights or warriors having a sword fight. My father's training all those years ago was useful. In an unexpected way it was quite exhilarating. Once again, Ruth pulled him away and told him she was taking him home. I took the lull in the action and escaped into my sister Donna's home, which was located on the opposite side of Dad's garden.

I knocked on the door and was given permission to enter. Donna was smoking and the house reeked of it. She exclaimed how happy she was to see me. I managed to greet her, then told how our nephew had attacked me. She said she knew he had problems. She went on to ask about my flight as though nothing had happened. I expected the Twilight Zone music to start at any moment. I said, "He threw a knife at me. I am very concerned about this." I did not feel safe going back to Mom's house. I felt traumatized and was pacing around and repeatedly watching out the window to see if he was coming.

Donna implied these incidents were commonplace, and there was no need to get upset over them. Her indifference was maddening. Ruth had brought him to physicians and counseling. She did not know what else to do. His father was absent and surely this left a void in his life that my father had filled until now. He was a handsome boy and looked older than his age primarily because of his size. Despite the fear I had felt, I grieved for my nephew. He must have been so upset to take things to the extent they had gone. Ruth and I had talked about him many times and my heart went out to her. She would give anything for him to be free of these episodes. At another level, I was angry to have flown on a plane all day and be put through this. After a while, I calmed down and managed to have a brief visit with Donna. Surely he was gone by now. My allergies could not tolerate the cigarette smoke, and in its own way the smoke attacked me also, so I decided to risk returning to my mom's house.

When I returned to my mom's house, I told her my feelings about what happened. After I had done so, she pointed and quietly mouthed to me. My nephew had not left and was hiding in the closet, afraid, because he knew he had gone too far. Amazed that mother had not interrupted me to tell about him hiding any sooner, I mouthed back, "With a knife?" She shook her head no. She was the concerned grandmother now. Knowing I had to get him to leave if I were to relax, I made a statement for him to hear. I announced, "It's all over now. Everyone is having a hard time right now. I did not like your behavior a while ago, but I still love you." There was silence.

I was not ready to talk with him yet. I needed some time to unwind from the adrenaline rush. I left to walk around the neighborhood where I had grown up. First I walked rapidly, then slowed. The walk was helping me to calm down. I was enjoying the variety in colors of petunias in the various yards. Bright pink was my favorite. The incident with my nephew left me very torn up inside. I hated what had happened because I could have been hurt. It worried me a great deal that a 9-year-old child could go to such extremes. He was every bit the future Special Forces recruit, intimidated by nothing. The look on his face and his demeanor told me he had no fear when in that mode. I was truly upset and everyone expected me to act like nothing had happened. George was never going to believe what happened. If I could, I would get on the next plane home and never look back. I heard a car pull up behind me and stop. Now what?

Chapter Eleven

I was afraid to turn and look given the day I was having. Curiosity finally got the better of me and I had to look. There was my sister Ruth and my nephew acting like this was just any day. They told me to come with them to get an ice cream cone. Surely they were kidding? Studying Ruth's face led me to believe it would be okay. I was nervous but climbed in. My nephew was in the back seat and I was settling into the passenger seat. I half expecting him to start choking me from the back seat at any time.

Ruth told me he had a gift for me. I refused to let my mind guess. They had gone to K-Mart and he bought me a silk flower. He gave it to me and I thanked him. He bought the flower because he knew he had upset me. He looked every bit the nine-year-old boy again. My mind whirled out of my own discomfort but also for my nephew who surely had a difficult life. I could not turn off my emotions and change gears so quickly. I needed time to adjust. As the ride continued, I calmed down quite a bit and understood my nephew's aggressive behavior had worn off.

After we got the ice cream cones, we stopped by the lake shore. My nephew got out to play on the large rocks and watch the waves. Ruth and I walked a little, then sat in the car. She said her son was having a difficult time because of Dad's illness. Mom let him think it was his fault. I wondered aloud if perhaps an accident occurred. Dad had a stroke previously and was hypertensive. There was no need to blame anyone for Dad's condition.

However, I asked if she understood how serious his behavior toward me had been. I suggested he go to an inpatient psychiatric treatment program. Even if he were playing, someone could have been seriously injured. If there was a problem it would be best to get to the bottom of it. I told her it was more difficult for me to tell her of my concern than act like nothing had happened. I wanted her to hear what I felt was best for her son based on my having counseled other families.

Ruth looked at me as though I were just another school official criticizing her child or her parenting abilities. I explained whatever was going on with him was probably biology or a hidden problem of which she was not aware. Despite his height, he was still a little boy of nine. I loved him but was fearful for him. When he was acting out, he had pure rage in his eyes. It was not just that he might hurt someone else. If he pulled that stunt with someone else they might not just defend themselves, they might fight back as aggressively. He saw a therapist on a regular basis and Ruth had put in a call. She relayed his response. He suggested my nephew was suffering from post traumatic stress and felt responsible for his grandpa's stroke. The therapist suggested he see for himself if his grandpa was okay. His grandpa was one of his only friends and always welcomed him when he visited. They went fishing and worked in the yard. Dad's stroke was traumatic for him. Dad's stroke was hard on everyone. Ruth had barely slept with all the worry and responsibility. She had spent long hours at the hospital. Also, Mom was distraught, so that was an additional concern for Ruth to bear. We were all stressed out. It was much harder to take than I ever imagined. While Dad struggled to live despite the brain attack, his family struggled for sanity amidst the chaos. One minute we would lean on each other, then the next we would be fussing. We all just plain hurt. Ruth and I had talked many times about her concern for her son. She faithfully had him attend counseling sessions, psychological testing, take medication, and lobbied at school meetings to obtain the best learning environment for him. He had been plagued by allergies and ear infections as a child, which affected his ability to hear. In addition he had problems with impulsivity and distractibility. He demonstrated attention-getting behavior, had mood swings and angry outbursts and was a discipline problem. Ruth had tried everything recommended. She was exhausted as a single parent trying to be a good mother. The incident was like a hundred other bad days she had for various reasons. Frequently someone at school criticized her parenting ability, yet they were without a plan to make things better. They needn't have criticized her. It did nothing to help. Besides no one could blame her any more than she blamed herself. Without clear answers blame always seemed to fill in the blanks.

    I thought over the situation as we drove back to Mom's house. With Dad struggling with his heart and possible stroke problems and Mom with her severe arthritis they were not in a position to baby-sit, especially for a child with hyperactivity. Mom and I discussed it some as I got ready for bed. She said it was too much for them to watch my nephew. With Dad in the hospital it was really a moot point. The baby-sitting days were over. So many changes all at once. I was glad to see the day wind down and before bedtime I phoned my husband.

When I heard George's voice at the other end of the phone, I wanted to cry. Why couldn't he be here with me? I shared with him the events of the day. Either one of us could have been seriously hurt, even by accident, and it is short of a miracle we had not been. It seemed like years since he had brought me to the airport. Maybe with some rest I could look at it all calmly in the morning. I hung up, looking forward to my trip home. The room was so stuffy it was uncomfortable to relax. The buzzing of a mosquito welcoming me back home managed to prevent me from dozing off as I would get up and flip the lights on every five minutes to try and track him down. I did not sleep well.

I was out of sorts in the morning. I had disrupted my life by abruptly stopping breast-feeding, which played havoc with my hormones. I experienced the discomfort of engorgement of my breasts. It was hard to be without my husband and children. I was lonely. My family was in crisis as Dad was in the hospital and Mom was unable to care for herself. I was so tired already and it was only the morning. My mosquito bites itched. It was the worst time I ever experienced back home. My family reunion was the equivalent of a category five hurricane. Now we were absolutely certain Dad would not be coming home. I talked with his neurologist on the phone. Mother wanted to stay in their home alone and have home health services. The home health social worker was coming to meet with Mom and me. Mom clearly needed to live with someone yet she was reluctant to make a change. But life had made a change for her. It was painful having to confront her with her limitations. In desperation I dusted furniture and picked up the carpet as best I could on my hands and knees. Their vacuum was long since useless. The closer it came to being time for the social worker the more determined I got. Piles of magazines were thrown into a drawer. No matter what I did, the home was still a modest home in need of repairs. I tried to look casual when she arrived. Then it occurred to me she had been to Mom's house before so she was past any shock at its simplicity. Mom and I and the home health social worker met to talk about Mom's situation. The conversation was enjoyable at first as we talked about matters of general interest. Once we focused on the situation at hand, tension joined us. When I tried to assist Mom in facing reality and how it was impossible for her to live alone, she quite sharply pointed out, "My Ruth will help me." I felt like I had been slapped for trying to solve the problem. Ruth was the one most opposed to Mom living alone. I was the one being punished. With her own family to care for Ruth would be run ragged trying to meet all of Mom's needs. Mom would not consider any other option. At that moment I was not in her good graces and it hurt me deeply. There was always a part of me which was unsure of her love; it seemed conditional. I never stopped trying though, the day being par for the course. The interview ended quickly after this. The social worker seemed to sense my pain. I hoped Mom would calm down and understand I was risking rejection for the ultimate good. It reminded me of the children's story, *The Emperor's New Clothes*. Someone needed to say the truth out loud.

Chapter Twelve

As Ruth and I drove to the hospital, we joked how despite all our worries and lost sleep Dad would probably be sitting up and chatting with people when we got to the hospital like nothing ever happened. As we walked in, Dad was sitting up in a wheelchair and at first glance looked quite fine. A smile lit up his face and he said, "My little girls." I noticed Dad was tied into the wheelchair. Ruth and I looked at each other and started to laugh. It was just like we thought, all the worry and Dad was fine. However, before we could begin our visit he looked worried and asked if he had a tube in his stomach. I thought he was referring to a feeding tube and told him no. Then he looked panicked and tried to get out of the chair to go into the bathroom. He had tears in his eyes as he frantically struggled and before I could help him he had fallen out of his chair. He then made a mess with diarrhea on the floor. Ruth and I were confused and embarrassed. Two nurses cleaned up the mess and helped him settle into his chair again. One glared at my sister and me as if we had caused the problem intentionally. He was slightly confused as we conversed. We talked about life in general and about some medical test which had been done. It was mentioned that there was a good probability he would be going to a Veterans' facility.

Dad had always been pleased with his treatment at the Veterans' Hospital. So going there was not objectionable to him. We filled Dad in on the well-being of family members. When we tired him, we ended the visit. There was so much to do and we needed to get started.

The first order of business was to stop by the Social Security office. We hoped to arrange direct deposit of my parents' Social Security checks to make things easier. While there we learned their checks had to be in separate accounts. Ruth offered to be the representative payee for both of them. This was not the agreement we had with Mom earlier in the day. We did not know the rules of management before.

We scheduled an appointment with the social worker at the Veterans nursing home for later in the day. We managed to get lunch at a Greek restaurant and talked over our feelings. We were both feeling the weight of the world on our shoulders. Ruth had been spending most of her free time shopping for our parents, cleaning and cutting their grass. Dad had always told us we could come home no matter what. Ruth agonized because we were not offering him the same choice. Logically we knew there really was no other choice. After Greek salads and iced tea, we were fortified to continue our day. Yet a gray cloud seem to follow us around

Since we had time before our appointment at the nursing home, we stopped to discuss a prepaid funeral plan with the funeral home the family had used. Initially it was for Catholics but now served everyone. The assistant funeral director kindly fit us in. We talked about how funerals worked and he showed us around. He was very knowledgeable. When we cried, he clearly understood and did not seem annoyed. We picked out some preliminary items such as a casket and stationery. We gave information for the obituary. It was emotionally draining. Yet if we did things today it would be one less burden for Ruth. Mom would not handle the stress of dealing with a funeral home well. It would fall on our shoulders. Because it was time for our next appointment we thanked the attendant and got back in the car.

The VA nursing home was formerly the hospital where Ruth was born. While we waited to meet with the social worker we walked around the facility to form our own opinions. One of the first people I saw was an elderly man tied into a wheelchair clutching a teddy bear. He looked vacant and was the only person in the activity room. As we wandered around, we were happy to notice how clean the place was. There were ample staff to care for the patients. It was the nicest facility in the area.

The social worker told us about the facility and how the financing would work. We discussed the way the facility was run. I broke down and cried as we talked about the activities for veterans. The social worker patiently listened as I explained how independent my Dad had been. He would not like being dependent. He informed me he had a facility full of independent people who were making the same adjustment. As the nursing home was full, Dad would first go to a Veterans' Hospital until there was an opening. This was a gift as we had no where else for Dad to go.

Ruth and I quietly made our way back to our car. We knew we were making the right decision. It was much more painful than I ever imagined.

We always expected Dad would die from a heart attack one day and it would all be over. There was no plan for him to die slowly. At least arranging the placement was over. We fell into silence, lost in our own thoughts. It hurt so badly. Out of nowhere, it seemed, Ruth and I began quarreling. It began with Ruth venting about her son and how she tired of people being critical of him. The worry etched in her face told me of her pain more than the words. I reminded her he was family and if I could help him in any way I would. I knew that was true for the rest of the family as well. Yesterday's events became one more incident to have to deal with along with a host of other problems going on. I am not sure if that was really the issue. With so much going on, fighting allowed us to temporarily forget the events of the day. Fighting was very unusual for us but was less painful than thinking about Dad. After all the abandonment Dad faced in his life, he would once again be left behind. Before it was his parents and now it was his wife and daughters.

Because of his confusion he would be put on an Alzheimer's unit. I don't know how his mother and dad felt when they left him behind but no doubt it was breaking Ruth's heart and mine. However, she also felt abandoned, as Dad had been there for her. She could always count on him to come through in a pinch. If the day had been difficult, this incident made it miserable. We were frustrated that Mom did not want to be a part of the planning. We needed her to be strong. Yet we worried she might have a stroke, as it ran in her family and she was so upset.

When we arrived at Mom's house, we opened the door to see my mother lying quietly in a chair. For a moment, it appeared she had had a stroke. Ruth and I both went pale. She had been so troubled. However, she opened her eyes and responded to us. We related the details of the day--of the funeral plan, nursing home and the visit to the Social Security office. The social worker at the Social Security office had called Mom and tried to explain how Ruth would be managing her check and my dad's checks. Mom said it was okay but I suspect it was all happening too fast. Ruth told Mom she would be the representative payee for both Mom and Dad. Mom seemed suspicious of this. Ruth told her how Dad's check and hers could not go into the same account. Mom felt she was losing more control. Trying to change the subject, we told her how pleased we were with the nursing home. As we continued with a description of the nursing home, Mom blurted out, "Can't you find a cheaper nursing home?"

I was stunned. I said, "He is my father and he will have a nice nursing home. I can't believe you. You don't really mean it." She then started to cry about how troubled she was. We assured her she would be cared for also. I knew Mother was distressed, but even so I wanted her to show more concern for him. I wanted her to fake concern for him, if necessary. Even though it had been rough at times I still wanted her to love my father dearly. After all the years together, she had to feel something for him. With Mother one could never be sure. She did not share feelings easily.

As the conversation continued, Mom reacted to something I said and held her twisted arthritic fingers in a fist. She looked furious and said, "I'll knock you for a hill of beans." While I have never understood the expression, it was clear she was angry. She had never been a physically violent person and obviously her health precluded her attacking me. Never in my life did Mom speak to me that way. It was not her style. She could straighten you out with one sentence or less and never raise her voice. Sometimes a sigh or facial expression took care of it. Something else had happened. For a brief span of time, I hated her right back. I wanted to slap her face but knew I would not allow myself to do so. I did not feel like myself. Feelings of rage shot through me. It baffled me how I could have a desire to be physically violent. I had never been strong physically and was used to solving problems verbally. We were all so tense. We all were hurting. Mom regretted leaving her home and all the decisions being made without time to think things through. It was all happening too fast. I did not have my usual patience. I had never felt rage as I did at that moment. There was so much business to take care of and no chance to rest.

Everyone was on my nerves and I wanted to go home to my husband and children. I did not feel well. I was tired and unsettled. My feelings of frustration were nearing the surface and I feared I might throw a giant tantrum if things did not slow down.

My feelings of anger were the strongest I had ever experienced. It was unlike me to physically act out anger but I knew it would not take much to push my button. Remembering all the advice I knew about stressful situations, I tried to counsel myself. Mom and her requests grated on me. I felt she was wrong to keep asking so much from me. The mood I experienced on the visit would later fit into a picture of mental illness getting a firm grip on me but not yet wrestling me out of control.

Our whole family was in crisis and we were running out of shoulders to cry on. The anger I felt toward my mother frightened me. Mother and I had always gotten along. We had always been civil and I usually enjoyed her company. There had been moments of hurt feelings but the fights my friends had with their mothers seemed unusual to me. I had always treated my mom with respect and consideration.

I always wanted a mom who had nice clothes, high heels and a stylish hairdo, like the moms on TV. Each evening there would be a great meal on the table and a clean house. When she wasn't mending or ironing my clothes, she would be making special desserts out of pudding and whipping cream. She would not be intimidated by the educated people at school if they were unfair to one of her babies. She would spend weeks shopping for my birthday gift so it would be just right.

Mom was not all I wanted her to be. No one ever is. People are a mixture of good and bad traits. Mom was not a drinker or a drug user. Given the poverty she endured she did the best she could. She risked the wrath of my father going behind his back to take out loans to buy school clothes for us. The loan would have an outrageous interest rate. There would be lots of screaming and criticism if Dad found out. He always found out, usually because the day would come when Dad got the mail first.

She woke at 5 a.m. to go to work at a job of extreme physical labor only to come home and start her second shift. She had several kinds of arthritis and her body hurt so much of the time. From day to day, supporting the family was the goal. There was not extra money for pampering. Mom certainly didn't pamper herself. As I matured, I realized making sure you can feed your children and have a roof over their heads was admirable. Loving your children, not abandoning them and encouraging them as best you can is beautiful. Taking them to church and Sunday school demonstrated devotion. Buying your little girls their own geranium to care for was sweet. Bringing home a treat for your darlings from the Tupperware party was thoughtful. Going to your daughter's teacher's conference in a worn uniform, with no pantyhose, torn shoes, hair colored with your roots grown out, and missing two hours' pay, was divine.

Chapter Thirteen

In many ways Mom had been extremely competent, finding summer jobs or scholarships for me. She never met an application or form which intimidated her. If a matter of importance was in the local newspaper, Mom tracked it down. She was up-to-date on current affairs. Her advice was usually on target. Mom was from the school of thought, "If you have something unpleasant to face, get it over with." The lesson has aided me many times and eliminated the wasted energy of worrying needlessly.

Mom was a family oriented person and came from a loving, close knit family. She grew up with five siblings and spent every Sunday with her extended family, who were Dutch immigrants. Her mother gave birth to seven other children who died at birth. Mom dropped out of high school to attend beauty school. She later joined the Women's Army Core and became a sergeant. Her IQ was tested in the army and was 120. Her mom died before I was born so I never met her. Mom was around age 21 and was in the army at the time. Mom was very close to her mother and shared her love for flowers. My mom never got over her death and missed her mother a great deal. It was very upsetting to my mother when her father remarried. Yet she understood he had young children who needed a mother. I did meet her father and I remember him as a handsome, soft spoken man, who made little jokes, and loved to read, mostly westerns.

Mom and Dad met after the World War II. Mom was a quiet person, shy even. She attended church regularly and had dreams of becoming a missionary. My father was a very expressive and outgoing person. Their personalities complimented each other and they were very much in love. Marrying Dad meant leaving her family. Mom and Dad's move to the upper peninsula of Michigan had been quite difficult for Mom. Lake Superior had unquestionable beauty. My father's passion for hunting and fishing thrived in this country. He had his family near him. Yet, the winters were cold and harsh. My mother missed her family. Her sisters meant the world to her. She was able to see them for about one week each summer. I looked forward to the visits also. While I did not know my mom's brother well, I have many fond memories of her sisters and their families. My Aunt Eleanor was the best cook in the world and she made the very best roast beef, served with fresh vegetables from her garden. My Aunt Gladys was a very generous person and had the greatest sense of humor. We stayed with her and my Uncle John at their summer place many times and it was always a treat. My Aunt Dee was so pretty and dressed so lovely. I remember her as a very elegant lady with a warm, friendly smile. My Aunt Joyce was always fun to be around. She was the most down to earth person I've ever met. It was always fun to go to her family farm because she had lots of children and my cousins and I got along well. Sadly, two of her children would not live to be adults. I have never forgotten Bobby Joe and Randy and the happy times we spent together. I have always admired my Aunt Joyce who endured such heartbreak yet continued to be a wonderful mother to her other children. I could understand why Mom's family was so dear to her. They were remarkable people.

My father was Catholic and she was Protestant. In her day it was unacceptable to marry someone of a different religion. This made for a difficult beginning, yet she persevered. She had tired of her work as a beautician and now worked as a housekeeper for some of the wealthier families in town. She and my father had four little girls which kept her busy. My father's mood swings and angry outbursts had devastated her. She was not used to such displays. In their daily struggle for survival the tension of supporting a family amidst layoffs from the steel industry must have been extreme. Cleaning houses was not always reliable and Mom might be without work with little notice.

Mom eventually switched to working for institutions as kitchen help, which was more reliable. Living in poverty wore on her to no end. Washing clothing was hard work. Water had to be heated on the stove and poured into her old-time wringer washer. There was no dryer. The clothesline gave the clothes a heavenly scent. In the winter there was a light-colored wood rack to put clothes on. Many times my fingers were pulled into the wringer and the machine had to be stopped. I liked to help her. Eventually we graduated to the laundromat.

Going to the laundromat with my mother was our special time together. I loved the smell of detergent and bleach. Liquid fabric softener had to be added when the rinse cycle began. This required precision. The extractor was next. This was a separate machine which would draw out remaining water from the clothes so they would dry faster. While I watched the exaggerated version of a spin cycle I was filled with pride. We were being economical. I was indeed my father's daughter. The best part of the visit was when I got a bottle of Elson's creme soda or Elson's strawberry soda. I was never completely sure which until I stood before the pop machine and studied the flavors. Once I had my soft drink and had a few sips, I would set it aside. It was time to fold clothes. I loved the smell of the clothes fresh out of the dryer, although nothing could compete with the smell of clothes dried on a clothesline. Feeling the warm clothing was so comforting. Mom and I would chat as we folded the clothes. It was a peaceful and relaxing activity. It was a piece of time when I had mother all to myself. I was amazed by the things she knew about. Besides washing clothes she could cook and bake.

Mom cooked from scratch, as did almost everyone. My favorite was goulash but her macaroni and cheese or scalloped potatoes were astonishing also. She baked pineapple upside-down cake and blueberry pies. She fried doughnuts and made homemade bread and cinnamon rolls. To sit in the evening watching TV and smelling a treat baking was the nicest part of the day.

She also liked having her own kitchen so she could eat whenever she wanted. In many ways food had been her main comfort. It cheered her up and calmed her down. It motivated her and was a reward. The key to my mom's heart had always been food. Any situation was a good time to eat. The appliances for cooking were a close second to food itself in terms of Mom's favorite things. When the hamburger cooker presses were out, you would have thought we bought her a new car, she was so thrilled. Another favorite was the blender for whipping up chocolate milkshakes. The milkshakes preceded the diabetic period which focused her eating patterns in a new way. Then her favorite was the hot air popcorn machine.

When I was older, I finally understood my mother had an eating disorder. She was a binge eater and an addict to food. Food was a comfort to her. It also rewarded her and motivated her. It cheered her up and calmed her down. When she was eating something she enjoyed, she would have her mouth so full a big bulge would be in her cheek and her eyes would dance in ecstasy. She had been in a state of depression for much of my childhood. Her depression walked hand-in-hand with her eating disorder. She was every bit as powerless over food as any alcoholic was about alcohol. The symptoms of diabetes, especially thirst and hunger, contributed to her condition. When your body is sending you a signal of thirst, you drink something.

Eating was a short-term cure for her depression. It made her happy temporarily, then guilty and ashamed because once again, she had eaten too much and she would not lose weight eating so much. She hated being overweight, and given her limited wardrobe it was especially hard to look good. Despite the depression and limited resources she trudged on.

It was not until I was in high school and went out to eat with friends that I realized the average person did not gallop through the parking lot in hopes of beating someone else out of a seat. It was possible to quite simply walk into the restaurant without the feeding-frenzy attitude. There was also the binge-eating factor. While I was struggling with the annual candy sale for Freshman in high school, I came home to discover that ten to fifteen boxes of candy were missing. As I asked in disbelief what had happened, Mom confessed she had eaten them in the past couple days. She had just opened one box and lost control of her impulses. She agreed to pay for them and we thought of it as just another Mom incident. In a similar fashion Mom ate a gift box of candy sitting under the Christmas tree for someone else. The person showed up later than expected and I searched everywhere for the gift. Mom got a guilty smile and said, "Oh, I don't know if I should tell you. Now don't get mad, it was me. I mean it was just sitting there, so why not?"

There was an unspoken rule in our home. Any food not eaten at the time it became available became Mother's. If I saved a cupcake for the next day and if it was not nailed down it would be devoured before my head hit my pillow. Food had to be hidden or relinquished. There was an attitude of, "Eat while the eating is good." It was your tough luck if you were late to a meal or wanted to have your treat later. I would be puzzled when commercials advertised means of storing leftovers. There were never any leftovers. Sometimes Mom's hunger outweighed her desire to cook well. On those days the roast would be very undercooked. She just could not wait for it to finish cooking. Her blood sugar must have been low as she looked pale and desperate at those times.

Mom wanted to make better food choices. She had tried Weight Watchers meetings and did well for a while. Her budget did not allow for many of the recommended foods, but she still managed to lose weight. She had gone to a different group where if you did not lose weight you had to stand in a designated "pigpen" and people who had lost weight made oinking sounds at you. An evening of humiliation to be sure. No doubt Mom may have taken a different course if she had relief from the depression which so frequently visited her. The depression weighed on her and added to her feelings of worthlessness and helplessness. She attempted suicide once, by taking a bottle of aspirin. It may have been in protest of my father's abrupt moods or her financial situation. Eating was one of her pleasures. She lived from doughnut to doughnut. I would not be surprised to learn she had a biological basis for her compulsive behavior. Watching the news took her mind off of her troubles and distracted her from her worries. Her all-time favorite news show was *Nightline*. She found an escape reading Harlequin romance novels and they seemed to help her as much as anything. She also lived vicariously through her daughters.

When under pressure, Mom became dependent and fearful of making a decision. She became childlike. Perhaps it was because of the anxiety she would feel. My sisters and I took over in those moments while she retreated. Perhaps I learned to be a social worker in those moments of Mom's regression. Sometimes it was quite inconvenient for Mom to hand over a problem. During my wedding brunch, one of these incidents occurred. George and I posed for the photographer as we cut our wedding cake. Mom rushed up to me in a panic while I was posing and informed me one of my nephews was running up and down the hall outside the room where the brunch was being held. Despite all the times Mom came to me for help when she felt overwhelmed, this seemed the most insensitive. I told her, "Mother, I am cutting my wedding cake. Find someone else to help you!" Somehow I pushed her out of my mind and continued to pose. I was amazed she could not sense the reverence of the moment. Yet in her own way she was trying to help, as she feared my nephew might cause a scene.

She disliked emotional confrontations and cried when one occurred. My father would frequently yell and scream and undermined her confidence. In particular he would ask one of us to do the opposite of something Mom told us to do. He knew how to torture her. He would never touch her but would destroy her material possessions like pretty knickknacks or plates. She eventually gave her wedding gifts away because she did not want to see them broken. Often she would sit crying and shake her head saying, "I don't know what to do." Her helplessness was aggravated by this brutal behavior. To be such a quiet person living with my father's angry outbursts must have unsettled her peace of mind.

One Saturday morning, when I was in upper elementary school, I noticed my mom sitting on the floor packing boxes with food. There was not a lot of food to pack. Mom told me to go to Catechism. She said we were going to stay with her sisters. She could not stand living with my father. On the way to class I felt sad because I did not want to be away from my dad. He would get really upset sometimes but he was so good the rest of the time. I did not want to leave my school and stay with my mom's sisters. The secret burned in my heart through the nun's instruction. I was afraid. Right or wrong, I wanted my family to stay together. When I returned home, Dad was there and the boxes were put away. I felt such relief. Yet I knew Mom felt defeated. Her sisters had families of their own. How could she stay with them for long? There was really no place to go. For so many years, she wanted to go live near her family. How unfortunate now she could leave and did not want to.

Meanwhile, the visit continued and I felt consumed by frustration and disillusionment. No matter how I tried to turn my family members into a TV-type family it was not to be. I thought of another of Mom's expressions. "If wishes were horses, beggars would ride." Everything would not be solved in 30 minutes and some concerns might never be solved at all.

Chapter Fourteen

Later in the day, when only Mom and I were there, I sat looking around the house I grew up in. This had been the space our family shared. It always stunned me when I walked into the house of my childhood, that it was so much tinier than I remembered. The Seven Dwarfs could have lived there. The drapes had not been changed from the last remodeling effort in the 1970's. Their color was Toast. The rust-colored carpet was worn and stained. The furniture was spent, including the special lift chair for arthritic patients. The cord had been cut by a grandchild so it was unusable. The philosophy of the day was, "Why replace the cord? It will only happen again."

Mom's knickknacks from recent years sat on the same shelves as always. Somewhere along the way Dad had quit breaking things. The highlight of the room was the graduation pictures of the four girls. My picture had flecks of paint on it from one of the attempts to spruce things up. In rivalry with the graduation pictures for most special were the ship models Dad had painstakingly assembled. He had such pride in them.

My favorite window was in the front of the house. Often I watched sagging pine branches with gentle mounds of snow or cars with chains on their tires try to navigate the long, steep hill which ran alongside our home. My sisters and I sledded down the hill when it was free of cars. I felt very proud of my sled, as some might feel about a car. In addition to the sledding memories I recalled less cheerful events. Like the time I awoke to the sound of a dog getting hit by a car. I ran to the dog to see what could be done. Sadly he was dead. I provided a proper burial for him. Once, a drunken man staggered down the street and fell into the ditch alongside the road. Ours was a poor neighborhood. So many struggles to survive poverty, misery and defeat. Yet so much joy as well.

I thought back to elementary school which was so significant a force in my life. The success I had in school helped me to build a life outside of poverty. While in third grade my coat had a broken zipper. Each day the janitor used pliers to get my coat off. I felt he hated me and just about all the other children too. He was crabby and I hated going to see him in the boiler room. Yet it was too cold not to zip it up the part way it would go. It was my winter coat for the year and would have to last. Clothing was always in short supply. If we lost our mittens or they weren't dry we had to wear socks on our hands. Teresa's teacher brought in some of her own clothes for Teresa to wear. She wore them and it was a tad embarrassing but the clothes were so desperately needed there was no time to feel bad for long.

    Each lunch hour in elementary school Donna and I made our way home and we opened a can of tomato soup, measured a can full of milk and heated it up. On a good day, we had crackers and a glass of milk too. During good times, we might get ravioli. If it was wrong for two elementary-age children to make their own lunch, we knew no other way. One lunch hour was unusually stressful. The front door was accidentally locked. The back door was always locked. We debated whether we should wait out the lunch period standing in the shed. We decided we were too hungry to do so. Instead we each tried to crawl through the coal chute and get in the house through the basement. The coal bin was nearly empty. I was the smallest so I proceeded into the darkness and made it through and unlocked the door for my sister so we could have lunch. I felt good about getting in until I saw in the bathroom mirror that I looked like a chimney sweep. I changed clothes and washed up as well as I could. I made it through the afternoon at school without a confrontation by the teacher.

    After school, we were latchkey children until our older sister would be home and we would sit with Ruth and play her records. With absolute commitment we danced the twist, swim and pony. We were together so it was utterly bearable and quite fun. Dad came home in late afternoon unless he was working overtime or at the shoe repair shop. Mom would come home last.

    We all took turns making dinner. Most popular were goulash, tuna fish sandwiches, hamburgers, Sloppy Joes and macaroni and cheese. One of my favorite dishes was scalloped potatoes with ham. The first meal I remember cooking was goulash. I felt quite important preparing a meal for the family. Mom cooked sometimes and after working in a kitchen all day she probably was tired of cooking. I remember her wearing a white uniform. She only had one. Usually there were stains on it from the workplace by the end of the day. She would let her uniform soak a while and later would boil it on the stove. Eventually it would be left on a hanger to dry overnight.

The next day would begin with the clean uniform being slipped on at five a.m. and she would be gone after making oatmeal for Dad and the children and leaving it on the stove for us. Dad would get up and be gone next and would wake my oldest sister as he left. The tag team would continue until we were all off on our way. If we were sick we usually went to school anyway. If we stayed home we would be alone until our parents were through working.

I gazed into my parents' tiny bedroom and noted I had kept my parents well stocked in sheet sets. Mom and I had discussed many matters of importance as we sat on her bed. Mother was willing to discuss anything. She might not have the answer but directed the concern to whoever did. However, the only time she faltered was when I asked to see a psychologist because I thought I was going crazy. It had taken days to work myself up to tell her. I was terrified of whatever had a hold on me. On television doctors could fix anything. Mom was shocked and dismayed by my request.

Continuing on I told her of the odd feelings I had at school after gym class. I had used the toilet and flushed and left the stall. Yet moments later, I felt really bad and had to check if I had actually flushed the toilet. I had to go back and flush it again. It was as if something bad would happen if I didn't go back. The ritual was repeated until the bad feelings lessened enough for me to move on. The look on my mom's face told me she was stunned by this information. She looked worried as I unloaded my concerns. Her voice was gentle as she tried to comfort me. Mom suggested I was a just a really clean person. She sincerely told me we could not afford a psychologist or psychiatrist. She offered that I must be nervous adjusting to seventh grade. There was nothing else to say once the words, "We can't afford it," were mentioned. Whatever was wrong would have to keep.

The next day my older sister had heard about my situation and informed me so. Mom had a habit of serving as a broker for problems. She would explain the problem to the person in the family most qualified to respond. She had chosen Donna in this instance. Donna asked if I were "nuts," and told me if I was I had to go to the state hospital and be locked up with other troubled folk. It was a frightening thought. I did not want to be crazy. Inside I knew I was different but would learn to conceal this strange behavior so no one else would know. It would be over 25 years before I told a psychiatrist about my obsessive-compulsive behavior. During the in-between years, I would try to mask my odd behavior by making some joke or self-deprecating comment.

My symptoms rose and fell with my stress level. Taking tests was an anxiety-provoking situation. I would have to tap my pen on the paper a set number of times. The frequency of the tapping would be whatever number popped into my mind. If the date was the fifth I would tap five times. Or if family was on my mind I might tap four times as there were four girls in my family. There were numerous variations on this theme. When reading a book I might have a bad thought about something scary. If I had such a thought I would have to start the sentence over or maybe even the chapter over to keep me safe from whatever force tormented me. Sometimes I felt compelled to say a word a set number of times. Then I had to fit the word into several sentences within a normal conversation. Schoolwork could take a long time when struggling with these issues.

Depression seemed to go part and parcel with the obsessive thoughts. My depressions could be triggered by a sad movie. When I had a sad response watching a dramatic movie, even if the event in the movie had nothing to do with me, I would start to feel depressed. My mind would seemingly get stuck in that part of my emotions like a broken record. Staying with the mood, my mind could always pull up an occasion from my life that made me sad, then another, and another. My ruminating would begin and I would be off suffering and hating myself. If I felt so bad I must have deserved it. No part of myself was off the hook. I fell short of perfection. I should have not missed one point on a test. What a terrible daughter I must have been to have quarreled with my father. Why couldn't my hair be prettier? Some people did not grasp my sense of humor. The self-loathing would go on for hours.

As an adult I asked George if my dark moods bothered him. More specifically I asked him what percentage of the time he enjoyed my company. I expected to hear five or ten percent of the time but he said about ninety to ninety-five percent of the time. Depression is sneaky. It can be a thought disorder as well as a mood disorder. With the mood came a mindset which basically felt like I will never be good enough at anything like a marriage or a career. Everyone else thinks so too. I should have caught every error I ever made and I may as well worry about things that could potentially happen not just proceed with solving real problems.

A psychologist who was my coworker once said to me, "Faye, you do not have trouble solving real problems. You tackle real problems with little difficulty. It's just the problems you create in your mind to worry about that overwhelm you." He was so right. My untreated depression kept me distracted from my life. I spent useless time being troubled over irrelevant or distorted concerns.

Before I sought help from a physician I discovered my own way to comfort myself and calm my anxiety. When the bad feelings started, I would say, "Jesus help me." I knew that any other force would be less powerful. While some of the bad feelings stayed I was not afraid. Despite my obsessive-compulsive behavior I managed to do well in school and have friends. It was just part of my personality and I learned to live with it.

Despite all of my idiosyncrasies, I had a positive attitude. I believed in happy endings, apple pie and true love. I was glad to have my family most of the time. Even as a child I enjoyed being with the people I loved more than anything. We celebrated each others' victories. The holidays were eagerly anticipated as we tried to do them all with style. We had watermelon for the Fourth of July or corned beef and cabbage for St. Patrick's Day. We took vacations and when we didn't we would camp out in a tent in our yard. As a group we went blueberry picking or to pick out our Christmas tree. During the holidays, we picked cedar and had our own seasonal wreath business. We would get the neighbor kid to sell them and split the profit. We also took orders door to door. We had a fine reputation and deservedly so. I learned about business from these experiences. Most of time I remember being happy.

Now I was the adult visitor to my childhood home. It was frustrating to be there. Nothing they had lasted the tiniest length of time. It was frustrating to keep fixing up their home. Had they given up so long ago on having nice things or did the grandchildren really wreck everything? The house was warm as it was July. There was no air conditioner, just a fan that Mom pointed at herself to stay cool. The air did not seem to move and felt heavy. Mom had a screened window with holes in it next to her bed. The night air would make her more comfortable and the mosquitoes would keep her company.

To do a load of wash I had to walk down rickety back steps and into the basement, a dark cave-like setting which held the base of the coal chute. Besides the coal chute was a furnace and a small work area where Dad kept his tools. Along the walls were shelves for the food we canned and various odds and ends. Beside the furnace was a washing machine I had spent hours trying to talk Dad into purchasing years before. He was so rigid and uncompromising when a change was suggested, especially if money was involved. I explained it would be less than the cost of the laundromat and would pay for itself, never mind be a convenience. Somehow he came around. Of course with time it was all his idea. Who cared, as long as he did it?

He had never bought a dryer because it would be too expensive. So wet clothing was hung on nails in the basement. In the summer they could be hung on the line outside. Dad eventually did the wash himself and hung up the clothes, with mother's disability more pronounced than ever. Dad was not particularly convinced of anyone's illnesses but his own. If he did not see blood and lots of it or total physical deformity, the illness did not matter. There would not be respect given to acknowledge the illness.

However, once he was certain you had a legitimate illness, he would be quite kind. When a window slammed down on my little sister's hand, Dad freed her hand and drove her to the doctor. If he had to he would have battled his way through. Since Dad was off work around three o'clock each day, he was usually the one to bring us to the pediatrician. Once, Teresa and I had scarlatina and Dad was most kind to us with our fevers and bought us some cool drinks. With babies Dad was especially attentive. For teething pain he would hold and comfort a baby or small child for hours if necessary.

Looking about the house there was a lack of personal hygiene products and cleaning supplies. A sliver of Ivory soap was the extent of available self-cleaning items. An SOS pad with the color washed out of it was available to provide the edge against baked-on stains. They did not cook much. They relied on Meals On Wheels for most of their meals. They loved the service and the food. The luncheon portion was divided with half saved for the evening meal. Perhaps that was why food was in short supply.

I considered the tiny bathroom. For a long time, there was no hot tap water. We had to fill a large pan with water and set it on the stove. After the water boiled, it was carried with makeshift potholders into the bathroom and poured in the tub. The drain was stopped with toilet paper and a plug which never fit but was never replaced. Cold water from the tap was added to reach a pleasant temperature. Then you settled into a bath with about four inches of water. Amazingly, we were never burned carrying the water. Fortunately, by high school we had hot tap water and even electric heat downstairs. We felt like royalty.

I loved to study the Breck shampoo bottle and wanted to look like the Breck girl. I would look at myself in the reflection of the bathroom window to see if a transformation had taken place. Sometimes I thought I had changed a little. Usually I would console myself with believing, "Maybe next time." Besides, there were other products. With Prell I would shape my hair into a tall mound on my head as in the commercial. The details are scarce but somehow this made me a princess. The neighbors had Mr. Bubble bubble bath. We never had it but I longed for it. Our bubble bath at Christmas came out of bright bottles, shaped like an animal, usually a poodle, and smelled like perfume.

Fortunately, with hot tap water and heat we could bathe every day. Before the heat we had to sit by the metal grate where the vent was from the furnace. We would sit around it as though it was a campfire and dry our hair. The coal furnace could put out some heat. It was inconsistent, though. Upstairs there had been no heat. My sisters and I slept in a dorm-type room. We had the option of sleeping downstairs but we were used to our arrangements. As it was all we had ever known, it did not seem unreasonable.

It wasn't until I was older that we finished off the room where we slept with wallboard and painted it pink. Before then it had been intended as an attic. The walls had not been finished on the inside. Some mornings as a little girl I could wake up and see frost on the nails where roofing had been attached. A "frosty nail day" would be a cold one. Part of the room had pink fiberglass insulation with brown paper on the outside. The pink reminded me of cotton candy but I knew better than to eat it. The insulation made me itch if I brushed against it. Once, it even got in my bed, and it was awful. Somehow I managed to cover it to protect me from the irritating material and bathed to get the fiberglass off my skin. I learned to be flexible and roll with the punches. I learned to adjust to my circumstances as need be. I really didn't mind the way it looked as a child. As I grew older, I felt embarrassed for anyone to see our room. By then I had been to other homes and seen what my friends' rooms were like.

In the backyard I looked at the sacred ground of my animal graveyard. My favorite dog was Lisa. She must have been part Scottie and whatever jumped the fence. When I was ten, Lisa and I were inseparable. She slept at my feet every night. There were her puppies who had distemper that were buried and other dead animals I came upon. Whenever I visited, I prayed for them and fashioned a new cross out of the materials at hand. I loved all of them and cherished their memory. Soon the property would belong to someone else so I had to say goodbye. Future owners would never know how much the spot meant to a little girl, who even as a grownup made an annual pilgrimage to honor these creatures who had been part of her life. Nearby was a tree house we never quite finished but had a great time working on just the same. Taking my last look around the yard was bittersweet.

I was glad for my adult life and the nice home I had. Yet there was beauty in this yard where I had grown up. There was the creek I floated boats in, cattails and wildflowers, birds, chipmunks and an occasional skunk. The garden had been my Dad's pet project. My favorite produce was strawberries, with cucumbers a close second. We canned homemade bread-and-butter pickles. In later years he would grow mainly raspberries and had different varieties. He especially like the white raspberries. In the "picnic area" we used to grill hot dogs and roast marshmallows. I learned to love nature because my dad did. We had a very simple life. There was so much enjoyment to be found just being in the yard.

My whole life I had been told that someday the land would belong to my sisters and me. When we had nothing else, Dad would remind us how he would save the land for us. He saved it all those years. Now we learned the land was worth less than we expected because a creek ran through the property. All those years my parents struggled to pay taxes they barely could afford. Dad sold a diamond ring he had inherited so he could pay the taxes. He had been so proud of the ring. With Dad going into a nursing home and Mom unable to live alone, there would be no money to pay the taxes and upkeep, and money would be needed for their care. It seemed nothing ever worked out for us. It was a cruel joke. I was glad Dad would not know about the land, because if the stroke did not kill him, the news of selling the property would.

Chapter Fifteen

As my visit continued, I found my money was running out. It did not take long to go through the cash I brought with me and any other money I could get my hands on. I wondered if I had been generous enough with them. Most of the sheet sets I had sent Mom were neatly folded in a dresser. Sheets were definitely not a problem. Clothing I had given Dad was evident. They had dishes from me. As their daughter I was responsible for them. I missed my husband and children. I was in over my head trying to rescue my parents. Mom wanted constant attention. In one weekend I was supposed to make up for all the time I lived out of state and was not there for her. It was unbearable, perhaps because I was still waiting for her to make up to me for all the years I had to take care of myself.

My mother was coming around to accept reality. I told her it was exhausting to be there and I was spent. It was clear now Mom would leave. She would stay with Teresa. We were packing and discarding items. It might have been the end of the world. Mom suggested I take a vase from a floral bouquet I sent her. It was lovely but I told her to keep it for now. Later, I would regret not taking it. I did take some decorative glasses she wanted me to have, and packed them and sent them to my home. Also I was given two of my father's hunting rifles and sent them to my husband for the boys to hunt with someday. I looked at my mother so vulnerable and crippled. I loved my mother. There were just too many changes at once.

When my Aunt Kay came over and I was packing up a couple of Dad's rifles, I felt ashamed. He was not dead yet, although he would never hunt again. Dad always said he wanted his hunting rifles to go to his children. In no uncertain terms he requested they not go to anyone else. With the instinct I had about my family, if I did not get mine now, they would be gone. I wanted something of my dad's. However, they were not really for me. My husband would use them and otherwise they would be stored empty, with trigger locks, separate from the ammunition, in a locked safe.

Aunt Kay was actually my great aunt. I realized I was only projecting my feelings onto her. She was not a judgmental person. She was always there for our family. As I grew older, I especially came to admire her for her good deeds and genuine happiness for others to succeed. She was so pleased when I graduated from college and planned to go to graduate school. Now her face was sad as she talked about Dad. She had been at the hospital with him. She truly loved him and I was not sure Dad even realized it. His self-esteem was so low most of the time.

My obsessive-compulsive symptoms were worsening from all the pressure I was under. A phrase kept coming to me, over and over. The phrase was "bone picker." I had heard the expression from my husband, an anthropologist with knowledge of ancient Native American charnel house tribal practices, but it reminded me of buzzards cleaning up after finding a carcass. It was an unpleasant thought. Yet they had their purpose too in the grand scheme of things.

When our company left, Mom and I were subdued. She looked so frail. The past few days had been impossible for all of us. We were a family in crisis. My father's stroke was devastating. What was most significant and was the true "keepsake" of the day were the memories of the life we shared together. Not just holidays and graduations, but the everyday existence. The little things made up a family.

Mom put a decoupage picture of Hawaii I made in Junior Achievement in a place of honor by the phone. She would have a look of absolute adoration for any project we made in school. To her it was as fine as any Picasso. She listened to my stories about school or work. She lived vicariously through my sisters and me. When I got a job at Hardees, Mom and Teresa would show up in the evenings, Mom purchasing coffee and Teresa getting a soft drink, and sit at a table and watch me work. It may as well have been a ballet performance. They seemed so proud. It was embarrassing to a teen-aged girl yet sweet at the same time. Mom would sit with the biggest smile. It tickled her to see her little girl working in an orange uniform and scarf and ringing up orders on a cash register. The same look would appear when I would get up to dance at a reception. She told me how cute I was out there dancing. Mom was very much a family person. Anything her girls did mattered to her. She was a shy person and not particularly expressive or confident. Yet it was clear as a bell how she felt when she looked on with such pride. There were not enough times in her life for her to look so pleased.

In high school I was chosen to attend Girls' State. This was a week-long program to teach a select group of high school students about the American Government. The students were assigned to make- believe cities and elected governmental representatives. Only a few people from each high school were chosen. The American Legion was a sponsor. I was chosen to be a delegate and enjoyed the experience. I was the mayor of my city.

My parents were proud of me. My picture was in the paper and Mom sent a picture to every relative we had. She went to the newspaper office and bought some in bulk. We all were so happy about it. When I was getting ready to leave, I had spent the day before putting seeds in the ground for flowers to enjoy later on. While I was away Dad went out and bought several trays of petunias and planted them where I had put the seeds. He found such delight in how I would be amazed to see the flowers had grown so fast, especially since I had planted marigolds! He also brought me an armful of dried grass and said it was hay for the Mayor, which was a word play for "mare."

Upon my return, there was a banquet for me and the boy who went to Boys' State from our district. The speech I gave was probably the best speech I ever did. The boy who went before me was polite and basically said thank you. The host teased me when he introduced me because he knew I would have plenty to say. When I had concluded my speech, he said to the audience, "Told ya!" While I was giving the speech I saw my parents sitting there, all smiles, happiness radiating from them, like they had just won a million dollars. I was glad I had given them an evening of pride.

As people began to leave the banquet hall, Mom held back and whispered to me her slip had come undone. She only had one slip and she had fastened it with a safety pin. Our host of the evening spotted us and came over to us to escort us to our car. Mom and I made up every excuse we could think of. Finally, Mom's slip fell down and was around her ankles. I hated for that evening to be one more source of embarrassment in our lives. It had been so special. So we would not let it be. We leveled with the man who discreetly abandoned us and we laughed as we surreptitiously made our way to the car. On the way home Mom told me at least ten times how "cute and smart" I was.

Dad commented about the whole experience as, "That was something," and there was no higher praise in our world.

Eventually Mom had a taste of life as a homemaker. She was able to quit working because of her arthritis. She was eligible for disability. Now that she could be at home, she would wake us in the morning. She had not had the luxury of that in earlier days. My parents had more money on disability than they had when they worked. The quality of their lives improved. Groceries were not as hard to come by. If I had a test, Mom made scrambled eggs and link sausage and waved goodbye after breakfast, telling me, "Have luck." When I became sick, she waited on me and made me chicken noodle soup. She was trying to be all she would have liked to have been. Better late than never.

These were all things I would have liked when I was younger. Mom and I eventually talked about her quiet, reserved nature. I told her it hurt me how she seldom said, "I love you." She said she was not taught or encouraged to show emotions as her family had strict religious beliefs. You were supposed to know your parents love you because they worked hard to provide for you. From that day forward she told me she loved me at our partings. She looked shy as she worked up to it. She never missed saying it again.

Without having accomplished all I intended, it was time to go home. Mom was calmer. My younger sister Teresa was coming to help Ruth with lap two of the crisis. They were going to tackle tearing down the garage as it was an eyesore and unsafe. It had been a very difficult visit. My energy had been sucked out of me. Lots had been solved but there was still so much to do. Ruth had made it clear she would be making all the future financial decisions on her own. She was taking over. Being the oldest and living in town I supposed it made sense for her to do the legwork. She ignored my suggestions. A door had been slammed in my face. There would be no discussion of managing our parents' estate. Ruth would do all the deciding. Inside me was a struggle to either hang on tighter or let go of my desire to be a part of the planning. As a social worker I had seen families fight over a loved one's belongings or disposition before. I never imagined my family would be just as difficult and unyielding. These thoughts weighed on my mind as I drove to the hospital. I went to see Dad for what I knew would be the last time I would see him alive.

Chapter Sixteen

Dad was clearly affected by the stroke. He was tied into a wheelchair and not his usual self. Yet he looked at me, sounding like he had just come home from a vacation, and told me, "The baby is fine." He proceeded to list all the relatives he had visited, all of whom where dead in the recent past, as well as his grandmother who he said was taking care of him. While I knew stroke victims could be quite confused, it was still awesome listening to him. For a while, I just sat regarding him.

Dad asked me when he was going home and watched me with eyes as innocent as a child. It was one of the most difficult questions of my life. I knew he was never going home again. After saying, "I'm not sure," guilt feelings flared up inside of me. How do you tell someone that their life as they knew it was over, their spouse would be living in another state and their house and car would be sold? In addition, I would be leaving the state as well to go back where I lived and this would be our last farewell in this life. How could I tell him I would not be with him to hold his hand or feed him in the days to come as he had once done for me?

I closed my eyes in part to hold off any tears which wanted to be expressed. Too late they appeared anyway. I wanted to disappear. I feared he would read my face where I wear my feelings quite transparently. Yet why torture him with upsetting news if in five minutes he would not have remembered the visit? I gave him a kiss on the forehead and told him I loved him. With certainty I realized I would never see Daddy alive again. It occurred to me this was the same hospital where we had shared our first kiss. Only that time I was the helpless one and he was taking me home.

He rocked me, fed me and kept me warm. Most importantly he loved me. Even amidst his rages and frugal ways, he loved me. Of that I was certain. I walked away wanting to get out of the hospital quickly. Inside I was suffocating with the intensity of my feelings. As I made my way through the parking lot, I stopped for a moment, searching for his hospital room amidst the many windows of the brick building. With all my heart I tried to send him the message, "Daddy, I will love you through eternity. You will always be a part of me. I will remember you as the guy who let me ride on his shoulders across a trout stream, advised me never to do drugs and would check my eyes when I came home at night to be sure, and walked me down the aisle to join up with my husband. Mostly, though, I remember you as my daddy who picked me up and sat me on your lap and comforted me when I fell on concrete and busted open my lip I asked you if I was going to die and you assured me I was not. I would be fine.

"But, Daddy, we are all going to die, and it seems your time is near. Inside me are memories I shall share with my children about you. I hope, as you leave this world, you are glad I was one of your daughters. Because despite the difficult moments, the angry words, and never having enough money, I am glad you were my daddy. You worked long hours in the bitter cold, went without possessions of your own so I could have some and sat with me when I was sick or sad. Thank you for being my daddy. I always knew you loved me. Please know now that I will always love you too."

Leaving for the return trip home was a blessing. There would be no good to come out of a longer stay. I did not feel the usual feelings of being sad to leave yet eager to go home. I could not wait to leave. I wanted to be as far from those people as I could get. My mind quickly tried to sort through the circumstances. It was similar to a juke box sifting through the choices to get the song chosen. Tons of choices to choose and it was all done so quickly. My mind was working so fast I almost felt dizzy.

So many memories and feelings were upon me at once. My sister Teresa had her thyroid removed. It had been a rough time. The surgeon had not shown up because he went out of town at the last moment. It was one of those days when things just went wrong. They found a different doctor to operate, but it was unsettling. She had already been anesthetized and had to remain so until an alternate surgeon could operate. That evening Teresa's respirator malfunctioned and was caught in the nick of time. The hospital called my parents and Teresa was afraid to go back to sleep for fear she would suffocate. My parents had not been allowed to stay the night. My Dad decided common sense would prevail. He went to the hospital and insisted he be with my sister. He sat awake and held her hand for the rest of the night. Teresa told me Dad's comforting her meant the world to her as she did not feel safe with the medical personnel.

Dad came through for me too, on a long night of orthodontic misery. I was in college before I had braces. My braces had been adjusted by a new orthodontist one afternoon. My mouth was sensitive as it was sometimes after an adjustment. However, as the evening progressed I was suffering. It felt tender as I took a pain reliever and went to bed. In the middle of the night I woke up feeling like my mouth was in labor. I was having a rhythmic waxing and waning of pain every few minutes. It did not occur to us to call the orthodontist. We did not know how to reach him and did not realize there was an emergency number as we never needed it before. We also thought the emergency room would not be able to do anything for dental pain.

As I sat with my dad, crying and holding his hand, I remembered the pain medicine I was given when I had oral surgery. There was some left and I took it. My dad sat up in a chair and laid his hand on my forehead. He did not have a washcloth, just his cool hand. He asked if that was comforting and I told him it was. He said his grandmother used to do that and he felt so soothing to him. I finally rested some and we called the orthodontist's office first thing in the morning. We were seen immediately. The orthodontist was apologetic and told me I should have called him in the middle of the night. It was clear to him from the expression on my face I had been in agony. He made adjustments and the pain ceased. Later, two of the affected teeth needed root canals. I appreciated his comforting me.

Dad was supportive and kind most of the time. We knew if he could do for us he would. We also knew if there is not money for something it would be immediately forgotten. As children we were aware of our financial station in life. Teresa's birthday was right after Christmas. On her birthday Dad brought her to the dime store. There she spied a doll and buggy which captivated her. It was the finest looking toy she had ever seen. She played with it a bit, then walked away to pick up a coloring book for her gift. It was just a fact of life we could not have nice toys like that. There was no self-pity in my sister's choice of gifts. Dad had watched the scene and called on a sales clerk for help. He brought Teresa to the register with the coloring book. Dad paid the cashier and Teresa walked away with her bag containing a coloring book. Before they left the store Dad called Teresa back and told her she had forgotten something. He presented her with the doll and buggy. It had given Dad so much joy, to just once give his little girl the kind of present she deserved.

It was so sweet for Teresa to repay a kindness years later. On Teresa's first Christmas away from home she gave Dad a small diamond ring in a black setting. She had remembered through the years how special the other ring was to him, the one he had to sell. He cherished the ring and her thoughtfulness to buy it for him. We had our share of Hallmark moments. Mom had received a bottle of her favorite White Shoulders perfume. She sobbed and declared Teresa loved her father more, but even that could not spoil the joy. The gift from Teresa was not as large as the other ring but the thought that went into the gift was priceless.

Dad's life was made up of so many little pieces all woven together. There was always the dichotomy of the loving and protective father who would wrestle a bear with his bare hands to protect us, and the angry decompensated man who would scream at us and have temper tantrums when his frustration level reached its limit. At heart my father was a good man. The impatience he displayed was a manifestation of his psychiatric illness which was untreated during my childhood. It was confusing to know how I should feel about him. I would do anything to please him and honor him. At other times he was intolerable. I did know underneath it all I loved him. Right, wrong or indifferent he was there doing his job as father. He kept showing up for his job, day after day.

When I finally reached a feeling of peace with my thoughts of my father, I paused to drink my complimentary beverage the stewardess had brought me. Coca Cola on ice was refreshing. The meal did not interest me. The plane ride home was uneventful except for the trance-like feeling I had. Throughout it all I felt a calmness as I tackled tough concerns. There was so much to process. All the way home my mind ran in high gear. I thought about every relative we had and started drawing conclusions about their lives because I was suddenly gifted with a special ability to evaluate situations. There were no family secrets because I was capable of figuring everything out. I had never understood this well before. I knew everything. For every unanswered question I had the correct answer. Something had happened to me. I was clairvoyant. Finally, I found a degree of comfort and control. There was not a happy feeling, though. I felt I had been put through the wringer. In retrospect the plane ride was a glimpse of the illness which would eventually overtake me. As I neared home, I reduced my thinking of deep thoughts and started to relax. It would be great to be in my home again.

When my plane touched down on my return trip home, George was waiting for me. My haggard appearance was like something the cat dragged in. As I hugged him, I whispered, "George, it was just awful." Now it seemed George and the boys were the only family I had and at that moment the only one I wanted. Daddy was not the only one I was losing. Sadness enveloped me and I could not shake it off. The burden of my family relationships was wearing on me; it crushed my spirit. Had I never really known my family for this trip to be so hurtful? Or were we a family in crisis? These were difficult times. I was too tired to see things clearly. Or maybe what I was seeing was making me weary.

I was elated to see my children. Hugging the boys made me feel happy inside again. Clutching their Happy Meal toys in one hand they tried to climb up either side of me. They were sweet, adorable and so happy to see me. My mood improved the longer I was around George and the boys. After I passed out my "thinking of you" gifts, I sat back and enjoyed my family. What a blessing they were. Waiting on children was nothing compared to what I had just been through. Despite the disadvantages of my life, I had a beautiful family. I slept well that night and began to feel more like myself.

With morning came the realization I was still troubled about the conflict with Ruth. We had always been so close. What had always been a pathway to serenity had become a brick wall. I did not know what to do with the anger I felt at her for shutting me out. I was a member of the family and I deserved the right to be heard. I just wanted to discuss it. As a social worker I had vast knowledge of these issues. Mom had been more demanding than usual and I felt angry with her also. Of course Dad being so weak and vulnerable wore on me. It was still difficult to fathom that he needed to be in a nursing home. It had never crossed my mind Dad would have a lingering illness. So many losses and a few resolutions. She had not seen him up to that point and the unknown was anxiety-producing. I needed to resolve some of these issues.

I made a phone call the next morning with the intention of repairing my relationship with Ruth. The phone call left me feeling even further away. Losing my big sister's support was devastating to me. She was my confidante.

It was clear to me she would not meet me halfway at this time. She would handle my parents' affairs. My input was unwelcome. There would be no explanations. I was so angry. I made a decision to consciously withdraw. Trying any harder at this point would only frustrate me more. I was losing three of the people I loved most in this world. Dad was a stroke victim, Mom was an invalid and psychologically regressed, Ruth seemed distant and unapproachable. If losing Benjamin had been strike one, then my father's decline and my family's response was strike two of my ability to cope.

I was grateful my husband and children loved me in a way that could never be shaken. I believed these sad times would pass. The only thing you can be sure of is that things will change. Unfortunately, instead of experiencing a positive uplifting change, we went from the frying pan into the fire.

Chapter Seventeen

While reading the newspaper in January of 1995, I noticed an article about people dying because of defective pacemaker wires. "How unfortunate," I thought. My husband had to get a pacemaker one and a half years before. He was 38 at the time. His heart rhythm was too slow and was discovered at an initial check up at a cardiologist's office. He was immediately admitted to the hospital. He had recovered well and we seldom thought about the pacemaker any more. I started to share the story with George, then froze as I realized the name of the company seemed oddly familiar. Trying not to panic, I asked George to see the pacemaker card he carried in his wallet. It was the same company and model. This was impossible. I felt I might suffocate. There was not enough air in the room for me. I felt claustrophobic. There was nowhere to escape. My husband could die instantly from his pacemaker wire breaking and piercing his aorta. In the morning I could ask the doctors or nurses at the hospital. I worked with the cardiology staff as their social worker. We were in shock. The pacemaker was supposed to make things better, not be potentially lethal. Not only did I worry about my husband but all the patients I knew at the hospital. We phoned George's parents and shared the news. My father-in-law had read a similar article and wondered about George, but he was not sure of the brand name. Because he was a retired physician he probably understood even more than the rest of us the gravity of the situation. Clearly his parents were as worried as we were. I began to feel a level of agitation in my stomach and tension in my muscles. I could cry at the drop of a hat. I was a problem solver and usually took any situation head on. But I knew the wire would probably have to come out. There was no simple way. Other than finding out where the surgery could be performed and scheduling an appointment, there was little I could do to control the situation. George's parents shared in my frustration.

George initially said he would not have the wire removed. The surgery frightened George. It frightened me too, but I had inquired around and felt it was the only way. He was a young man and I could not live waiting for the other shoe to drop. The problem needed to be faced. I talked to him and his parents talked to him. We had reached a stalemate. George no longer wanted to discuss it. A phone call from George's sister Ann finally persuaded him to have the surgery. She pointed out that leaving it in was dangerous and the hospital he would receive treatment from was part of a medical center that specialized in this procedure. The most convincing part of the conversation was when she stressed he needed to do this so he would be there for his sons as they grew up. She reminded him to pray as she and the rest of the family would. I was grateful to Ann for her effort. An appointment was scheduled for the middle of February. We would drive to Baylor Medical Center in Dallas for the corrective surgery.

Sleep was next to impossible in the days before the surgery. A sinus infection left me feeling drained and added to my difficulty sleeping. Most nights I lay awake or would sit up and watch George sleep. He could die at any moment and there would be nothing I could do except call for help. If the wire cracked it could kill him outright. It comforted me to watch his chest rise and fall. For that breath I could relax. The strain of his medical problem wore at me. Feeling irritable and exhausted I had difficulty working because my mind was so frequently on George. My husband's doctor's nurse offered me some medicine for my anxiety. Having always prided myself on my strength I declined. I had enough problems without getting hooked on an anti-anxiety agent. Instead I toughed it out, feeling miserable and looking worse. Surely people would admire my stoic stance.

One day at lunch, I sat with my boss Kim and coworker Jamie going over the details about George for the hundredth time. I started to cry. Then I heard a subtle popping sound inside my head. Then I burst out laughing uncontrollably and could not compose myself. When I stopped laughing, I immediately began crying again. Never had I experienced anything like the mood swing I was having. I half expected someone to slap my face as they do in the movies with hysterical people. The strain was really getting to me. Talking about it brought me some relief. Basically I was a pool of emotions trying to concentrate and complete tasks. There was no relief. It was upsetting to work on a cardiac floor and hear stories about other patients struggling with the same dilemma, and having to reassure them when I was so afraid myself. Some of the cardiologists were extremely stressed about the news as well. It wasn't their fault the product was defective. Everyone knew that. They were so dedicated to their work it was unsettling to have patients so distraught. A great amount of effort went in to distributing information as quickly as possible.

I phoned my mother to let her know. It was hard to keep my voice steady. She said it was a shame and told me to call her when it was over. Mother was not the person to call in a crisis. Yet in telling her I felt a little better. I did not know where to turn. First I lose my son, then my father lays on the brink of death, and now my husband might die and leave me to rear the boys on my own. All the significant males in my life were either lost or in peril. I felt a hundred years old.

George's parents would be watching the children for us in our absence. They had come a little early for moral support. They were scared and were terrified they could lose their baby. Their concern for him was lovely. Unfortunately, as they strengthened their parent-child bond I felt pushed out of the circle. It comforted them to be with him and pamper him. George was so pleased they had come. I felt each comment I uttered and each gesture I made was being evaluated by his parents to determine if I were as loving as they were. We were all trying to get through the nightmare the defective product had created for our lives. I didn't know of any book which told the reader how to survive a medical catastrophe. What is the proper thing to say to your spouse when you are not sure he will survive a surgery? Does a crisis have to be the time to impress your in-laws? Who can you tell your fears to when everyone else is just as afraid? I prayed. I cried. I prayed some more.

Chapter Eighteen

The drive to Dallas was calm. George and I stopped for Mexican food along the way. As we munched on tortilla chips and salsa, I wondered about our return trip. Would George make it, or would I be going home alone? Was this to be our last day together? I tried to act natural to calm him. The social worker in me wanted to encourage him to express his feelings. Surely there was fear, anger and sadness. I had so many feelings of my own which I did not care to feel. Cheerful optimism or restrained concern ruled the day. Surely if I said it enough times it really would all turn out in a good way.

Meeting George had been a wish come true. We met in graduate school at a dance. We danced to a couple of Donna Summer's songs. He was everything I ever wanted. His blonde hair and tan skin set off his muscular body. With his casual but quality clothes he could have stepped right out of an Eddie Bauer catalogue. His field of study was anthropology and archaeology and he was earning a doctorate. Nice, intelligent, polite and easygoing, George's nature seemed a good balance to my own outgoing, exuberant and intense personality. He was comfortable listening and I had plenty to talk about. There was nothing pretentious about George. He was a confident man and a simple man. In his presence I felt all things were possible. He was the kind of guy every parent would want their daughter to bring home, clean-cut and ambitious. We both loved the outdoors, movies and going out to eat. It took no effort to relax around him.

On our very first date he showed up at my dorm room wearing an outfit exactly matching mine. I had a navy blue blazer, white blouse and khaki skirt. He had a navy blue jacket on over a white shirt with khaki pants. We looked like we could have been in a mixed choir. Also we each had an injury to a finger which had mildly deformed a finger, his as a result of a football injury and mine from my fingers being slammed in a car door. To me it was destiny.

On one of our first dates we had gone to a steak house. While I was ordering George very sweetly suggested I try a nicer cut of meat. The truth was I did not know about the differences in steak. Mostly though I was in awe. Quite likely it was the moment I decided to marry George. No one in my life had ever encouraged me to choose something nicer or more expensive. It seemed like so many of my dates were looking for the cheapest way out. They seemed relieved if I choose the least expensive item and often would make comments along that line. One guy marveled how if I got a Coke instead of wine the bill was much less expensive. Not being much of a drinker I was thrilled to please my date by ordering Coke. In time I likely would have switched to water to earn more points with him. Once, on a double date with this same man, I ordered chicken, thinking it would please my date as it was a low-priced item. After dinner, I commented on how the other lady had ordered lobster. Instead of praise for my being economical, my date responded that she ordered lobster because she had class. My definition of class was not buying the most expensive item; it was putting another person at ease and considering their feelings in a situation.

My parents adored George from the first moment they laid eyes on him. He loved to hunt and fish and to my dad that was the ultimate plus. Mom thought he was polite and nice-looking. He brought her a gift of butter-coated pecans and this was like hitting a home run with Mom. She asked questions about a rock she had found. Although she seemed to think he was a geologist it worked out because he had taken plenty of geology courses. In the past Mom suggested I not pamper my boyfriends so much. She told me not to smother them with, "I'm thinking of you" gifts. So I used restraint, which worked well because I was broke from having just finished graduate study.

Despite my worry over George being repulsed in some way by our poverty, he did not seem surprised or disappointed. I told him my sister had a shower and she lived just up the street. He responded that our little tub was just fine for him. After the weeks of stress, trying to get the house in order, I realized he was dating me because he liked me. He was quite respectful to my parents. Even when Dad brought George into the basement, about ten minutes after his arrival, and despite days of me pleading not to take him down there, I got over it. When George spilled fish blood on his jeans, he asked my mom if she could wash them for him. She told him it would be an honor. Even though I was embarrassed we did not have a dryer and had to put them on the clothesline in the back yard, everything went well. My fears of rejection disappeared.

After George's visit was almost over, Mom pulled me aside and whispered, "If he asks you to marry him, say YES!" I was way ahead of her. I had already decided I wanted to marry him. Mom and Dad had never encouraged me to marry anyone else. Perhaps Mom was swayed by the buttered pecans gift package he gave her. None had ever impressed them as George did. It was not just his education that impressed them, though it didn't hurt. The clincher was how he was such a nice guy. My parents had come to view me as having passed my prime for marriage. Once, Mom had told me a guy I dated was better than nothing. I had not agreed. Waiting it out for the right one had paid off. After all the searching, here was a man who made every other man I had ever known fade from my memory and every man I would ever meet pale by comparison.

The next week we stayed with George's parents. One of my first memories of them was walking into the living room and seeing George's dad helping his mom by making a surgical knot where she had been sewing on a doll body. They both seemed much less intimidating after that. He was a surgeon, which seemed awesome before I met him--before the knot on the doll that is. Now he seemed approachable. I admired him a great deal just the same.

Mrs. Shannon made dolls with ceramic faces, hands and feet. The bodies she would sew. She said it was her therapy. It was clear she truly enjoyed them. She also enjoyed giving them as gifts and they were given to her dentist, doctor, friends and family. Sometimes she sold them in booths at craft fairs.

Mrs. Shannon immediately struck me as a friendly person. Down-to-earth and unpretentious, it was easy to be in her presence. Dr. Shannon was incredibly dapper with his finely pressed clothing, not a hair out of place. He loved to watch the news and was very knowledgeable about current affairs. It took me a while to feel at ease with him. Apparently they had been told I had braces and tried to put me at ease by sharing how one of their daughters had braces in the past. They remarked it was a good thing. I was a little old for braces, as I had gotten them in college and paid for them myself. My sister Teresa suggested I get them. She felt they would enhance my appearance and give me confidence once they were taken off. I knew I would ultimately be glad I got them.

It was clear George was adored by his parents, as were all their children. As I sat on the sofa chatting, I wondered if they would be my in-laws and if one day we could talk without so much effort. Our lives had been different in many ways, not the least of which being they were Southerners and I was a Northerner. Our food, accents and expressions were different. We had a common interest, though; we both loved George.

They had more comforts than I was used to having. There was a bathroom in my guest room and as I washed up for bed I peaked into the drawers of the bathroom cabinet. In the drawer were no less than twenty-seven toothbrush packages. In addition there were many packs of soap, with Cashmere Bouquet being the most popular one. I had never seen so many personal hygiene products in one place outside of a store. A remedy could be found for any malady. There was an abundance of all things. It was such a contrast to what I had known. If we ran out of something, we had to wait until payday to replace it. Anything one could crave was in there. I lacked money to stock up on such items. There were even various perfumes. On the walls of my room were huge framed bridal pictures of George's sisters. They were so beautiful. The bed I slept in had belonged to George's grandparents. It was a brass and iron bed. The bed had a white ruffled comforter and dust ruffle and pillow shams. I did not think people really had things like that in their homes. I felt like a princess. It was even more special because I had new pajamas to wear.

The first night I had gone to bed leaving George and his dad in the next room. I heard his dad ask what our house was like. I held my breath waiting for George's response. George said we had a nice little house. I felt so relieved. It was a major hang-up for me. A day or two later, George's mom and I were chatting. I learned she had grown up during the Great Depression. The day would come when we would try and outdo each other with our poverty stories. If I were at peace with myself the rest would fall into place. Besides, I had worked hard for everything I ever accomplished and nothing had ever been handed to me. I had made my own way. I was secure in my abilities to adjust to situations accordingly.

My reflections shifted to when George and I had only been dating a short while. I went with my mom and sisters to visit my dad's sister, Aunt Betty. She could always be counted on to be at every family function and to organize the routine of a sick relative. She was born to handle a crisis. When my mom was in the hospital for gall bladder surgery when I was in fourth grade, Aunt Betty came to help out. Since it was the first day of the school year, she accompanied me to my class. I was so proud of her because she dressed so nicely and wore a yellow dress with a flaring bottom. She had a matching little jacket, high heels and a beaded necklace. Her figure was in good shape and to me she might have been a movie star. Her confidence entered the room in front of her. Things ran smoothly when she was in charge.

No visit to Aunt Betty's was ever dull. This visit on a warm summer afternoon was no different. Mostly I thought about George since he would be visiting me soon. Being as colorful as the rest of us, Aunt Betty took out her fortune teller's cards and worked up our fortunes. She told me to think of someone but not say who it was. I picked George and my question was, quite predictably, will I marry him? The answer was yes. She then began to relate my future. There were love, money and many obstacles to overcome. Despite the struggle the cards always showed, "The lovers come out on top." George did not put much credence in fortune telling, but he liked the phrase and would bring it up after we had tackled a difficult problem. It was such a positive inspiration.

I brought my mind back to the present pacemaker wire crisis. George was too young to have to face an ordeal like this. He just had to be okay. We needed him. The other question which loomed over us besides life or death was, who was going to pay for it? The hospital where I worked and where the initial procedure had been done had only implanted a device they thought was safe. We registered at the hospital nervous about payment but knowing we needed to proceed and would sign over our home if necessary. Whatever it would take.

I quietly worried and prayed. Trying to be sure the details were in order I busied myself with forms and fine print. I quietly reassured George. His doctor comforted George and me while meeting with him. He did not seem afraid to do the surgery. I felt a sense of hope. Yet the operation loomed before us as like a rapid moving stream we had to cross. While in many situations I could be dramatic and demonstrative, when it came to the really big stuff I wore my feelings in my eyes. Quietly I whispered to him my positive thoughts and with tears in my eyes kissed him on the cheek. He was brave, at least on the surface. When he went to surgery, I felt relieved. We got him here and we were doing everything we knew of to do.

I entertained myself while George was in surgery by wandering around the hospital halls, never veering far from the waiting room. The waiting room was like the one at the hospital where I worked. Family members supported each other and became fast friends. If a phone message was left it was guarded until the visiting family was found. There were a lot of prayers and tears as anxious family members waited for news of their loved one. I overheard as families met with their doctor and imagined how I would feel hearing good news. However, I practiced in my mind how I would respond if the news was bad.

When the good news arrived, I could have kissed the doctor. He was my hero and I was so impressed by his skill. George was grateful and pleased as well. We returned home with hope and gratitude. We also left with rain and overcast skies. I drove as George certainly could not. It was a gloomy and rainy day. I was lost before we left Dallas. Hating to drive, especially in the city, the drive took forever. George was sore and tired. I was just plain exhausted.

As soon as we arrived home, we were greeted by my in-laws, who were clearly relieved by the results of the operation. I was happy for them as well as for myself and the boys. No head of state ever received more tender loving care than George did as he recovered. It was great having someone else running the house. I was weary of the strain. At the same time I am certain his parents were ready to rest after watching the boys. Still, something was wrong with me. I could not focus on tasks. I was so tired most of the time. George's parents doted on him, which was quite logical given the ordeal we had been through. My energy wavered and I felt his parents were annoyed because I was not being nurturing enough to George. Never mind that George was playing it for all it was worth. I did not do things he was capable of doing for himself.

Each evening while they were visiting I ate a small dinner and went for an after-dinner walk. The walks increased in length and time. Soon, I was walking for miles in the dark to meet my goal to lose weight. George's parents were very health conscious and I felt self-conscious about being out of shape. Also it was expected the walk would help me relax. It was nice to have a break from the children. I was surprised no one praised me but instead suggested I was gone too long. There was a tension between George's parents and me which usually was not there.

As I walked, I would compose letters, speeches and research reports on the effects of a medical crisis on families and hospital staff. I would be a specialist in the area of defective medical equipment trauma to patients and families. Since I worked with heart patients, some of whom were facing the same ordeal George and I had, who better? It was the best part of my day. I was consumed with the topic, perhaps because I still saw patients on a daily basis who faced the surgery. Everyday I had an instant replay of my own fearful moments. The good news was George was recovering well.

George's parents left and some tension remained. I loved George's parents as they had been quite good to me over the years. They had said for a long time that I was their fifth daughter. Now I was not sure they even liked me. It made me sad, but on a deeper level, I was too exhausted to care. I no longer had energy enough to care about a lot of things.

My collection of people who I felt estranged from was growing. My sister and I had clashed about the management of our parents' affairs. We were barely speaking but forced ourselves to because Dad was dying. Mom was ill herself and basically unavailable. In my heart I knew all my fantasies of Mom making up to me for all the disappointments of childhood would never come to pass. Even George irritated me. I felt angry towards him. He had been doted on enough in my opinion. He was going to be fine. I seemed to lose more support each day and I felt very alone. There was no one to comfort me. I felt like I had lost everyone and it was just as well because no one was sincere. Besides my children there was no one else who loved me. It was a very lonely time.

I decided to take care of myself. Since my sinus infection had ruled my life for several months, I pursued treatment. After giving me a CT scan of my sinuses and finding some of them blocked, it was recommended I have a sinus wash to cleanse my infected sinus. After declining George's offer to accompany me, I went alone. I was doing some major feeling sorry for myself and was a little afraid as I headed for the ENT's office.

The procedure was successful but I really could have used help getting home. It tired me out more than expected. It was difficult to drive with my nose still draining. The fluid was making spots on my dress. I was angry at George for not coming. When he asked if he needed to come, I said no, but hoped he would come anyway. He owed me, I figured, after all I had done for him. I was run down and could not regain my strength. I was being pulled downstream without a root or a branch to hold on to. In every way I had come undone.

I was given antibiotics and steroid nasal sprays to help me recover. Weary of steroids, I was somewhat apprehensive. After a steroid shot months previously, I had not slept well and became extremely fragile and labile with my moods. I yelled at my husband and father-in-law in public. The prescription for a Medrol dose pack was not filled due to my worry over my moods being altered. Using steroid sprays seemed harmless. I did not discuss my concerns with my doctor. Later, I would consider they may have aggravated my mood swings.

Sleep had not come easily since I learned of George's medical concern, and my insomnia persisted. The over-the-counter sleeping aid only worked for 4 hours. Since it had the same ingredient as Benadryl I could not continue to take it. My doctor told me not to take Benadryl. It dried up my sinuses instead of allowing them to drain. My nightly shortage of sleep continued. I had not slept through the night in two months. The time I did not spend sleeping gave me more time to think and perhaps ruminate about my life. I made an attempt to solve my lack of sleep and asked a physician I knew for an antidepressant. News of my father dying was all around the hospital. The samples I received were for one of the newer antidepressants. I was proud to put aside the shame and acknowledge I was depressed. But like the steroid sprays, I would later call this a mistake because of the possibility of antidepressant medication triggering manic symptoms in someone predisposed to mood disorders without also taking a mood stabilizer.

Chapter Nineteen

Once again, sleep eluded me as it had every night for quite some time. Four hours of sleep a night was about the maximum. Yet I could not lie quietly and relax. My mind raced through topics examining any idea or person I thought about, seemingly in every way all at once. Now Dad was the subject. My mind was flooded with images of him. I wrote my father's eulogy in my mind. So many impressions of him came to me: Daddy teaching me to fish, teaching me to make a sundial, taking me to the day-old bread shop for Persian rolls. Dad would sit at night and cut up leftover pantyhose into little squares and put a small portion of spawn on each square. He then took thread and tied it off so it made a round ball. He stored them in empty baby food jars in the refrigerator to use for bait.

It intrigued me to watch Daddy search through his tackle box the way a doctor looked through his black bag. He knew each piece of tackle and what it was capable of in his pursuit of fish. I enjoyed the shiny items. My favorite was a silver spinner with red and white paint on it. At times he would share how his grandfather had taught him to fish. He still had some lures his grandfather had given him. No matter what people thought of my father there was never a question whether he fished well.

Sitting atop my father's shoulders as we waded across a trout stream, Dad's waders keeping him dry, was a great way to pass the time. I felt like a woodland princess when Dad would identify the plants and trees for me. The land near the trout stream was my kingdom. My love of nature began on those outings. On a rainy night another adventure was to get a flashlight and an empty cottage cheese container and walk down the road after the rain to look for night crawlers. I would spot them but let Dad pick them up. He was considerate that way.

In so many ways he was a wonderful father. I especially appreciated him waking at night if it was extremely cold and building a new fire if the fire went out. We had a coal furnace. At other times, in addition to the fire, he would get coats to lay on us over our blankets. He said he could never stand for his babies to get cold.

He had a majestic smile, beautiful white teeth, big blue eyes and a handsome face. When he smiled, his whole face would light up and his eyes would sparkle. As he aged, his dark hair turned white and was quite becoming. When he came into a room, you noticed, whether he was in fishing clothes or dressed up. He had presence. He loved to tease and make corny jokes. When he teased you, it was his way of showing affection. There were times he did not sense appropriately when it was time to stop. A joke can be carried too far as to be painful in repetition.

As a teenager, I pretended to be annoyed when he would try to be funny. His Quasi Modo imitation was quite believable to be sure. He loved to tell my friends, and eventually dates, stories about me as a little girl. There was a "Faye as a little girl running away from home" story. This was not to be confused with the "Faye reciting the Longfellow poem about a little girl, having a curl, right in the middle of her forehead" story. It was embarrassing to me, yet I was secretly glad for the attention. Externally I rolled my eyes and sighed.

To this day, it is impossible to see strawberry ice cream and not think of Dad. Of course there were numerous trips to get banana splits or dip-top cones at the Tastee Freeze. An occasional change from ice cream was a frosted mug of root beer at the A&W. One pleasure we shared as a family was eating. Whether we went blueberry picking and made blueberry pie or grew cucumbers for bread-and-butter pickles, preparing and eating was often a family affair. Dad knew about living off the land at a time when many people were modifying their lifestyle to the more modern way.

Dad initiated planning for a camping trip out west because I had told him about all the different states I had learned about in Geography. We bought a large blue tent from Montgomery Wards and a sleeping bag for each of us. We joked about the tent being large enough for the circus. We saved for the trip and bought something each payday. My bag was navy blue on the outside and had ducks on a yellow background on the inside. Mine was the most unique but no one seemed jealous. We hitched Dad's boat and trailer to the back of the car and loaded up our gear. A canvas covered it and it worked out reasonably well. A high point in the vacation was riding past the Cody, Wyoming, Chamber of Commerce because they had answered a letter I wrote to them. They even sent me brochures. We did not stop for me to introduce myself and to inform them I was indeed a tourist in their town. Maybe next time I was in town.

I went home with a black cowboy hat and memories of my family having a good time. I had captured the memories with my Christmas present, a Polaroid camera which took black and white pictures I could develop instantly. It was priceless to see Mt. Rushmore, painted canyons and Old Faithful, the geyser in Yellowstone National Park. The biggest thrill was Custer's Last Stand. I remember looking at the exhibits and reading from a journal a soldier had written in throughout his tour with General Custer. Museums and history fascinated me and my family. We stopped at every museum we could afford to see. Dad had planned the trip to please me. We were studying American History in school. It was nice having someone plan a trip especially for you.

It also felt special to have your father track down a neighbor boy who had thrown a rock at you. The boy was told to follow my father to our home. On my front porch Curtis looked at me with the utmost of sincerity and apologized repeatedly. He never threw a rock at me again. Nor did anyone else in the neighborhood.

Dad was our protector. If there was a knock on the door in the night, my father would answer the door with a shotgun. He had been in World War II and was always prepared. We never had any trouble. He was not a big man, only five foot six, but he had plenty of common sense and intuition about people. He was a survivor of his parents' divorce and abandonment. His father never returned to be a part of his life. His mother did and saw his children and spent time with him after he grew up. The scars of those relationships were branded on Dad's heart.

I have never had a satisfactory answer as to why his mom could not care for the children. Someone thought it was alcohol. After hearing she died in a state mental institution, I felt it was probably mental illness. My aunt swears the treatment she had was for diabetes and heart problems. She said at that time the hospital admitted regular patients. I did obtain the death certificate and it cited diabetes, heart disease and renal failure. She may well have been diabetic, but there must have been more to the story. I barely remember her. Mom said she worried about me because I was so frail and Donna used to pound on me as older children tend to do.

Reportedly she was a brilliant lady who was fluent in several languages.

She did not take care of my dad for most of his life. I hated that my dad grew up wondering what was wrong with him because his parents were not there. The details about his father were also sketchy. After his parents divorced, his dad moved away to the Detroit area.

We heard from relatives he worked designing car doors for one of the major automobile companies and did quite well for himself. I never met him, yet he was a significant force in our lives even after his death. When Dad was in an argument and someone expressed displeasure about his behavior, he would say, "Yeah, well, my father did not want me either. He walked away from a little boy who did not know what he did wrong." The pain was always in his heart.

Dad rebounded fairly well and after the war he met and married my mother. They dated for a year. Mom's father gave her away. Dad's grandmother, who reared him, was there for him. Mom's aunts gave her the wedding as her mother had died. They look happy in their wedding photos, young and hopeful with a world fill of opportunities, looking fresh and strong before life slapped them in the face. Mom wanted to live near her sisters. Dad wanted to return to his hometown and felt he had the best chance of employment there. They lived where Dad decided to live.

Dad was charming, funny and handsome. Mom was shy, fun-loving and pretty. Dad swore Mom owed everybody in town when he married her and said he paid them all off. Mom never refuted this claim. Money would always be an unresolved issue between them. Mom would think Dad much too controlling and tight and he saw her as an impulsive spendthrift. Perhaps somewhere in the middle was about right. Ultimately they never had enough money to live on.

They were of different religions which was a serious difference in those days. Dad was Catholic and Mom was Protestant. Dad always felt Mom's family did not consider him good enough. Allegedly they doubted the marriage would last six months. Dad was determined to make a life with my mother. Mother was a saint to him in many ways. He had the enthusiasm and the drive for hard work. In his heart was the foundation of love to build a family on. There had been another side to Dad, though. The endless demands for money and food wore on him. No doubt he worried where our next meal would come from. He had a bad temper to be sure. Especially if he was tired. Working two jobs, he was tired a lot.

Chapter Twenty

Dad tended a vegetable garden and hunted or fished to supply many of our meals. When times were hard, Dad would come home from work and scream about the dishes not being done or another domestic crime. He would yell for a while, eventually throwing dishes or anything else he could get his hands on. Mom usually deflected any criticism coming her way to us. She usually blamed us for whatever the offending behavior had been; the kids did not clean up, the kids did not put that away, or the kids did not do the dishes. Perhaps we should have. Mom had arthritis and was tired after her day of physical labor. She cleaned houses or worked in the kitchen of various institutions.

When Dad yelled, his face looked scary. His eyes popped out and his face got red. At times he took his belt off and hit us with it. It wasn't so bad if it hit our bottom but if he missed and got our backs or legs it was quite painful. He never hit Mom, although the verbal tirade usually punished her. He would finally exit and go outside to cool off. Mom always cried and said she could not take it. My sisters and I would comfort her. She seemed so miserable and overwhelmed. Why Dad had to upset her all the time did not seem fair.

The beginning of my social work career had been counseling Mom at these times. Most of her adult life she had probably been depressed. It was as if she just gave up one day and decided to coast through the rest of life. She sat around waiting for someone to give her the next push.

To consider both sides, Mom was not an energetic housekeeper, nor did she teach us any kind of discipline to approach housework. We also did not have hot water and at times only well water. Cleaning supplies were scarce, food was more essential. Many of our dishes were chipped or broken due to Dad's fits or from children handling them. There was little in our home that was not fit to be discarded or burned. There was not enough linen for the beds so we slept on bare mattresses at times. My little sister did not have a bed until she was in 4th grade. She slept on the couch with coats to keep her warm. There was an antiquated washing machine but clothes had to be hung on the line or in the house to dry. There were countless obstacles to overcome and some days it did not seem worth it to try. Mom said she did not want pretty knickknacks as Dad would probably break them anyway. Often Mom would give things away or sell them at a ridiculously low price. While in elementary school I was playing with a floor-to-ceiling lamp and spinning it. One of the three glass globes broke. I felt so bad because it was Mom's favorite thing. Besides, she had already lost so many things because of my dad. Now I was adding to the list of casualties. I waited up to confess but fell asleep on the easy chair. When Mom came home, I sat up half-asleep and told her. She did not seem disturbed and told me she could replace it. She was so understanding.

Our family pet Spike was a black and tan dog who was as meek as they come. We adored Spike as he had a gentle disposition you could not ruffle. Spike was known to stand at attention when my sister Donna came into the room and started singing the melody of an Italian song from a spaghetti commercial. Spike would immediately break into a little dog dance shuffling on his paws and turning in circles. He did this throughout the eighteen years we had him, even after he went blind.

When Dad would start on a tirade, Spike would walk straight up to him, tail wagging, and stand in front of Dad. Dad would immediately soften and bend over and pat Spike on the head and say, "Look, he's afraid I'll hurt the kids. It's OK. The kids will be fine." Dad loved the dog. When Spike approached him in this manner, it calmed my father and helped him get past his bad mood. This worked except for once, when Dad became enraged over some matter related to money. He sat protesting the latest twist of a financial crisis which never seemed to end. He continued on with his complaints and not finding relief for his rage, he reached over to Spike. He started choking and shaking the dog. Spike did not return the aggression in any way. Dad stopped upon the screams of my sisters and I, and let Spike go. Spike cowered and hid by my sisters and me. There was absolute silence for a time while we comforted Spike and glared at my Dad. This was unacceptable to us. We silently filed out of the room with Spike. Dad instantly regretted it, I could tell. He shook his head. Sadly, taking his anger out on the dog did not make his problems go away. If Spike had been a sacrifice it had all been for naught.

I suspected Dad wanted to cry but could not have done so in front of us. I know he worried so about the bills. He needed someone to turn to. Mom did listen to him ruminate about bills. She was very patient that way. He was troubled and everyday stresses were too much for him. He needed comfort and somewhere to turn.

I wish the Catholic nuns at Dad's school had not criticized and beaten him so much. Since Dad would not allow us to use the word "stupid" to describe anybody, I suspect the nuns had told him he was stupid. What a shame, since I think he had a learning disability. He would have trouble separating the way the nuns treated him from a positive relationship with God. He often said "More wars have been fought in the name of religion than anything else." Perhaps that generalized to punishment in general. While it was human beings who treated him harshly, they justified their behavior in the name of God. They were representatives of God. His Catholic school was a source of trauma for him. If he was in trouble at school he would be in trouble when he got home because his grandparents did whatever the nuns suggested. He would get another switch when he got home.

When he tried to get closer to the church as an adult, I suspect he would remember the brutality and back away. Perhaps he generalized the abandonment of his biological father to that of his heavenly father. His own father left and never looked back. He was not a comforting and supportive source. While Dad was spiritual, I wish he could have found a greater sense of peace during the hard times.

Spike returned to his revered status in our household. Now he was a martyr and if necessary we would defend him in anyway possible. Unfortunately Spike was not the only one to be treated in such a manner. I attended the Catholic church and catechism class on Saturday. On Palm Sunday we were given new palms. We were told to dispose of the old ones which we kept behind pictures and put the new ones up. I mentioned to Dad I was going to take care of the palms. One way was to burn them and another was to bury them. Instead of doing it his way I did what the nuns had said.

Dad asked me later what I did with the palm leaves. I told the truth. We were standing behind the wreck that was our garage. I had defied him in favor of the church. He became irate. He reached over to me, cursing as he put his hands around my throat and shook me. Inside I was panicked. He had never done anything like this before. The strangulation attempt seemed to go on forever. I did not think he would kill me intentionally, but I knew he could without intending to do so. He was so strong. It was like Dad exited his body at these times and someone else took over. The differences were so extreme. He might patiently help you work on a project for days yet in a tantrum destroy it in a matter of seconds. At almost any other moment Dad would have died defending me from harm. But when the crazed behavior appeared all bets were off.

When I was released, I made tracks to get as far away as I could. I took the martyr approach in my mind. I had stood for the church and what was right. The Catholic church was right and so was I for following the teaching of the church. I must have overlooked the "Honor Thy Father" commandment. It hurt to have disappointed Dad. His approval meant everything to me. His behavior was something I accepted about him. It was the way he was. I did not like it, but it did not occur to me he was out of line to hurt me. Perhaps even more painful than being choked or watching Dad strangle the dog was when Dad would stand in front of the mirror and choke himself. He would say we were killing him and ask repeatedly if we were happy now.

Without missing a beat he would comment about his father not wanting him and it was no surprise we did not care either. He was the breadwinner of our family and our protector from everyone but himself. If my father wanted to die because of the burden we presented for him, it was a very sad day indeed. It was all too much for him. I felt responsible. As soon as I could I began baby-sitting, selling seeds, peeling logs or any other respectable work to pay my own way. In junior high I bought my own clothing and entertainment. When I was older, I paid for my own braces. He would not consider welfare; he was too proud. Every day he faced the world. At times I suspect he was afraid where the next meal would come from. He had responsibility and did his best to rise to the occasion.

My father's outbursts would coincide with where we were in the paycheck cycle. On payday all was well. Dad bought Paprika chicken and potato salad from the deli at the IGA. All sins were forgiven and there was hope.

The further we went along having to make ends meet the more troubled Dad would become. He paid all his bills in cash and would drive to each business to pay them.

Going out to a social function always led to my dad throwing a fit. However, once he blew off steam, we would go and have a nice time. The only hard part was as we drove to the event I was still mad. While Dad bopped around greeting people I was trying to lighten my own mood. Usually if we were going out it was to a wedding reception. I would usually be wrapping the gift when the griping began. Perhaps the price of the gift would upset him. He always wanted to give a good gift because he believed someone was keeping track and would eventually return the favor to his daughters at their weddings. Yet the gift would cut into grocery money. We really could not afford to give the gift, which was always nicer than anything we had at our house.

I didn't know if it was the gift or the idea of socializing with others that created the tension. We rarely had nice dress-up clothes. I know it bothered my mother. Or maybe running into acquaintances was stressful. It may have been feeling excited about going out that pushed the button. I never figured it out for sure. But I did know there would be the Saturday Night Special, episode of rage. Once past this, the evening usually was very nice. Dad would dance extremely well. He enjoyed the music and food.

Dad's tantrum behavior also manifested itself outside the home. While riding in the car Dad would be pleasant and talkative most of the time. He would dim his lights and courteously let other cars cut into the traffic flow if he saw they were really trapped. Sometimes he would sing and tell stories. But then there was the fifteen percent of the time when he was overtired or angry about something. He became a scary guy. He did not direct his anger at other drivers, though.

If he felt his opinion or directives were being challenged or did not like one of the suggestions we would toss out, he would get furious faster than you could blink. He would grip the steering wheel firmly and announce, "I am going to kill us all!" and he would floor the gas pedal and start choosing a tree to hit.

Mother would beg, "Don, don't! Calm down!" and in the nick of time he would slow down and drive appropriately. He had made his point and we could move on.

While it should have been so obvious, it was years before I pieced together how my father had been mentally ill most of my childhood. He was functional though and that made it trickier to determine. He held a job and even had Blue Cross insurance. So many times I had tried to push it out of mind or find a way to make it logical. I thought he just had a bad temper. I did not think of him as abusive. We never were deprived of a meal. He would never let one of his children or their friends have to walk home after a movie or school event. He never systematically tortured us as I would read about some parents doing. We never walked around with bruises or burns.

When we were little, we would be hit on the hindquarters with a belt. This was a common practice in the families of my peers as well in the early 1960's. That stopped while we were still in elementary school. From time to time there was the choking thing. My sisters and I remembered. I never knew the basis for the behavior. Ruth said when she was in arguments with her husband or with anyone she would be really angry with, she found herself having trouble speaking loudly. She would clutch her throat as if some impediment were there. Years later, I would be attending a workshop on group therapy and the man leading the class commented about different participants. When I was described, he said there was a lady in red with her hand at her throat. I had been too afraid to express my feelings during the class discussions. Remnants of Dad's emotional storms lived within us.

One of Dad's strange habits happened when we had a journey of any length in the winter months. Most men would go out to the car, brush off the snow so they could see, and warm it up, allowing the windows to defrost. When the car was of adequate temperature, they would signal to their womenfolk to come to the car. Dad had a different take on this. His style was to go to the car, brush the snow off and sit in the car until the last person emerged from the house and got in the car. This could be five minutes in extremely cold weather. When the car door closed after the last person entered the car, then and only then was the car started. The car was not warmed but immediately driven, with Dad seeing through a peephole where he had cleared ice and snow away.

Chapter Twenty-One

One of Dad's most embarrassing ventures to me was the worm farm he kept in the basement. Worms were advertised for sale on a haphazard sign in front of the house. I cringed when anyone came to the door wanting worms. If Dad was not home it was a no-go. No way was I sticking my hand in the dirt for a worm. Worse than the contact was the knowledge we made money selling worms. It distressed me.

Another of Dad's unique interests was that he loved to speak the German he had learned in the war in front of my friends when he picked us up after a movie or skating. His all-time favorite words were "mach schnell," which is the German equivalent of "hurry". Sometimes he spoke it to me if we were waiting in line at a store together. It was not clear if speaking German was supposed to impress people or amuse them. I studied German for three years but he had an ear for it, and was better at applying it to casual situations. I learned to request that someone, usually Hans or Fritz, go to the blackboard, to the map on the wall, or to the library. The applications for German in my everyday life were thin. Dad, however, was a legend, and some of my friends may have never realized he could speak English.

Thoughts about my dad stayed on my mind. The pieces started to come together--his anger, his eccentric behavior and his excessively talkative nature. The talking was the most comforting to label, somehow. It had been a source of embarrassment for years. If the family went for a ride to look at Lake Superior and get an ice cream cone we often stopped to allow Dad to chat with the fishermen. He would walk on the dock or on the shore. He would begin a conversation which was a nonstop monologue. Or if some acquaintance passed by him in the grocery store Dad would chat interminably. At my graduation from graduate school my dad cornered a classmate of mine and my classmate seem to be suffering and without the considerable tact it would take to end the conversation. It was nothing for Dad to chat half an hour or more with a virtual stranger.

Later in life, I would see a man who attended some community functions and talked endlessly. It was difficult to be polite to him because if you kindly listened he would never leave. I witnessed a conversation between this man and a physician after a gathering. The physician was so polite and never interrupted or seemed annoyed. The gentleman went on and on, never reaching the point. He reminded me of my dad. It hurt to think of him as the village eccentric. In a way he reminded me of Belle's father in *Beauty and the Beast*. Belle's father was an inventor and clearly marched to a different drummer. I wondered as I watched him if there was really a genius inside trying to get out. My dad was always coming up with little ways to make improvements. When we had our wreath business at Christmas time, Dad found ways to keep improving our product by changing how we attached the cedar, what we attached it to, and so on. Show him a problem and he could physically demonstrate a solution, by drawing it or building it, with great detail. He enjoyed quiet time for working on his projects and he enjoyed being the center of attention.

There was a time when Dad did have his bit of celebrity. He was asked to call out bingo numbers for the Catholic church bingo night. The host of the game was in control, got to talk the most and everyone wanted to be his friend. He enjoyed it and was becoming the mild celebrity host but it all ended when the regular fellow returned. It was like Dad had found his niche and then he had to give it up. He also had his picture in the paper for catching the largest coho salmon anyone had seen in a while.

It was disturbing to think so much about Dad's life and how it would soon end. I had always been linked with my father in a spiritual way. When he was harmed, I instinctively felt it. One night, he was later than usual coming home. I announced that Dad had been in an accident before the phone rang. I could feel it. Also, I knew he was all right. Now the tie was gone. The connection was broken. I felt the essence of my father had made a departure.

Chapter Twenty-Two

When I did not sleep well, I would go to another bedroom so as not to disturb George. I would look in on the boys. Then after my early morning awakening I tried to make peace with the sadness of my past. The feeling of being unloved dominated my thoughts. My dad had questioned his grandmother's love, just as I was questioning if I were loved by any of the people I loved. He always felt she cared more for his big brother. It was nice to know that when Dad died he would be buried next to his grandmother. My aunt owned the site and gave it to him as her family already had other ones. There was poetic justice after all. Dad ended up in the place of honor. Life had so many twists and turns.

I was confused about my feelings. It seemed like all my relationships had shifted to less positive than before. I wondered if they had changed or if I had. The most likely thought to me was that all the others had changed or I was much wiser now and could read people more clearly. There were so many questions on my mind. Sadness weighed heavily on my shoulders. I was not sure of anything.

On one of my evening walks, I looked up at the sky so predictable with the dark, clear sky and the stars appearing with their white lights. As I raised my eyes, I remembered about wishing on stars, particularly the first one. I wished for someone to love me, understand me and comfort me. I felt so alone and unwanted. I desperately needed a friend. Perhaps more significantly, I prayed as well. I was afraid life would never be all right for me again. George's close call had just about killed me. On top of Dad's dying, the threat of losing him was horrifying. I knew the pacemaker problem wasn't his fault. I was still very afraid. I had lost Benjamin, I would soon lose Dad, and I did not want George to leave me too. Maybe some distance would help. Maybe I could protect myself if I was not so involved. Besides, we had been quarreling. He said I was irritable. He said I was talking to myself more than usual. I always had a little. My thoughts were coming faster now and it was hard to communicate my feelings to George.

I kept forgetting little things like where I left my keys, my purse or even my car. My energy level fluctuated from none to plenty. I still could not sleep through the night. George was becoming my enemy. He told me I was talking to myself more than usual. I always had a little. Each day I thought of more reasons why he did not deserve me. I imagined my life away from him to be much more fulfilling. Feelings were blended together and generalized. My thoughts began to come rapidly and I pondered so many thoughts at once. I thought it was just an adjustment to the stress.

A few evenings later, I lay on the floor of the room we called our library, I felt very sad and unable to cope. I turned the lights off and lay face down on the floor and pushed the *Cosmopolitan* magazine to the side. It had a love quiz and my life was so confusing. The magazine was a hand-me-down. I would have felt uncomfortable buying the magazine as I had historically been conservative in my choice of magazines. I read an article and tried to think about it and felt a need to refer back to a passage. But when I did the article was changed. It happened more than once. This frustrated me. All of a sudden life was overwhelming to a degree I had never experienced before. I rose and turned off the light to keep my thoughts from spinning and lay on the floor. George opened the door a while later and switched on the light. He seemed puzzled by my situation. He suggested I go to bed.

I went to the guest bedroom and dressed for bed. I dressed up in one of my finer gowns. Now I had the light on and was looking around the room. I fixed my hair and put perfume on. I felt like royalty. I started to get the giggles. I thought how absurd life was. I was caught up in thoughts that confused me but beckoned me to keep searching for their meaning. George came into the room and just looked at me. I reminded him I wanted to sleep alone now. When I chuckled in the midst of our conversation, he just looked at me for a long time. This only led me to burst out laughing. He was the one who was weird as far as I was concerned. I held my secret thoughts for company.

Some of the thoughts were far-fetched. Thoughts like how I was being studied by a team at the FBI and how they wanted to hire me to assist them in the Mental Health Division. Also when I had bathed I was hypnotized by the light reflecting from the ceiling light on the chrome fixture of the tub. I would then be interrogated for long periods of time about all sorts of things so they could learn all they needed to know of me. The more I thought about them the more believable they seemed. While I slept he whispered questions to me about my childhood, adolescence and college years an I unwittingly replied.

That evening there was a hailstorm. Hailstones the size of golf balls were falling. I went our onto our porch and watched the storm. I was wearing a white cotton nightgown with ruffles on the sleeves. During the storm, I twirled around like I was Stevie Nicks in one of her videos. Leaning against the pillar, the world seemed enchanting. Nature was still the master as I witnessed the hail hitting our cars. Everyone in the neighborhood was in bed, as far as I could tell. It was close to midnight. This moment existed only for me. I felt like I was in a trance.

For some reason I thought of Edna St. Vincent Millay and a poem I had read to my American Literature class in high school. The poem was *Renascence*. The words flooded my mind. I felt like I was in the poem and all of the description identified where I was. I looked in an old set of encyclopedias and read about her. One of her works listed was *Conversation at Midnight*. The title intrigued me. Most of my new and confusing thoughts had occurred around midnight. She must have titled the work to reach out to me over the years. She knew I would come along and identify with the title. I alone would understand what this conversation really was. She too must have had an admirer who sent messages into her mind. Suddenly I knew she could understand all the strange feelings and thoughts I had been having, for surely she had them too. I was needed to help mankind. I was up to the challenge of the mission on which I would embark. I stopped questioning the thoughts, stopped resisting the seduction to be a better person. The odd ideas took hold. I was psychotic, my manic depressive illness had me pinned to the mat and was about to take me on a magic carpet ride through hell.

Chapter Twenty-Three

"George is threatening to poison me," I told my friend at work. "He bought fire ant poison. He left it on the counter. It worried me because the children could have gotten into it. Then I realized he intended it to be a warning to me. If I did not stop talking about leaving him he might hurt the children or me. Sure, he did not come straight out and tell me what he would do. He was too smart for that."

I did not think we were compatible and I was considering a divorce. There was such a well of anger inside me. Everything he did disturbed me. Just because he had been sick he expected me to pamper him forever. When was it my turn to be pampered? His presence was like an evil eye wanting to know the slightest move I made. He would poison the children or me if I continued to pull away from him and the ant poisoning on the counter was the message. The fact there were numerous ant piles in the yard did not occur to me. Each day seem to overwhelm me more. I was not sleeping and the strain of exhaustion taxed my reserves of patience and rational thinking.

It seemed George was determined to humiliate me at every turn. He left a gift in my car. It was a tiny hippopotamus with a poem. I saw red. He must have thought I was too dumb to see his subliminal message. I was supposed to understand I was fat and no one else would ever want me so I should stay married to him. He had always bought me tiny animals as I collect them, and I had loved adding to my collection. But it felt different. I believed he wanted to humiliate me.

What ticked me off the most was the songs he would sing in my presence. After I told George of my plan to leave him, I could hear him in the shower singing Kenny Rogers' hit, "Lucille". If he was trying to make he feel guilty it did not work. The only feelings I had for him were anger and rage. He initially minimized my protests but when he found a card for an attorney in my purse he took my threats seriously. Why he felt justified looking through my purse was another matter. He had never done that before. He always seemed to be studying me as of late. His expression was puzzled and irritated.

Surely I deserved a kind man who would pamper me and value me for being myself. It just so happened there was such a man. Someone did adore me and worship me. Every hour of the day I was on his mind. No detail was too small. This was love at last. For once, someone really knew me and loved me.

I had not told a soul because I needed time to plan. A man was listening to me with listening devices. At first I thought it was just at work but with a growing realization I figured out he was listening to me at home and in my car also. During my bath, I had been hypnotized by the light in the bathroom and was interrogated while in the tub. No words were spoken out loud but mine. Questions would appear in my mind about some aspect of my life. One question was, "Would I leave my family and go to work for the FBI Mental Health Division if they cured my sister of schizophrenia?" I said I would. Much of the interview was blocked out of my memory. A team of FBI professionals listened to me. I was initially mad when I found out.

Once I realized the monitoring was a compliment, it did not upset me any more. I was an outstanding person to be observed in this way. Since my observers were a team of professionals and I would soon be one of them, I relaxed. It was frustrating, though, to get mixed signals about when my day of departure would be. I would feel an impulse to go meet with him when I would hear someone mention a time of day. I was certain it was a signal to me. So I would head out in my car just driving around until I felt an inclination to turn. If and advertisement on the radio caught my attention it would become my destination because he was sending me the message as he controlled the radio announcer.

Every time I set out to meet him, he would not be there. Once, I went to a bookstore and once, to the mall parking lot. On the visit to the bookstore I wandered around looking for him. I was drawn to the Poetry section and felt compelled to open a poetry book. There I would find poems he had placed there just for me. After waiting inside, I went back to my car. A car passed in front of me and it occurred to me it might be him. I was in pursuit and followed the car for miles. Before long, the car disappeared. So I suspected we were playing hide and seek. I would turn down side streets randomly. I kept going further away from the city and had an urge to turn right down a back road. The road was bumpy and dark. There were no lights anywhere and it occurred to me I had no idea where I was. I was mad and just a little worried. I knew he would see me home, though. I fussed at him and told him how I felt about his absence.

"You could at least show up! I have been sitting on pins and needles expecting you to come to me. I keep a Tic Tac in my mouth at all times so my breath will be fresh. Today I swallowed one whole. I wish you would present yourself. I am beginning to think I am psychotic. Anyone else would think so if I tried to explain our relationship." Not long after scolding him I saw a light in the distance. He had come through for me. I knew he would. I just had to remember he monitored me at all times. I pulled into a driveway and while I was wondering if I would finally be meeting up with my dear friend I noticed a man and woman staring at my car from the window of the house I had pulled up near. For some reason I felt afraid and turned the car around and left to make my way out of the forest. Amazingly I made my way home. I decided the no-show was a test of some sort. I was on a need-to-know basis and he would eventually explain it all. Since it seemed I was about out of people who loved me, I needed him more than ever.

Chapter Twenty-Four

There had been a close call at work. It was when I first realized he was watching me as well as listening. This became apparent when my coworkers were talking to me. Their words were messages from my secret pal. They complimented my outfit. That is how I realized he could view me. I ran to shut the light off in the office I shared with two other people. I was sulking because he had not told me he could visually observe me. What if I had acted weird or something or my makeup was smudged. What if he could see me in the Ladies room. As I stood in the dark waiting to forgive him, my boss appeared and told me she had called my husband.

Kim told me I was acting strangely because I had sat at my desk all morning staring into space. I had worn the outfit I had bought for my father's funeral and she thought that was odd since he had not died yet and most people save a new outfit for the event. Also, it was unusual for me to stand in the dark muttering to myself. The muttering to myself part was not totally unusual, but doing it in the dark was a change.

When George arrived, I did not want to see him. He and Kim persuaded me to leave. The whole time I protested I was fine. I wanted to stay and communicate with my new friend. Then I realized I could do that at home just as well. Of course I did not tell them about my admirer. George asked me on the way to the car, "Do you have schizophrenia, like your sister?"

I could not have been more insulted. When he mentioned my seeing a doctor, I hit the roof. "I do not need to see a doctor."

George added, "When you went into the bathroom, the cleaning lady walked out and said there was a woman in the bathroom talking to herself. Faye, if this is a joke or some attempt to get out of work, you'd better stop it right now! You might lose your job. This is not funny or cute!"

My story was it had all been a misunderstanding. He was overreacting and so was my boss. I knew I would need a cover story for Kim, but I had until Monday to come up with one. George suggested I talk to a psychiatrist we knew. I told George that would not be a good idea. I was just stressed.

If I talked to the doctor and told him of my behavior he might think I was psychotic, because it sounded like I was. Since I was certain I was not, I took a bath to relax, to be followed by a nap. That should placate my husband. I had not been sleeping well and George knew that. Maybe a nap would make me a new woman.

George interrupted my bath and ruminations. He said, "I'd better sit with you. Kim told me some pretty weird stuff you were doing. Turning the lights off and talking to yourself and telling people there are listening devices. I think we should call a doctor. Jamie said to call a psychiatrist. I feel like I should watch you. You might try to drown yourself."

I said, "I don't think it is possible and I have no intention of harming myself, I promise. There was a misunderstanding and I will straighten it out on Monday. I just need a bath to relax and a nap." What I could not tell him was there was a new life awaiting me. I was not completely sure how, but I knew big things were coming. There was a man who loved me now, so I had every reason to live. The details were not clear yet because I was on a need-to-know basis. Any time now might be the moment. He was not just any man, he was an operative with the FBI. My life was suddenly as exciting as a movie. It was also a delicate situation. Absolute secrecy was needed by me to protect this covert operation.

The situation had begun as a routine assignment for a gifted FBI employee. He was supposed to study me and my reaction to stress. There was a secret project with high school graduates from the year 1975 being studied. It was a coincidence my high school reunion was that year and the packet I received sat on my desk. I had been selected, as many others had, to be studied. The agent had to observe me and learn everything he could about me. If deficiencies occurred they were corrected by the agent whispering to me so quietly the suggestions would appear as thoughts in my mind.

The agent had patiently studied me for some time. I was not specifically sure of the duration of time. He decided I was the most wonderful person he had ever observed. His conclusion was I was cute, kind, generous, smart and truly gave my best to situations. He of course noticed I was hard on myself but that had its charm also. He believed I was fabulous and I desperately wanted someone to think so. Here at last was unconditional regard. The identity of this man changed throughout this time period. Sometimes it was a boy I went to junior high school with who grew up to be a genius with computers and had introduced the program to the FBI behavioral scientists. Just as I had grown accustomed to this identity a thought would send me to my yearbook to double-check all the males I knew in any grade level. No particular identity seemed to stick. I eventually threw some of the yearbooks away.

George and I went shopping. It seemed like a good idea to get out and relax. We split up as we usually did. Instructions appeared in my mind. I was to select a wedding outfit for myself and the guy. He would come behind me and purchase the wardrobe after I selected it. As I made rounds of the store, I found a lovely cream colored suit which would be tasteful for a second wedding. For the groom-to-be I chose a brown suit. When it was time to meet George at our designated meeting spot, I was on time and face aglow. I was supremely happy. It would not be long now. Besides the wedding clothes I had examined some other pieces of clothing and suspected my better-half-to-be would surprise me with them. My life would be like that from now on.

When the agent's identity changed, it was not to upset me. It had been necessary to withhold information for the well-being of the project. Whoever he was, he was the best thing in my life and he had come to me as my daddy was leaving me. I pretty much felt Dad was the only person who loved me, besides my children. Now there was someone to lean on and to see me through. I was really important to him. He was with me all the time and I felt comforted. The loneliness that enveloped me at times was dissolving.

In those dark days of my father's illness, George's health situation and the general unrest with my sisters, he was a shining star of hope. He was smart too. Of course it is easier as an observer sometimes to notice solutions. He knew I felt overwhelmed by the expense of our home. He gave me the idea to sell it and buy a smaller home. I took his advice and pressured George to agree. There was merit to the idea. George saw this as a chance to placate me and went along. What George did not know was I might be leaving at any time. The day scheduled for an open house I was wearing pajamas when the Realtor arrived. At any moment I expected the staff of my observer to arrive and groom me for my departure. Then a limousine would appear, like in the movie *Pretty Woman* and I would be swept away to a land where there are no problems which cannot be solved. The open house was canceled and I lay on the dining room floor weary and disappointed.

I had not been picked up yet. Like the other times, he was a no-show. However, I overcame the minor setback because the timing must not be right. I had to be patient. I was in the big leagues now and could not appear weak. Besides I wanted to be an outstanding person and that required sacrifice. There was an opportunity to serve my country and be happy at the same time.

When I returned to work the following Monday, I made my way into my boss's office. She was kind and I am sure she knew it was awkward for me. I proceeded to tell her a long story which was supposed to explain the incident a few days before. As creative as I could be at times, it was difficult to fabricate a cover story. She seemed to accept it, but would tell me later the whole time I talked to her I kept looking around her office for cameras. I was watched by boss and coworkers. I tried to act as normal as possible. There were moments I pulled it off, but not very many. Kim had received calls from several people who were worried about me. Kim told me to take all my vacation time and get myself together. Fortunately and perhaps divinely, I was blessed with a graduate student from Grambling State University. Linda had an extremely pleasant personality and was a quick study. She hit the ground running and took on many of my responsibilities so patient care was never compromised. Meanwhile I was told to not come back to work until I had seen a medical doctor.

I now blamed everything on George and this seemed to placate people. I had made a concerted effort to demolish George's reputation so if I divorced him, there would be no criticism. Indeed everybody would be happy for me to find a kinder man. They did not know I already had. With the momentum building in the trash-George campaign I moved out of my home an into an apartment with my coworker Jamie and her daughter. Jamie said as a Christian she felt it was right to help a friend in need. For days, I had been pouring out my heart to her about the misery in my life. She kindly offered to take in me and the boys until I got things straightened out. I doubt she had any idea of what she had gotten herself into. The day I left my house I went to Jamie's. I managed to bring Hunter with me but George had already been picked up at daycare by his dad.

As I sat outside my friend's apartment, I had a temporary change of heart. I did not want to be there. I wanted to go home and have my life back. It was scary and lonely. I missed my family and wanted all of it to go away.

But then my mind changed again. It was necessary to do this so I could have a better life. The night before I had knelt on the floor and prayed to God and confided what I intended to do. However, I said if it was wrong to end my marriage I hoped he would lead me on the right path. I had made a vow to my husband and I tried to honor my commitments. If it was wrong, then no matter what I would stay in the marriage.

I wasn't enjoying myself being home. Staying at my friend's apartment was difficult. It was so nice she had offered to help me out. I read several books. It seemed each time I opened a book at random the passage I found was about me. Even articles in magazines were put there for me. My friend at the FBI must have done it. He was very powerful.

While driving in my car I would have conversations because I knew the agent was listening. At times I would tell him stories and laugh and gesture. While at a stop light in the midst of a particularly funny moment I looked to my side to see the lady in the next car was staring at me. I expected her eyes to pop out of her head. She could not seem to turn away, as though she was mesmerized. I knew I must have looked unusual yet its not like I needed to explain myself to her. After a while, I wondered if she was staring at me to ridicule me. Finally, the stop light changed and we went our separate ways. I felt a little embarrassed but soon remembered it was not significant because I would soon be serving mankind. One horrified expression would not chip away at my self-esteem. It would take many horrified expressions to do that.

Chapter Twenty-Five

    Instead of giving George my usual share of money toward the house payment, I leased an apartment instead. As I was given a tour by the apartment manager, I giggled as I followed her around the complex. There were no worries as I believed I could afford any apartment in the world. Everywhere I looked was a message from my observer. Even the apartment numbers were a code for me to break and I pondered the significance of each number. No number was incidental, they each had a meaning to my life. A number 3 was because I had three sons, number 57 was the year I was born. When I combined the numbers and related meanings, I put them together for my unique interpretations. The numbers had to be just right so I would know it was the apartment I should pick. I had thought my days of apartment living were over. I did not much care for them. However, I would only be there a short while before my new life began, so not to worry.

    As I waited for the day I could move into my own apartment, the call came that my father had died. I was temporarily staying with Jamie, who had been kind enough to take me in. So many times I had wondered where I would be when I learned Dad died. I had always thought it would be at work. Never did I think I would be living in an apartment with a coworker and without my husband and children.

    I picked up the phone and asked for the details. Ruth had received the call a short time ago that Dad had passed away. It was a blessing as he had been so sick. The head nurse told me later she prayed every morning Dad would be dead when she came to work as he struggled so with his chronic obstructive pulmonary disease and congestive heart failure. I felt a cushion around me so my feelings were protected. It had finally happened. Surely the world should stop revolving at least for a little while. My daddy was dead. I had prepared for the news since high school when he had his first heart attack. Reality is just never the way you think it will be. It was supposed to be all over at once, not a year of misery.

    George and I were fighting like cats and dogs. He was glad to take

Hunter while I was gone. He seemed angry each time I spoke with him. I screamed at him and hung up on him when he was rude to me. He would not buy me a ticket to fly home to Michigan to my dad's funeral. This made no sense to me. How dare he act like that in the face of my father's death? He had canceled all of my credit cards. How was I supposed to go back home? Even through psychosis I understood the financial situation I left him in and the expenses we had. It was so unlike us to mess up our bills. I had left George on the spot financially by withholding funds. Also, since I always paid the bills, George was unaccustomed to my records. It was so confusing. I wanted George to be there for me yet at the same time I never wanted to talk to him again. Our finances resembled my dad's at the very end of his life. Eventually he called me back and had the means for me to go home. By then I had found help from my church.

There was a female minister at our church who had counseled me when Benjamin died. I asked her for help. She arranged to get me the ticket. I had seldom asked for help and it was so nice to receive it. A few weeks before, George had talked with her about my unusual behavior. She had recommended a marriage counselor. I had many excuses not to attend the session. By then I was already well into my delusion so I was not open to solving our marital problems. I insisted George and I had no chance to reconcile. She suggested I leave the door open as she had seen other improbable situations resolved in a positive way.

Meanwhile, Jamie had gone to the hospital where I worked and collected money for me. It was touching to see how much money she gathered. Some of the people gave checks and my peers in the Social Work office had given so generously. It was all so awful. There should not have been such a scene. George said his mother had asked him if she should send flowers to the funeral. George had told her not to send them. Under the circumstances it made sense. At a deeper level I had been friends with George's mom for so long I missed her support during this horrible time. Jamie dropped me off at the airport. Feeling exhaustion and some relief as Dad's suffering was over, I flew home.

Chapter Twenty-Six

When Ruth picked me up at the airport, it was like we had never fought. She was my big sister again. She dropped me off at our parents' home. I went to bed as it was the evening. A few hours later, she returned with my niece Jessica and sister Teresa. They woke me up and we all went out to Mr. Donut to visit. It was fun sitting there at one a.m. and cutting up. After a while, I said it was time to get down to serious matters. I asked everyone what their favorite memory of Dad was. Since I was giving the eulogy, I needed to know. Teresa was the first to chime in, "I especially enjoyed being hit with a belt, myself!"

Ruth countered with, "I cherish the memory of my prom date's headlights shining into the garage with the rickety doors falling off. I begged Dad to fix it."

I added, "I looked so forward to Dad's endless advice. For financial advice he would say, 'Make it while you can make it, kid' or 'You make money with your head, not your hands'. For advice on cooperation it would be, 'If we work together we can move mountains.'"

Jessica brought us all to a more reverent spirit when she shared how Grandpa had been good to her. We got quiet then. How could Lake Superior lap against the shore without Dad there to fish for coho salmon? He loved the woods and probably could have survived a winter in the wilderness with just a Swiss army knife and his understanding of nature. Our moment of silence was interrupted by the drunken ravings of a local high school teacher who was sitting at the counter of the doughnut shop. It was great to be home again! We decided our lives had not been so bad after all. At least Dad did not drink.

As I sat with two of my sisters and my niece, I felt loved. Perhaps the crisis of Dad's illness had brought out the worst in all of us. We had a bond. We grew up together and had a history. Despite the sadness of the funeral the next few days we spent together were some of the best. I persuaded them to be mad at George. When I tried to share about my other relationship, they grew quiet.

I told them a man just worshipped me and cared so much about me. I think they doubted my story. The really difficult to believe part I left out. Since he and I had never had a date or even had coffee and I knew nothing about his personal life, my sister Ruth could not follow why I was sure he wanted to marry me. Surely it would not be a good idea to tell them about the cameras and all. It was okay if they did not believe me completely because it would not be long before we would be together. I would bring him to meet them. Then they would be shown my word was good. I would not rub it in, though. It probably was hard to believe such a fabulous relationship had happened to me. It had felt right to tell them no matter what they believed. As usual I would come out with a neat solution for my life. I had to be patient with them because they were not capable of understanding the great things my life was about.

I told them I talked to a doctor and that he had given me an antidepressant. In all fairness I should have made an appointment and gone in for an appointment and reviewed my history with the doctor, instead of a phone call. Since I had talked to a doctor they left me alone. Dad's death was hard on all of us. Nothing seemed normal anymore.

My other sister Donna had listened to my desire to divorce George and my numerous complaints. She had schizophrenia but was incredibly empathetic most of the time. She did not support my idea of divorcing George. In her opinion evil forces were at work and I was not thinking clearly. She thought I should try to work it out. It annoyed me I could not sway her. Her opinion mattered. She was like the conscience of the family.

Dad always said there would be no one at his funeral. He had been so wrong. I was amazed at the people who came to honor his memory and to support the family. I was especially touched by a man who had known my father as a little boy. He said when the lights would be shut off at the local ice arena Dad and his brother would climb up a post and put the lights back on so they could keep skating. He also said Dad loved to build boats. The man was so impressed that Dad had built a beautiful boat from scraps of wood. This was a hobby Dad carried into his later years. The ships he made were now at Ruth's home.

The funeral and the visitation were held all in one afternoon. Mom had surgery on her hip the day before Dad had died, so she was absent from the funeral. She was in Idaho and recovering in a Veterans' hospital. It occurred to me she must find it difficult to miss Dad's funeral. Maybe it worked out the way it was supposed to be. Her health prevented attendance at family functions so many times. She might be relieved to miss the funeral. It had been a long time since I considered what Mom's feeling for Dad were. They had been married nearly 50 years but there had been a multitude of hurts along the way. She had been unable to care for him at the end, but I also suspected she did not want to have to wait on him and would not have considered it.

My Aunt Kay sat with us and several people thought she was our mother. I appreciated Aunt Kay so much. She had supported all of our school fundraisers and probably purchased whatever candy Mom could not get to first. She was widowed while her children were little and had to be all things to them. She reared two sons into becoming wonderful men and they had the greatest respect for her. As she sat with us, I remembered how she had often been quietly in the background offering support through many traumas. When Dad had bypass surgery, she stayed near him and cared for my mom. Surely there is a special place in heaven for Aunt Kay. She looked great too.

My sisters and nieces also looked good. Teresa, Ruth and I had gone to the mall earlier in the day. Ruth had her hair done and I had a makeup session at Merle Norman's. I had lost weight and was pleased with the black crepe suit I had bought for the funeral. It was elegant. After so many years of scraping by, it felt good to stand before the visitors with the confidence that comes from feeling good about your appearance. My nephew who had been so troubled on a previous visit looked cute in a white dress shirt and dark trousers. His hair was combed back with water. He seemed more at peace and behaved fine throughout the visit. I decided he would do well in the medical field someday because he had such energy under stress. He was also such a smart kid, with an IQ of 130.

Donna and her family came but did not want to sit in the main room and instead sat off in a side room. I was delighted she and her family had come. Most of the people I loved were together.

Chapter Twenty-Seven

I slipped out of the funeral home during a lag time to get something to eat just down the street. I limped down the street because my black patent leather shoes did not fit well. There was nowhere to sit so I left with my meal. When I returned to the funeral home, I had a slice of pizza in my hand and a Coke. Just as I was ready to take my first bite, the funeral home director approached me looking irritated. No doubt he saw his beautiful carpet and plush furnishings about to be stained with tomato sauce. He said it was against the state law to eat food too near a corpse or something like that. He told me I could eat in the smoking area. Since I am allergic to smoke, I tossed the food in the trash.

My best friend Jackie had arrived to witness my being confronted. She smiled her best, "Oh, Faye is into something again," smile. The Ethel to Lucy, "I don't believe this" look. We chatted and quipped comments. I had decided by now the funeral director must hate me. However, I also believed every man I saw that day was hopelessly attracted to me. Since the ceremony would be starting soon, I excused myself to put on more lipstick. Since I had already applied lipstick several times, it was probably unnecessary. Yet I wanted to look nice. The entire staff of Behavioral Studies at the FBI would be watching me give the talk. Could you really have too much lipstick?

I had selected a list of my father's favorite songs to be played before the service. The songs that reminded me of my father most, due to his frequency of singing them, were "El Paso", sung by Marty Robbins, and "The Green, Green Grass of Home", sung by Tom Jones. I announced they would be playing a polka also. I expected either the "Beer Barrel Polka" or the "Too Fat Polka", as I had requested them and Dad loved both songs. He taught me to dance with the "Too Fat Polka", and when the song would start, he would call to my mother, saying they were playing her song. There was no polka. The absence of accordions should have been my first clue. No one challenged me about the obviously unlikely judgment of playing a polka anywhere you could not eat pizza.

There had been so many flowers one of the florists sent an extra rose as was their policy for multiple orders. I knew though that it had been arranged by my friend. I whispered, "Thank you," discreetly, as I got ready to talk. The talk flowed freely and for a while I felt like my usual self doing another public speaking gig. Despite my almost relentless anger towards George I hesitated to tell anyone I had filed for divorce. For a few moments, I did not want it to be true. It had not been so long ago that I had been happily married. I did not want them to think I had failed or had been wrong all those years ago.

Strangely I did not think I had been wrong. I was always proud of George's accomplishments and my family had always been proud of him also. Yet I began focusing on my delusion again and its presence won out. It was like being possessed in the movies. You are not running the show, your disease is.

I was calm as I began the eulogy but then a point would hit home and I would become more emotional. At those moments I realized my daddy was really dead and then I would slip back into the denial veneer. When it was over, my cousin said he had never heard a eulogy quite like the one I gave. One minute he would be laughing and the next minute crying. It pretty much described my moods, and my life.

George had written a eulogy for my father. It was well written and kind. He asked me to read it at the funeral. I implied I would but tossed it into a drawer to save for the boys. The boys would not be at the funeral anyhow and I decided George was undeserving to be a eulogist for my father. He had given it to me before I moved out. It just did not seem right for George to be part of the funeral with the way things were. Dad liked George, but my wishes were more significant at this time.

Teresa, my "baby" sister, was patient when I assigned the task of reading from the book *Lifetimes* to her preteen daughter, Jessica. Teresa was divorced from Jessica's father and had basically brought Jessica up herself. Her daughter backed out after I had tutored her on the matter. Perhaps it was a little much to spring on someone who knew nothing about it beforehand. I was determined it must be read. Teresa gracefully stepped in and read it. She told Ruth she did it, although reluctantly, because it clearly meant so much to me.

Teresa was dear to me and we had many wonderful times. It upset me terribly when Teresa came home shortly before her graduation from high school and announced she had joined the Navy. A recruiter had been talking to her and sold her on the idea. She wanted to see the world. My parents had not been included in any planning. I was so disappointed because I had dreamed we might attend the same college. I was going to attend graduate school in the fall at Michigan State. She had not sought out my opinion about this and I felt angry.

Her choosing to make decisions independent of family members was the most difficult part of Teresa to accept. It seemed she would take the word of a total stranger over her own family. We had been so close. It was unthinkable to me how she would not be around to shop, ride bikes or go out to eat. She was my friend as well as my sister. She was ready to take wing. I knew each of us had to travel our own path. Teresa had a way of communicating her feelings so intensely with her big blue eyes. They held wonder. I had to let her go.

The day she left my father, Teresa and I stood in the yard in front of the dilapidated garage. Dad turned away as she prepared to leave and tried to hide his tears. He understood, in a way I did not, she would not be the same person when we saw her again. Life would lead us in different directions. Our family unit had changed. The girls would be gone. She was grown now as was I. When Teresa left, my tears were for the sadness of the departure. In my mind I would just pick up where we left off the next time I saw her. It was like she was going away for summer camp or something. I was naive. The totality of the situation did not register with me.

When my first boyfriend broke up with me, Teresa listened to my sadness and comforted my fears. With her help I faced the reality that the relationship ended. What good could come from being with someone who did not love you? She told me there would be another man who would complete before me. She was sure of it. He would buy me a nice house and as we drove around town she would point to houses and say I would have a house that nice. She convinced me there would be a man who truly loved me and not to give up. The part which was the clincher was when she said we would have children and in the back yard we would have one of those tacky patio tables with an umbrella on it. She was certain my husband and children would be crazy about it. I would tolerate it because of their joy. I believed her. Whenever she gets that tone of voice and expression, I still do. Now she was the one with the tears and Dad was leaving. This time she and I knew life would never be the same.

After the funeral was over, I waited for everyone to clear out so I could have a moment alone with my dad. I bent over and kissed his forehead and said goodbye. I felt like someone was watching me and I don't mean the FBI surveillance. When I stood up after kissing my father, I turned to see the funeral director watching me. He looked at me as though I was peculiar. It was as though at any moment he expected me to twirl a baton on fire and march around the coffin. I resented the intrusion. I was a social worker and I knew people did much stranger things than kiss a deceased loved one on the forehead at funerals.

At the reception following, I updated Jackie about the state of my marriage. I left out the part about my intended. Sitting at the table amidst relatives and friends, I listed George's transgressions. The more private the better. I wanted everyone's blessing when I married again. Our sex life, financial status and disagreements were an open book whether people wanted to hear about it or not. No detail was too small, indelicate or irrelevant.

Chapter Twenty-Eight

One of the people sitting near us was my father's friend Paul. He was actually our godfather. As we were growing up, Paul was a welcome presence in our home. He would sit around and talk and could easily be begged into buying us a treat. If we needed a ride home we could call on him if Mom or Dad were busy. Every Christmas he would come to our home after my sisters and I had gone to sleep and leave a gift for us, just like Santa. In the early years it had been candy and toys. In the later years, it was money. He was single and I once tried to fix him up with the mother of one of my sorority sisters. They were not compatible. He had always been appropriate with his behavior and kind. He was like an uncle to me.

When I graduated from graduate school at twenty-four, I returned home thinking about a new job and my delight over having met George. Paul gave me a card and a generous amount of money for graduation. I told him about George and he seemed happy for me as always. A friend of mine had invited me to visit. I needed a ride to the Mackinaw Bridge and my friend would meet me there outside a restaurant. Paul said he would drive me to meet my friend. He picked me up two hours early for the three hour ride. He drove slowly all the time so this was not unusual. We had not reached the outskirts of town when he turned to me and said "Faye, I like you a lot." I responded, "I like you too, Uncle Pauly." He said, "I want to marry you." My response was visceral. It was like someone had just injected me with every major virus known to mankind and I had only seconds until I collapsed.

Life seemed to be in slow motion after what he said. I felt afraid for the first time in his presence. Here I was in his vehicle feeling trapped as we had traveled down the road enough to be in a deserted area. He had never said anything like that to me before. Besides, Teresa was always his favorite person. I had to say something so I said, "I love you as a friend who was very good to me while I was growing up. I have a boyfriend who I hope to marry."

In the hours that followed, the car was mostly quiet. He drove slowly as usual, never going over forty miles an hour. The slow speed drove me crazy as I wanted to get this drive over with and be out of the car and away from him. He did not make a move to touch me in any way, yet I was afraid he might.

I buttoned the top button on my blouse just to be sure my camp shirt and khakis were not too appealing. Throughout the rest of the drive I was in shock. I felt as though I had been abducted by a diabolical person. It is a wonder I did not throw up. While I did not sense he wanted to touch me, the concept of us being married disturbed me. The conversation was so unlike him I thought him capable of anything. If he had taken out a weapon to use against me I would not have been surprised. The unknown was the worst part. For the five hours of the trip, I prepared to escape if I needed to do so. My mother would ask me later why I didn't jump out of the car. I remembered it was so desolate, just miles of trees and sparsely populated. Just the pure disbelief made me hesitate. I kept hoping I had not heard correctly. Another part of me thought how it was about right that I finally met a great guy and had finished graduate school and now Paul was going to ruin it all. His words were such a blow to me. I worried what I had said or done to ever make him think of me that way. Nothing came to mind. I was sad too, because this man who had been so kind for so many years would never be close to me again. Ruth told me later she did not think he was thinking of me as sexually being a wife to him. She felt it was more an "I want to protect you" thing. I ultimately did not care about his motive. That car trip was on the fourth of July. For years, I would dread the holiday as it brought back traumatic feelings. His truck was light blue and I could not wear or purchase anything of that color as it disturbed me so.

When my friend arrived to pick me up at the restaurant, I made a mad dash to get out of Paul's way. I felt better when Paul drove away. My visit was ruined, though. I was upset all weekend. When I sat in a boat watching fireworks, I just replayed the scene over and over in my mind. It should have been such a nice weekend. For days, I had looked forward to relaxing. Instead I felt so traumatized I did not think I could ever feel okay again. He had not touched me or spoken of vile things. Yet I felt so victimized. He was supposed to pick me up at the restaurant in a couple of days. I called my parents and told them what happened. It was decided I would take a bus home. The ticket would take all the money I had brought for the visit. After I got off the bus and saw my parents, I felt better. I was embarrassed to tell anyone because I felt it sounded stupid. I did not know what to label the situation. He had not touched me but I felt sick as if he had. He had betrayed me.

I had bad dreams about him kidnapping me. He phoned the day I came back from the trip and I tensed when I recognized his voice. He apologized to me. I said I forgave him, but I wanted him to stay away from me. For a while, I thought that was the end of it. But I was not dealing with a sane person at the time. My parents did not know what to make of the situation. My mother was very troubled by his behavior but Dad, trying to help, said I should be flattered. I expressed how I did not feel flattered because it gave me the creeps. I stated how I hated Paul, and Dad asked me what I wanted him to do. If he had touched me Dad would kill him for me. But he had proposed to me. Dad said I should forgive him because I might make a mistake in my life and need to be forgiven. I said, "I would never do anything like that."

Dad said, "You never know." I was upset my dad should suggest such a thing. For a while, I was more angry at my dad than Paul. His comment traumatized me again. Now instead of just feeling guilty I might have sent an incorrect signal to Paul; I felt I was cursed. I would be punished for not instantly forgiving someone who hurt me. My punishment would be for me to worry about hurting someone else someday and for me not to find closure easily. My potentially hurting someone else superseded any need I had to feel angry or troubled. Everyone else mattered and I did not. I could not decide if I had a reason to be so upset. My thoughts tortured me. I felt I was damaged and I did not know how to feel any better. I felt embarrassed and did not think a counselor would understand. Maybe they would think I was crazy for letting it upset me so. My instincts told me to be afraid, but logic did not.

For a break I went for a ride on my bike. I tried to clear my head because George would be visiting me next week and I wanted to feel as happy as I had about seeing him. After a while, I began to feel a little better. As I approached my house, I noticed Paul's truck. I had asked him to stay away. I was mad he did not follow my wishes. The logical thing to do was to go to my sister Donna's house and wait for him to leave. He stayed quite a long time. I stayed at my sister's even longer. When he eventually left, I returned home frustrated I could not be in my own home without his presence. These surprise visits continued. I managed to avoid him every time. I was angry my parents did not just throw him out. Instead they would pretend they were going to bed so he would have to leave. I resented his feelings being more important than mine. He had hurt me. When George arrived, I told him what had happened and I knew he would protect me.

    Yet I did not expect physical harm. It was more like he wanted to lock me up and keep me like a pet or something. He was stalking me. It was the worst feeling I had experienced up until that moment. I resented it had happened just when my life was magical since I met George. I visited George's family for a couple of weeks. It was uncomfortable meeting new people and desperately wanting them to like me when I felt so troubled inside. I gave it my best shot, though.

    That summer I stayed with my Aunt Eleanor and Uncle Gerald on a farm which close to the Grand Rapids area. My aunt and uncle were great to me and helped me get to a job interview and showed me about farm life. It helped me relax to work on a farm and go to church with them. They tried to entertain me and introduce me to their friends.

    I wish I could have told them but I felt they would have thought less of me. Later, I would realize the opposite would be true. They were truly compassionate people. I went for a day trip to a local university to look for a job. I passed the counseling department and agonized over whether or not I should ask for someone to see me. Since it seemed like I would likely get a job on the other side of the state, I thought it might be worth a try. Maybe someone could help me. Then I backed away and thought there would be a chart about me and decided it was unacceptable. I kept the bad feelings inside.

    When the summer was over, I accepted a job a couple of hours away from George, who was still pursuing his doctorate at Michigan State. I was able to see George on the weekends so I had something to look forward to each week. He agreed to drive me up to see my family in the Upper Peninsula. I was excited as we approached our home until I saw the infamous truck of Paul's. My parents had let it slip I was coming home. I was angry they did not just get rid of him. I was tired of hiding. George and I went into the house and I spoke to my parents and ignored Paul. Since he was not supposed to be there, I felt no reason to be polite. George standing by me with his arm draped over my shoulders could not have hurt either, as he was a very tall, strong man. Paul was a little man. I went up to my room for a spell and while I did Paul left. I hoped it would be over now.

The next day Dad and George went fishing. They were two peas in a pod about fishing. George told me later how they had seen Paul when they were fishing. Paul was trying to invite himself over and my dad made it clear he was not invited. It was troubling having this man trying to be around me. I worried he might hurt George out of jealousy. His presence in my parents' home put a damper on the weekend. I resented not being able to just relax and do as I pleased. When I went out to eat with Jackie, it was a lot of fun. As the outing was winding down, I would get tense just thinking about returning to my parents' house. I left to return down state and was relieved. Yet I worried that he might get my address and come to find me.

When I returned to my apartment, I received a phone call from my mother saying Paul wanted back the TV set he had lent me years before and other items I never heard of. There were shades of a rejected suitor. He wanted a rocking chair which I knew nothing about. I told Mom I would bring the TV next time I went home. I had a TV and had not been using his and wished I had a way to get it out of my apartment sooner than my next visit. It worried me how Paul kept intruding in my life. I had nightmares he was waiting outside my home to kidnap me.

No one seemed to understand my fears. I wanted to go to a counselor but felt ashamed to do that. It hurt me so terribly but everyone seemed to act like it was no big deal. So I suffered and eventually the uncomfortable behavior stopped. I never saw or spoke to him again until Dad's funeral. When he withdrew his delusion, I felt more at peace but still troubled. I asked George if I could ever get over it. His response was almost silly but it helped. I have reflected on his words many times since. With the sincerity of Gibran he shared the words of the song "You Can't Roller Skate in a Buffalo Herd", that Roger Miller made famous. George the positive thinker. He made me believe I could be happy again.

It was not until a staff meeting when I worked at a mental health center, that I finally was able to forgive Paul. During the meeting, a patient who was delusional was described and had behaved the very same way. I knew then that Paul had been delusional. He had a false belief about me. His mind was mixed up At the same time I remembered he was a patient at the mental health clinic back home. Perhaps all the years of kind behavior had been genuine and the weird behavior had been because of an illness. The man who upset me was so different than the man I knew in my childhood who I was never afraid of and only brought good feelings to my life

When my sisters and I were greeting guests, who appeared but Paul. For a moment, I winced. Then, since I knew he was just human, and since he had not bothered me again, I decided to show him my forgiveness. With Teresa and Ruth on either side of me I extended my hand and said, "I am glad you came. Dad would have appreciated it." I knew then I truly had forgiven him.

I then got busy talking to someone else, but Ruth and Teresa told me later it had been very kind of me to greet him as he had been a friend of Dad's, despite how strange he had been to me. I had not thought about him in a long while. During the eulogy, when I talked of how Dad had comforted me as a child, Paul and I looked at each other. He had tears in his eyes and he did not seem scary, just frail. Through the grapevine I had heard he had heart surgery. It had been 14 years since the ride in his truck. I felt at peace about it now. I tried to remember the man who had been my friend for so many years, the man I loved. Yet, to be sure, I did not allow him the opportunity to chat with me individually, just in case he had missed his medications lately.

Later, I would think back and consider the likelihood of my greeting Paul, who had once had a probable psychotic delusion about me, while I was having a psychotic and romantic delusion of my own about someone else. I thought back to my dad's words about forgiveness and to do so because someday you might need it yourself. While it would be a while before I put the pieces together and recognized the parallel, I was sure that forgiving him was the right thing to do.

When it was all over, we went back to Ruth's house. We had many plants to carry home. Without realizing it, I chose a plant to take back to my apartment because I thought it was silk. I told every employee of the airlines it was silk and they believed me. You are not supposed to transport plants across state lines or something like that. Seeing it had clearly come from a funeral, bearing a ribbon saying father, I think they did not want to put much effort into examining it. It wasn't until Jamie picked me up at the airport and complimented the plant that the issue was raised. I told her it was silk and she said it wasn't. There had been some silk flowers in it, though. The ivy was real. It was hard to imagine I had missed the difference as I am usually quite perceptive. It had been harder to concentrate lately.

I felt a sense of relief that Dad's suffering was over. I thought of him lying in bed struggling for breath and so weak from his cardiomyopathy he could not stand. Before he died he said the angels had been talking to him. They had been with him all night. Dad's obvious anger problems aside, I always knew he loved me. I had seen him sacrifice for us. He would go without clothing he needed or any luxuries so our family could meet some of its needs. He worked overtime in his job at the steel company, even though the area he worked in was a far from comfortable experience. It would be bitter cold at times. He also tried a shoe repair business. He did a great job on the work but was not trained as a business man. He felt sorry for everyone and would give them work for free or reduced the fee. He worked 18 hours a day for some time.

While he did not say it to me, he told everyone else repeatedly how proud he was of me. He bragged about my going to college. During one of my psychology classes, I was doing an experiment on memory. I asked him to memorize some words, then read out loud from a book for a couple of minutes. He remembered the words but would not read out loud. My reaction was anger. Why wouldn't he cooperate? We did not finish the exercise. I felt he was deliberately trying to mess me up and I was frustrated.

Later, when I was fussing, my mom told me Dad could not read well and was embarrassed to read in front of me as he only had an eighth-grade education. As I mulled it over, I did not know what to say. It was a moment of importance. I had never really thought about it. I never saw Dad read a newspaper or a book. His friend gave him used hunting and fishing magazines. I knew he looked through them. When we had gone on vacation out west, Dad would dictate to me what he wanted me to write on the postcard we sent his friends. I had felt honored to do it at the time, feeling I was a big help. How difficult it must be to go through life not able to read well. Dad was functionally illiterate.

My feelings were such a weaving of good and bad aspects of my regard for people. I suppose I was seeing what it was to be human. For every fault my father had I could think of two plusses. But the totality of the feelings made the truth. I began to take subjective and harsh moral inventory of myself. Surely like everyone else I had good and bad traits. Depending on the circumstances they might be the same trait. However, I felt I had very few good points. What a horrid creature I was. Energy left me as I found it hard to complete tasks. Driving home from Jamie's church I got lost and rode around the same block numerous times. My two children were with me. They were all quite patient. Jamie's daughter said she was hungry as we had been driving nowhere for a while. Somehow by riding around long enough I made it back to Jamie's. We were late and she had her family over to eat and we held everyone up.

    Later that day, I moved into my apartment with the boys. George was waiting there when I arrived. He was standing with a box of supermarket fried chicken. He wanted to be a family again. For a moment, I considered letting it all go. He stood so sweetly by my door with a stupid box of chicken. I hated supermarket fried chicken and he was clueless about this. Like so many things I had told him repeatedly it went over his head. If I had adored him I would not want the supermarket fried chicken. He always seemed to miss the point.

    He was quietly accessible. He stood there like nothing was wrong, when only a few weeks ago, by his own admission, he was going to have a private detective follow me. What a task that would have been. Any report about me in that state would be fascinating. I hated his guts. How dare he stand there like all was well with a box of greasy fried chicken and dry rolls.

    We argued about anything and everything. He was quick to find his "I am going to make you pay" attitude, and he left. He took his meal offering with him. Jamie unpacked my stuff out of her car and soon left also. I sat on the floor of the apartment too exhausted to stand. Sort of like Dad with his heart disease I suppose, but for different reasons. I was depressed. The boys ran out on the sidewalk of the parking lot and I could not find the strength to go get them. Walking across the room to get them juice felt like I was in the last mile of a marathon and everyone else had crossed the finish line an hour ago.

    I brought them for a walk around the apartment building. Hunter's diaper started falling off but I kept us walking knowing if I stopped it would most likely be impossible to get up. The diaper was completely off when we completed the walk. I sat and cried. Whatever was wrong with me felt horrible. By the end of the day I could not take it. The neighbor ladies introduced themselves. They asked if they could do something for me. They agreed to get Happy Meals for the boys. Before they returned I knew I could not care for my boys.

With my last bit of energy I drove to Jamie's with the boys and asked if I could stay overnight. She did not say she minded but I could see the last thing she needed was me overwhelmed again. I knew I could not handle the children. She took us in and cared for us. The next day George took the boys. I had said all along I could not handle the boys. But everyone said, "Keep them if you want custody." The legal assistant had said, "If you can't care for the children go into the hospital." I did not consider her advice for a moment.

As confused as I was, I knew something was wrong with me. My moods were like a pendulum. They ranged from ecstatic to agony. The down side was crippling. I would lay on the floor of my apartment and feel like I had been weighted down with bricks chained to me. I wallowed in self-loathing. Life was miserable. Later in the day or the next day, I might get in my car and drive with the radio blaring, feeling all the songs were written for me.

Having worked at the hospital for some time I had friends from various areas. One of my favorite people was a nurse for a cardiology group. Beverly was very approachable and we often swapped stories about our children. She also had a lot of common sense. I told her my inkling that I might try lithium. She was nonjudgmental and supportive. From our conversation I realized taking medication in itself would not make me an outcast. At the time I did not realize that it's what you don't do about a mental illness that gets you in trouble. Her permission meant so much to me. If Beverly said it was okay, then I knew it was. It was time to solve what I perceived as a little problem.

I pursued a doctor's appointment with my family practitioner. I asked for lithium and told her I thought I was manic-depressive. She gave me an excuse from work and said she would contact a psychiatrist in our health plan. She did not treat my condition. She did not give me lithium. It would take about 10 days before I was seen by a psychiatrist.

I called several psychiatrists but they did not have appointments available for over a month. It did not occur to me I could be seen instantly if I had presented at the hospital. That was for psychotic or severely depressed people. Surely I was not that bad. Besides, the only psychiatric hospital covered was one I had worked at a few years earlier and I still had contact with the staff as we worked for the same hospital service. That is where I eventually went to see the psychiatrist at his hospital office.

During the time I saw my family practice doctor and until I saw the psychiatrist I had phenomenal mood swings. George asked me to come for dinner and see the kids. I probably would not have had dinner otherwise. I was out of food. When I walked into the tiny cottage he had moved into, it looked like a trapper's cottage and had initially been a cabin for a church camp. My little sweethearts were living in this dump with nothing. It seemed impossible after how hard we had worked to give the boys a decent, even fine home. It was because of me.

There was not enough room for the furniture. It had one bedroom and was 800 square feet. The sink and bathtub had huge rust deposits. There was no stove but George had a microwave set up. It was drafty and old. George had found a snakeskin when he moved in. He had set up one double bed in the kitchen area. Upon the kitchen bed the boys watched children's videos at length. It was not safe for them to play outside, as the cottage was built right near the edge of a 100 foot cliff. Despite the wire fence children might find a weak spot in the fence. The good news was it was free. The bad news was I had sentenced my beautiful children to a miserable existence.

George had been left to support the children and pay the bills with his income. We had budgeted for two incomes when we had made purchases. In a sad way he was lucky to get the place rent-free due to the kindness of a minister he knew. My dreams for the children had never included this. The house I grew up in was equal to or perhaps better than this cabin. A cruel twist of fate placed them here.

I felt so sad and tired thinking of it. I lay on the sofa as George grilled vegetables. George suggested I rest for a while. He lay a blanket over me as I laid and cried. My three and a half year old son George came and said, "Momma, it's all right." It was so pitiful, my little boy trying to comfort me. I had been the little child once, with the crying depressed mother. It's too much to put on them. I hated myself for it. But I loved my little boys so; I wanted to be worthy of them.

Nothing could have prepared me for the sound of two beautiful little boys crying as I left to go home. They were so heartbroken and wailing from their soul. I told myself in the long run it would turn out to be a good thing and it would be fine. The children were a gift. I adored them. Since I had given so much effort to be a good mother over the few years of their life, I hoped they would understand. But the echoes of the tears they cried, as I walked away, would ring in my ears forever.

I was not happy with their father. I knew he would be good to the boys though. He cherished them. They were always my pride and joy too. My efforts were supposed to bring a better life for them as well as myself. I wished it would hurry up and get here. Trying to push the disturbing thoughts out of my mind I drove away with music blaring. Everywhere I traveled there was music with the volume on the highest level possible.

Of course the love song on the radio made me think of my adoring FBI person. My mood improved and I started driving around. The driving excursions at night were more frequent. Usually I would go to sleep, then wake up around 3 a.m. and drive. When I thought about him, I felt excitement and joy. It frustrated me how he never came to talk with me or hug me. Patience was the answer. Really wonderful things do not come easy. Our time would come. Everything would turn out great. The children would be given back a decent home and George would have his worries eased. All would be well and although others could not understand what was going on, soon they would. I was even trying to set George up with a nurse I knew.

I had started driving faster now as my FBI friend had control of my car. He was really driving it and making me press on the gas. Few people were on the road. Proving to my FBI guy I was totally committed to my relationship with him, I sped up to 100 miles an hour to demonstrate one hundred percent commitment. Then I would drop it back down. I would drive this way for a few more days until I was stopped by a police officer in the middle of my acceleration. He clocked me at 85 miles per hour.

The reason I was speeding was I was on my way to pay back the gas station attendant on a country road who let me put gas in my car on my word I would pay her before the end of her shift. He said that was nice but there was no reason to speed. I then presented him other explanations. He finally just looked me in the eyes and said, "You do not need to speed no matter where you are going." He handed me a ticket and I politely accepted it.

I stopped the speeding behavior once it was pointed out and did not do it again. I drove away at a lawful speed. I had always been a very safe driver.

The FBI guy was in trouble now. My trust had been violated. Then I realized he was trying to show me not to assume he is controlling every aspect. Common sense would be required by me. However, there were so many confusing messages. I wanted to keep up with him so he would know I was worthy. It was hard to stay mad for long since we were a team. Feeling tired and wanting my life to feel better, I needed him to present himself to me in person. I was certain everything would go well from then on out.

When I arrived back at the gas station, I paid the lady back before her shift ended. It wasn't until I got back to the apartment I realized I was on empty again because of the trip to return the money. At least now I was home and out of gas and not on the road somewhere. There would be a check coming the next day, thank God.

I started buying the deluxe version of everything. Even though I did not have the money to pay my car payment I bought a TV and VCR combo. When I got my cable hooked up, I went for the extra movie channels, even though I was not concentrating well enough to sit through one. The phone company was offering caller ID's on special. I bought one and actually hooked it on to my phone. A cookbook on vegetarian cooking caught my eye. It occurred to me I should become a vegetarian. Of course I also wanted to know more about the *Bible* so I bought a book to explain it to me. It was the time to gather the richness of life. I would no longer deprive myself of merchandise which could be fulfilling to me. Money was not a problem, it would all work out fine. My admirer would see to it.

Unlike some of my other purchases, I really used the caller ID. Whenever George or people from work called, I would sit next to the phone and let it ring. Hiding out made me feel in control. I also felt everyone must be sick of me by now. It did not occur to me people might be worrying about me. I knew I was being gossiped about at work. Surely some people were taking advantage of my absence, as is human nature. Responsibilities which had been mine were being redistributed. I had made quite a stir.

Chapter Twenty-Nine

The day after Memorial Day, I went to see the psychiatrist. I wore a floral one-piece pantsuit. Since I had lost weight, had a great tan, had lightened my hair and wore makeup I felt reasonably confident. Usually I did not try to draw attention to myself in terms of looks or clothing. My personality style usually brought me all the attention I could use, unless I was depressed. Then I faded into the woodwork.

I felt good about myself. In fact I had been looking at magazine covers and noticing I looked exactly like the cover models. Why did I not notice this before? I guess it was because I was truly in love now and my beloved had made me take care of myself. To go on to a new life with him, seeing the doctor was what was expected. He was still trying to do his job. If you are sick, see a doctor. It was good to care for your health and appearance. He represented all good things in life. It was refreshing after the horrible past few months.

The women's group I had attended each week throughout the ordeal had been very supportive to me. In this group even my story about George allegedly wanting to poison me was small potatoes. Some of these women had been through the mill. Their situations were so much worse but they made me feel special anyway. The ladies in the group reminded me of my sisters. We gave each other advice and encouragement. One lady talked about her mother never being very available during difficult times. The group had been an anchor through the storm. They were there for me.

These women had courage and some had been in life-or-death situations with their male partner. Other than the poisoning allegations, I never thought George would physically harm me. But he had broken my heart at times. Sometimes his evil twin would show up and rub out any closeness I had for him. He did this most when he was depressed over something. One negative expression from George could wipe out days, weeks and even months of intimacy. He had a look which communicated to me, "You disgust me."

One evening at the end of group some church members from Church of

Christ brought us chocolate chip cookies. It was the kindest thing anyone had done for me in a long time. They stood and watched us divvy up the cookies. They seemed as happy as we were. I do not think kindness is ever really wasted, even if the person does not thank you right away. We thanked them for those great cookies. Somebody I did not know had made cookies for me. It was such a beautiful gesture from a complete stranger. I was a child of God and even a stranger felt I had a right to exist. I credited the FBI guy with commanding the church people to make the cookies. A few years later, I would make twelve dozen chocolate chip cookies for a prison ministry. I felt it was my turn to give back. Maybe it would make someone's day as someone had made mine on a lonely summer night in 1995.

The doctor would agree with my attendance at a support group. He would realize I had been the perfect wife trying to have the perfect divorce. Learning more about myself was constructive. There were similarities in our mothers. We had been the strong ones. We never counted on our mothers to solve our problems as they had enough of their own they could not solve. Both of our mothers had clearly been depressed throughout a good bit of our lifetimes and their own. I wondered if the doctor would want to know my observations. I had an opinion about everything. Maybe I could impress him with my vast knowledge.

I was undecided about telling the psychiatrist about my romance with the FBI guy. It would be hard to keep it secret. I thought he might think I was crazy or if he did believe me he might check out my story. Of course it would be true, but I did not want to put my admirer on the spot. It was essential I be discreet. I could not afford to blow things now. We were so close to our new life. Perhaps after I tried the medicine and came back I could confide in him. I was proud of our relationship. But I knew how psychiatrists were. They often took statements out of proportion.

It was not as bad as I thought sitting in the waiting area. A nurse I knew came and talked with me. I told him I thought I was manic depressive. I was not sure if it was to be nice or he meant it, but he said, "Oh, it's just your personality style." He said if I took lithium they would have to do blood tests to determine the lithium level. By his chatting with me I became relaxed. To have a former coworker sit and talk with me at such a scary time meant the world to me. He told me about his life. The time passed. Finally, I could see the doctor.

Feeling nervous and confident I walked in the psychiatrist's office. He sat at his desk charting notes. He greeted me warmly and clearly knew who I was. I looked around his office, then focused on his desk. So much paperwork. We chatted about his life a little. I didn't really want to be there. I asked him questions. He answered my questions and then switched the conversation to me.

I thought I was quite rational and told him I wanted lithium because I wanted to rule out whether or not I was manic-depressive. My moods vacillated to extremes. In one day I could be delighted with every aspect of life and hours later be screaming and in tears or lying on the floor face down unable to rise. Also, my sister who was schizophrenic but whom I believed was actually schizoaffective, had been tried on lithium. Coworkers were telling me I was talking louder and faster than usual, which was pretty fast. The subject matter was rushing out. The content kept changing.

I told him I was writing a book. Quickly changing ideas I remembered I had been prescribed steroid nasal sprays in the beginning of this and I knew manics were said to have problems with steroids. When I had a shot of Celestone, I could sleep only part of the night and had become unbelievably irritable. I had seen a movie about Patty Duke and her reaction to steroids and that was my biggest clue I might be manic.

There was obvious stress in my life. We talked for a while. I gave him my form to be off work and offered to fill it out for him. When I had worked with him, I had assisted with his paperwork. He said, "No, I can do this."

I told him he could write, "rule out bipolar illness" as a diagnosis. He said, "We can just put bipolar as a diagnosis. I looked at him with wide eyes. Even though I had shown up suggesting I was bipolar, at one level I had not believed I was. It was devastating. I now had a label. "I finally made it." I said, "For years, I thought I might be cyclothymic but not outright bipolar." I thought I had a tiny problem, and now, I was being told it was full blown. I felt upset about it. This was horrid. I wanted to be normal. There was a part of me, though, that had always known my moods were different. That I was different.

I would find out later the doctor had debated whether or not to admit me. Since I had worked on the unit, he knew it would be uncomfortable for me. He also knew I had plenty of pride. Finding out I had a mental illness was shocking. He wrote me a prescription for the lithium and sent me on my way.

I was to check in with him in a week. I do not think my doctor realized I was completely alone. I will always be grateful he did not admit me under those circumstances. In time I could handle a diagnosis I suspected. But being hospitalized with the people I had formerly worked with was unbearable. My doctor must have acted on his instincts and I am glad he did.

That day I took my first lithium capsules. Depression had hold of me and I was tearful. Having a diagnosis of manic-depression or bipolar illness hurt. I did not want to be different in that way. Yet I always had been different. Deep inside, there had always been a part of me which was eccentric. George came by to bring me some mail. I told him about my diagnosis. He was so sincere and sweet. He told me he was sorry I had the illness. He said the illness explained so much. I had already stopped at the library and picked up books to read on the topic. George asked if he could borrow a book and look through it. I was glad he wanted to. He left and I felt close to him for the first time in a long time.

I later stopped in to see my boss. I told her about my diagnosis and she was very kind and I appreciated it so very much. She said she had come to suspect, as everyone had including myself, that I was manic. She encouraged me to take my medicine and I assured her I intended to do just that.

When I went to bed that night, I slept through the night for the first time in several months. I woke up feeling good. George stopped by again a day or so later. He returned the book. He had read most of it and shared some of it with his parents on the phone. He seemed relieved at one level. However, underneath was a well of fury.

He was not there for more than a couple minutes before something I said annoyed him. He yelled at me how I had messed up his life. He demanded I apologize for the misery I had caused. I did not feel like apologizing to anyone since I had been through quite a bit myself. When I did not immediately beg his forgiveness, he screamed at me, "I hope you die in a mental institution." I had never told him my grandmother had done so. He left and I remembered why I was divorcing him. He could be so cruel. Surviving these days was taking all the energy I had.

When George left, I felt tired and hurt. What did he expect from me at this time? Why couldn't he see that my coping skills were on overload? In the past I talked out his problems with him and helped him find solutions. He had lost his confidante. When he criticized me, it took up the little energy I had to keep going. If he waited for me to comfort him and make it all better he had no clue how overwhelmed I was. His bad moods depleted me. It made me angry how he expected me to grovel for him to forgive me. It was time he started to solve his own problems. I could have used his help. No doubt caring for the boys must have been rough but I knew being diagnosed with a major mental illness was worse. He could not begin to know how absolutely horrible it had been.

As I continued my lithium, I noticed my sweetheart was not sending me as many messages. It did not trouble me, however. I no longer felt in a hurry to give away what few possessions I had. My plans for the future felt less certain. I continued to sleep at night. Things were moving at a slower pace. The medicine agreed with me. I allowed myself an hour each day at the pool. I limited my time because I did not want skin cancer. I would swim a mile, apply sunscreen, bask in the sun and talk with the neighbors from the apartment complex.

After four days on lithium, I talked to my mother. She told me I sounded better. I felt better too. She genuinely cared. Our family was shaken in every direction. Mom had not been at Dad's funeral because of her knee replacement surgery the day before he died. Ruth told me she had suffered from guilt and with not having closure to his death. She was given Zoloft and medicine for anxiety. Dad had been gone less than a month. We were all overwhelmed. I would later learn my youngest sister Teresa had been hospitalized for depression and suicidal ideation at this time. As I clearly had problems of my own, no one wanted to worry me.

What I had done at work began to worry me. But I thought I could smooth it over. I had to support myself now. The job was about all I had left. It was still unthinkable to imagine returning to work. Somehow I would make it all okay. It was difficult getting divorced amidst all the tragedy. Each day was so difficult. I had little money left and too many expenses. Having a diagnosis of manic depression was draining my feelings of hope.

Chapter Thirty

"Oh, my God!" It was a moment of clarity I shall never forget. It was like waking from a dream. Or falling asleep during a thunderstorm and waking up after the rain stopped. The delusions were over. There was no adorable boyfriend or a fabulous new career. No one would take me to a secret land of wonderful experiences, where everyday was sunshine. I had acted like an absolute fool and ruined my life, career and marriage. If I had intended to mess up my life, I could not have done so as completely. So many thoughts passed through my mind. So many horrible things had happened. It was not possible I had said and done those things. Or was it? I remembered the faces and tried to establish what their role had been with a mixed-up 38-year-old social worker over the past couple months. I wondered why it was not enough to have psychotic ideas, why was I compelled to draw attention to myself while in that state?

My sanity had always been taken for granted. I suppose this is true for most people. It seems like such a little task as we go about our lives to be able to reason, comprehend and remember. Of all the things I feared happening to me, insanity would have been near the bottom of the list. My older sister Donna had schizophrenia. I hated for her to have it. It was a relief thinking she had the misfortune of being the one in the family to get the lousy end of the gene pool. Surely only one case of schizophrenia per family. However, schizophrenia was not the only brain disease out there. Equally devastating, the mood disorder, manic depression, also known as bipolar illness, lay in the wings.

After a lifetime of trusting my mind, I did not know where to turn. Could I ever trust my mind again? A mind is a link to your soul. Our brain makes decisions and solves problems for us. A remarkable memory had won me praise and assisted me in obtaining good grades and a belief I could have any career I desired. My brain opened doors and opportunities which were otherwise unavailable to me. With an intense desire to learn I was welcome company in situations my financial status would have denied me, like college and graduate school. In my career I helped others to solve their problems. My mind led me to the man who was supposed to love me forever and helped us begin a life together. Together we had beautiful children. Wanting the very best for them, I learned to be the best parent possible.

Now I felt like I had been to Oz, my desire being to return home to the land of sanity while amidst a fascinating world where questions about love and competence were all about. People I knew had been there with me in the mysterious land of insanity, but not in their usual context. I had done so many embarrassing things. Matchmaking being one of my finer gifts whether you wanted it or not. For an entire day, I walked around telling people I knew only casually who their love match was. No less eventful was preaching and witnessing at work about my faith whenever I could corner some staff person with a free moment.

Distorted versions of my sex life were shared with people who merely said hi to me, people I hardly knew and who were unlucky enough to be in my path. Couldn't it all just go away? How could I ever face those people again? Tears rolled down my cheeks as I began to consider the consequences. Would anyone want me around? Much less in a professional position. I had been very, very sick.

My marriage, my home, and my job were all going or gone. My children were with their father who hated my guts. Daddy had died. Momma had moved in with Teresa in Washington state. I was penniless and had all kinds of bills. Maybe worst of all I had been diagnosed with a major mental illness, bipolar disorder. What did the future hold for me, insanity or isolation? I had definitely returned to sanity but how long would it last? My life was ruined. The longer I sat pondering the possibilities, the more regrettable memories appeared.

What happens when you have become a "mental patient?" No one was there to hold my hand and calmly tell me it would all be fine. It was like waking from a dream in the sense it was not quite real but then it really had happened. In addition to the losses of my reputation, self-esteem, and sense of well-being, perhaps the most difficult to reconcile was that there was no secret love affair. There was an imaginary friend who comforted me. Only the bad things were mostly true. The good memories were false. My life was screwed up for nothing. I took inventory of all the changes so I could begin sorting through the ruins which had become my life. The nursery rhyme about Humpty Dumpty came to mind. I hoped lithium could put me back together again.

Depression was no stranger to me, but I felt only the really depressed people took antidepressant medication. Since I was not taking one, I must be fine. Full of pride as a social worker I would not take an anti-depressant even when it was suggested to me on more than one occasion. For the life of me I could not think of one person who admired me for suffering all those years. No one had been impressed with all my ruminating and negative thoughts. The anguish could have been eliminated in a positive way.

I was not a better person for it. Suffering needlessly for years left me feeling alone and withdrawn. With the decreased energy level of depression I quit reaching out and with the pessimism of depression I convinced myself I was not worthy of extending my base of friendship. Now I was truly alone. Having worn out the friends from work with my antics, and my family and long time friends being so far away, there were few places to turn.

Not only did I feel alone physically, I also felt the loss of most of my possessions. Beyond the house which was for sale, most of my possessions had been given away in my manic state. Much of it had gone to charities and I felt good about that. However, the donations had been beyond reason. I had little clothing or shoes. Even some of my jewelry was gone. The baby clothes the children had worn were put to good use and were given to the Battered Women's clinic, Goodwill and some churches. Also, some expectant mothers were given clothes and books.

However, I did not just give away extra things. I had given away some heirlooms. As I am a very sentimental person, I was saddened by this. One white knit gown which tied at the bottom had been Benjamin's outfit to wear to come home from the hospital. It had never been used as he did not come home. I had saved it, never knowing what to do with it. There were other special outfits I had saved for when my nieces and nephews had children. Many of the children's toys had been given away. Granted they had a wide selection, but it hurt I had given away so much. Possessions I had taken for granted were gone. My favorite books were passed out in the office. Even the one I had signed by the author. I made a big production of presenting them to people. I had packaged up boxes of my possessions and what I did not bring to a clinic, I gave away to a passerby or I left a box on a stranger's doorstep.

As I looked around the apartment, I remembered taking my expensive teapot collection out to the dumpster of the apartment complex and smashing them one by one. Some high school yearbooks were tossed in the dumpster too. The book I had treasured which carefully listed all my wedding gifts and information about my showers and the rehearsal dinner had been tossed. The book had meant the world to me.

My exquisite wedding dress was packed in blue paper inside a dry cleaner box. I had carted it around to our different homes. I intended to pass it to some future relation. Before I brought it to try and sell, I had taken it out of the paper and held it up to me and looked in the mirror. The dress was lace and felt like satin against my skin. I had forgotten how beautiful it was and the rustle it made as I lifted it out of the box. I had seen it in the window of a bridal shop and knew it was the one for me. Since the store had only one, they took the dress out of the window and tailored it for me. I was thrilled to get a discount because it had been a store sample.

During my episode of insanity, I needed money, so I took the dress and veil and shoes and tried to sell them to a resale store. The owner told me she had a dress much like mine and did not need two. I felt so rejected. So I took it to Goodwill drop-off location. I tried to explain to the lady working how special this gown was. She looked bored, had little to say and just tossed it in with other dresses. Even in a manic state I knew I had made a mistake. However it did not stop me from driving to pawn shops to pawn my wedding ring set, finally selling it for one hundred dollars. I made jokes about George as he prepared to pay me. I knew a lady from the hospital who was in the store with me. I could not stop laughing as I walked away with a hundred dollars. Surely I had been so clever. The look of delight on the man who worked the counter's face made me briefly wonder if I had been cheated. Just as quickly as I thought it I knew the answer was no, because I had my special agent looking out for me.

There were a few boxes I had been packing when I started to take the lithium. With the medication I no longer felt compelled to give the clothes away. Looking around I cried all over again to see what had been given away. George had a share of the furnishings with him. Looking back while I was ill some people had resisted taking whatever I was offering at the moment. Some had not. Whatever the case, the dishes, books and miscellaneous items were gone. I felt like I had been robbed.

Wasn't it enough to walk around acting like a lunatic? Did I also have to lose valued possessions? The apartment was empty and I felt alone. My finances were a nightmare. There was no one locally I felt comfortable calling. I was not ready to face them while I was so disorganized. Knowing in a couple of weeks I could not have afforded to pay the rent on the apartment I would have moved into my car until they took it also. So this is why some people become homeless. It was unbelievable how an illness could disrupt your whole life.

Nothing besides losing Benjamin had ever knocked me off my feet like this. With Benjamin there had been support and comfort. Having a mental illness earned much less sympathy. People realized they could lose a loved one also. But insanity was not a state to which most people could relate. It was not glamorous or sentimental. The words "mental illness" made people wince. A variety of images could be conjured up, all of which one would chose to ignore and avoid.

I tried to call forth the strength of the person who had once been Faye. I was not sure she existed anymore. She would know what to do. She always did. There would be a reason to go on, a reason to live. Maybe I could even be happy again? The thoughts were there but there was no energy inside of me. I was tired and sad. I was so very alone. It felt good to be oriented again, but reality was painful. Despite my exhaustion I prepared to fight my way back to the world of sanity to recapture at least some of the self-esteem I once had. As I strategized, I wondered if I would be welcomed back to the life I had lived.

Chapter Thirty-One

I made my way to the phone and called my big sister Ruth. When in despair, call Ruth. As my eldest sister she had often seemed like a mother to me. Ruth could master any situation and was incredibly confident, at least about other people's problems. Always in the darkest hours I could talk to her and when I was through I knew I would make it through my crisis. Today would be no exception. Neither of us had the money for a plane ticket but Ruth's heart would be with me just the same.

I had to let someone know I had returned from the clutches of insanity. I could not afford to make a phone call but at this point what could it matter? Ruth was pleasant and relieved to know I was thinking clearly again. She did not make fun of me for my imaginary boyfriend. She did not need to, as humiliation was now my middle name. But she wouldn't have anyway. With her assistance I could start digging my way out of the ton of troubles that enveloped me. She assisted me in hammering out a tentative plan to get through the day. Ruth reminded me that when faced with adversity I always landed on my feet.

She cautioned me in her big sister way not to let people know what had really happened. She said people will use it against you. I countered that whoever gets there first is right. Better I break the news my way than have them hear a casual rumor. I responded how there were some people I would tell. For sure I would tell Jackie, my best friend since high school. Ruth advised against it. She did not know Jackie well. Jackie was one of my favorite people. I would certainly tell her.

When I first met Jackie, I was eating lunch in the school cafeteria and as she knew the girl I was with, she joined us. After some light banter, she threatened to spit on our mutual friend's mashed potatoes if our friend did not give her some. I was appalled but our mutual friend just smiled. I knew little of Jackie except that she had attended a parochial school until high school and had a prestigious job selling popcorn at the movie theater. Only the really confident girls worked there.

I said, "Hi," to her after that initial meeting and we started speaking by our lockers, which were near each other. At first I wasn't sure if she wanted to be my friend or if she was trying to secretly copy down my locker combination by distracting me. I ultimately decided she was a nice person. I helped her get a job at Hardees, where I worked. Apparently the popcorn business was not as luxurious as it seemed. Wearing a bright orange uniform and scarf in a fast food place was more our style. After high school, we went to college together along with some other girls from our home town. We had lots of fun. We usually went out hoping to meet boys and hardly ever did and would wind up the evening at Mr. Donut.

On one occasion I will never forget, Jackie and I were out riding around in my car and listening to the car radio. We had taken a short cut and drove through the university area which was closed for break. We noticed a woman walking alone in a very dark area and we were concerned. There had been a rapist terrorizing the town and women were encouraged not to go out alone. We agreed to be good citizens and offered the lady a ride. She shook her head no. We told her there was a rapist on the loose and she should be careful. I thought it odd the way she held her purse in front of her at chest level with both hands on the straps. As we looked more closely at the person, we realized it was a man wearing women's clothing. We decided to get out of there and tell the police what we saw. Maybe the rapist was disguising himself as a woman to have access to victims. As we started to drive away, I stopped the car and looked at Jackie and said, "Wait a minute. I think that was my cousin. It looks just like him."

Jackie looked puzzled only for a moment. She asked, "Your cousin dresses up in women's clothing?"

My response was, "No, not ever. He is a detective for the police department. I bet he is working undercover and trying to catch the rapist."

We decided to stay away from him in any case. As we made our way to Mr. Donut, we discussed the case with animated enthusiasm. As luck would have it, and maybe not so surprisingly, there was a police car at Mr. Donut. Jackie and I ran up to the police officer and told him what we saw. After we got to the point in the story where we realized the person was a man, the officer looked concerned. I then shared my thought it might be my cousin. The officer knew him and called in to the department to check on it. When he finished his communication with the department, he came to us and said he had passed the information along but he could not discuss it. I couldn't help myself from asking about my cousin. He then smiled at me and said to ask him about it next time I saw him. I did so and I had been correct as to the identity of the "lady." He said he did not recognize me and had written down my license plate, since we acted suspicious. As we chatted, I had a feeling that his peers had teased him about that assignment. Having watched lots of police shows on TV, I was fascinated by his work. He went on to an outstanding career in law enforcement and remains a source of pride for our family. We learned not to offer rides to strangers.

After the cousin episode, discussion of family members was routine. We both had colorful relatives. We regaled each other with the funniest or most outrageous things our family members said. My favorite story was about my dad. While traveling in Canada we searched forever to find a parking place in an historic area. I jumped out of the car to put money in the meter and realized I had no Canadian money. I asked my dad if American money would fit in the meter. He said, "It will if you pound it hard enough." To me it was extremely clever. Jackie suggested it must have been a "you had to be there" kind of thing.

Not all of our conversations were so lighthearted. Jackie and I sat in the student commons one winter afternoon, and she told me her older brother had schizophrenia. I could tell this troubled her but I did not know what to say. I thought schizophrenia meant you had multiple personalities. What she was describing did not sound that way. I was flattered she trusted me enough to tell me.

Even though I was truly unclear about his illness and its ramifications I cared because Jackie did. When I learned my sister had schizophrenia, I told her. It seemed impossible I would tell her of my own mental illness someday. She had an ability to be absolutely nonjudgmental. She might crack a joke, but it relieved the tension but did not criticize the person with a problem. I came to consider her as dear as my sisters.

We had a joke about dining at a favorite restaurant. Jackie would order breaded mushrooms and I would order fries. She would often distract me and grab a fry off my plate. I in turn would ask her to get me an extra napkin so I could get my fry back. I commented on her craving potato products which I had first noticed in high school. This became endless banter with us.

Jackie met my dad and he forever referred to her as the "little Finnish girl." He liked her pleasant disposition. He bumped into Jackie while at a conference center. He told her in detail about his heart bypass surgery. He offered to show her his scar. Jackie politely listened for what I am sure was a lengthy conversation. Dad always thought highly of Jackie. He was a good judge of character. I guess he did so because of her friendly and down-to-earth ways.

Jackie found a boyfriend first and married him. She dropped out of college. I felt lost without her as she had been my sidekick and I rarely saw her. She was clearly very happy. We stayed in touch, though, and eventually Ed and I became friends too. Ed is an extremely bright man, is quick to smile and a riot to be around. We are both talkative, but each learned to jump into the conversation when the other took a breath. Together we could have conversations about the most mundane topics and become engrossed with them.

Without fail, Jackie and Ed always had some excursion planned when we visited, like canoeing or bowling. It was fun knowing them. They met and approved of George and we spent some pleasant times together whenever I got back home to Upper Michigan. Ed said George and I had more degrees than the city of Negaunee, a mining community where they lived. Ed worked for the mining company. He impressed me with his skill in building. He built their home and one of his hobbies was to restore and repair cars which had been damaged. His striking blue eyes were as charming as Jackie's sparkling green eyes. Their lovely daughter would inherit her daddy's eyes, though. Most importantly, Ed adored Jackie and if ever there were soul mates they were it. As far as I knew Ed was willing to share fries with her.

I don't know if there were any potato dishes at our wedding brunch, but Jackie was there. She was my matron of honor. Ed was an usher. Her presence increased my joy, which was already considerable. The only weak moment was when I turned to her in the receiving line and smiled blankly saying, "I am so glad you could come," as I had to the many guests with whom I had chatted.

She patted my shoulder to help orient me and said, "Faye, I am in the wedding party."

Jackie could always be counted on to be compassionate. While I was in graduate school my father needed a heart catheterization to determine if he needed bypass surgery. At that time I was not familiar with medical procedures. The idea was upsetting to me and I shared my worries with my graduate school friends. With the utmost of sincerity I was told to face it-- Dad could die and I needed to prepare myself for the potential loss. Unable to sleep, I phoned Jackie. She had been asleep I think, but listened intently. She said Dad was where he needed to be and she felt he would probably be fine. After talking with her, I could then relax enough to fall asleep.

When our baby died, Jackie could not come for the funeral. This was quite understandable as my family could not come either. We had many phone calls, however, and she sent an arrowhead vine plant. The leaves looked like tiny hearts and it was adorned with white baby's breath and was spectacular. At Christmas she sent a beautiful angel Christmas ornament with Benjamin's name on it. The following spring we were chatting on the phone. I was in my new house and we commented how hard it was to never get to be with the people you care about. I said I knew people only got together like that if they were really rich or in a movie. I knew her thoughts were with me. It was so hard being far away. The house had taken my last dollar. We finished our call shortly after that. Within half an hour Jackie called me back and told me she wanted to verify some dates as she was booking a flight to visit me. I cried when she told me and several times afterward. The very idea she would go to such trouble and expense to visit me was such an honor. It was amazing to me how someone as wonderful as Jackie wanted to be my friend. How could I not tell Jackie about the latest development?

Chapter Thirty-Two

My family and friends had always been proud of me and my successes. Now I wondered how they would relate to a mentally ill Faye. I could not give up. I had to rebuild my life. My sisters were one reason, rubbing it in George's face was another, but most importantly I had two babies who needed a mother. Many times I had said I would do anything for my children. This time I would prove it. From somewhere inside I would find the strength. I had to do it for myself too. To climb out of the gutter, to take tiny steps to a new beginning. As I paced around the apartment, I would stop every few moments, put my hands in my hair and say, "This cannot be happening to me."

But it had happened to me. It had happened to my sister Donna. She was happily married, her three children were the joy of her life. She worked as a neonatal nurse. They had a lovely home. Donna busied herself with sewing quilts, baking after-school treats for her children, garage sales and being a wife and mother. In her early twenties she became psychotic for a short period of time. After a brief hospitalization in a psychiatric unit, she returned home to her family. Her life continued on for a while basically okay. She then got sick again. This time she was hospitalized longer, and came home a little more depressed.

She would begin a pattern to last for years, of psychotic or depressed episodes with periods of wellness in between. She had to retire from her career as a nurse. She spent more and more time living in her own world or realm as she would say. She was not compliant with her medications. She did not take her medicine as prescribed and through advice from the voices in her head, decided she did not need medicine. Once, when Donna was in court being committed by family members, she tried to persuade the judge not to order her to take medicine. She said , "The Lord told me I do not need medicine."

The judge very patiently responded, "That may be, but I am ordering you to take it."

As I thought back about growing up with Donna, I remembered she was an introverted person. She had few friends and was extremely shy. She could be brought out of her shell occasionally and she would be a lot of fun at those times. Starting at puberty and during her teen years she began having periods of angry outbursts. We had gotten along well until in her senior year of high school, when she took an extreme dislike to me. For reasons I never understood, she harassed me. If I was napping on the couch she would come into the room and put her stereo on full blast. For Christmas that year we drove down state to where Ruth, her husband and child lived. Mom and Dad's car was not running well so we ended up taking Donna's car. Throughout the trip she punished me at every turn. Mom told me to ignore her since we needed her car.

While she rode in the front seat she would deliberately flick ashes from her cigarettes to land on me. When she was through with a Coke can, it was targeted at my face. She argued with anything I said. One time Mom or Dad dared to disagree with her on my behalf because her criticism was so bizarre. It became the straw that broke the camel's back. Although it was freezing cold she had her boyfriend stop the car and put my parents, little sister and me out of the car and left us in a rural area without enough warm clothing. We stood for hours on the side of the road where some passerby told us the Greyhound bus went past.

We never saw a bus. I could not understand what her hatred for me was about unless it was jealousy. My life appeared more appealing as I had friends and got along with most people with ease. Donna and I had been close in the past. There was no event that I could recall to account for the change. I felt guilty because Mom, Dad, and Teresa were being punished because of me. At any moment I expected them to turn on me. They did not. Everyone knew something was terribly wrong with Donna. Nobody knew what to do about it. Eventually Donna and her boyfriend returned. I suspect because he knew things had gone too far. Standing in freezing temperatures in the middle of nowhere, uncertain if help would ever come was painful. Knowing someone you love deliberately left you there hurt even more. The conflicts between Donna and I became more physical. She would begin the fights and set out to hurt me as much as she could. Her fights were intimidating because of the expression she would get on her face. Blind rage.

During most fights, which began over nothing, she would pull my hair and scratch me with her long nails. She would add a punch or two when she could fit it in. My mom tried to intervene, usually getting scratched in the process. Usually I tried to cover my face and defend myself against her attacks. One day I had had it. I was dialing the phone and she came after me for whatever reason, maybe the room was too warm or something. She reached for me to harm me and I took the receiver of the phone and decided at that moment to fight back. As she got closer, I drew my hand up to hit her. Just as the phone was nearing Donna's face my mother jumped between us and I ended up hitting Mom. I was so mad. Finally, I was ready to back her off and Mom rescued her. Donna had it coming. If I hurt her she would back off.

Donna was a senior in high school when I was a freshman. My friends used to walk the halls in a group. Often we would pass our older siblings. Many of us had older siblings who were seniors. When I saw Donna, I cringed and hoped no one would notice her and know we were related. She made sure they saw her though and came over to me and shoved me against a locker and said a rude thing in my honor. Later that year, I had saved up and bought a pretty dress. I only had one pair of shoes and even I knew they were for pants, though I was far from being fashionable. Donna had a pair of black dress shoes. I did not have any. She usually locked up her possessions but she had forgotten. In the past we had shared clothes. I was pushing my luck but in the spirit of high school I did it anyway. Later that day, I was sitting in history class and it was announced over the loudspeaker that I must come to the principal's office. I did not think I was in trouble. When I walked into the office, the principal looked weary and said, "Faye, do you have your sister's shoes on?"

I was not sure exactly how we solved it but the shoes came off then and there. I was extremely embarrassed. It was a mistake I never made again.

It was troubling me to live in the same house with this person. These episodes would come and go. At least this time it made sense. I was not the only one she had fought. In the past she and Dad had a period where they had serious fights in the living room. Nothing was accomplished. Donna also took on the neighbor lady previously, in the lady's driveway, and definitely held her own. The goal for the fighting behavior was unclear.

Even for Donna this was extreme behavior. In childhood friendships eluded her. She was beyond shy. Often she was picked on. A boy in my class threw an icy snowball at her and hit her in the head. I knew it hurt from the sound it made. She did not respond but walked in front of me quietly holding her ear. I was not a great shot with a snowball so I turned to face this boy and let him have it. I remember some things my mom had said about their family and proceeded to lecture him with the weaknesses of his family. When I ran out of things to say, I started over until he could successfully distance himself from my words. When we got home, Donna burst into tears she had been holding back so as not to give the brat the pleasure of seeing her cry. I hated it when she cried. It was as if she hurt more than other people when she cried.

There was a whole part of Donna to which we did not have access. She was very withdrawn and suffered for lack of friendships. Mom always seemed to favor Donna but I later considered the situation and thought Mom was always trying to protect Donna, especially from herself. In eighth grade Donna was hit by a car on the way to school. She went to the hospital in an ambulance and for hours there was no word of her. I had considered staying home from school; I was not sure what the protocol was in such matters. After being sure Teresa could be with a neighbor, I went to class.

My teacher and the students were excited to see me. They had thought I was the one who had been struck. It was fun being a minor celebrity, but I worried she might die and I would not have her anymore. I loved her and hoped she would make it. Eventually I learned she was indeed alive and despite back injuries she was well in the hospital. The lady who hit her visited Donna in the hospital. It had truly been an accident and there was no blame. Anyone who knew about snow and icy roads knew what an accident was.

There was an insurance claim and Donna had a thousand dollars put in a trust fund for her until she became twenty-one. This trust fund seemed to help Donna's self-esteem. Nobody in our neighborhood had a trust fund. My parents were given a modest amount of money up front. They went grocery shopping and for once bought anything they wanted. They had spent a hundred dollars on groceries. When they came home, my sisters and I celebrated. We had Welch's grape juice, Oreos and fruit. It was like Christmas morning. Donna was home, my parents were relieved since Donna was okay and they had an unfamiliar luxury of a little extra cash and the security it brought.

Unfortunately Donna suffered painful neck spasms in the days that followed and was diagnosed with having a wry neck. We never knew how to help her when this happened. It seemed like when I got a "charley horse" in my leg muscles, it was the same kind of pain. We assumed the cramp was because of the accident, but never knew for sure.

I felt responsible in part for Donna's trouble. School came easily for me and I was naturally a talkative and outgoing child. Although we went to the same school with her three grades ahead, I was the one with the reputation. Her teachers asked if she was my sister. I was thought of as bright and she was left to stand in my shadow even though she was very bright herself.

Despite everything over the years I loved my sister and felt bad for the way life kept hurting her. While in nursing school, shortly before graduation, one of her instructors had commented to her that she was not warm and friendly enough with the patients. She may as well have asked her to grow another foot. Donna was a quiet person. Donna lay on the couch sobbing one night because she feared she would not get to be a nurse. It just would not be fair as she had worked so hard. She talked about wanting to kill herself. I felt so helpless as she cried. I wished I could take the test for her or talk to the patients or the teacher. I wanted her to be successful. She was my sister and was strange at times, but I loved her dearly. Her heart was so good and despite her periods of aggressiveness, was otherwise thoughtful and generous.

We coached her and practiced with her how she should be greeting patients. We told her to pretend to be more outgoing than she was. She pulled it off and graduated. We were so proud she had been to nursing school. Her life was looking hopeful again. Just as easily as Donna's dark mood appeared, it went away. Once again, I did not know why. While a month or two before I was not invited to her wedding, now I was not only invited to the wedding, I was to be the maid of honor. When she went to choose material for the bridesmaids' dresses, I was included. She was no longer mean to me and I felt she did not remember how she had been.

Her fiancee was a fine man and they were so happy together. They looked at each other with such devotion. Donna was happy. The wedding was beautiful. Donna made her own wedding dress and the bridesmaid dresses as well. The bridesmaids all wore dotted Swiss, with each bridesmaid having her own pastel color. I wore a pink dotted Swiss gown with a large white hat and pink ribbon around it. Their wedding reception was one of the nicest evenings of my life. The best man went on to medical school to be a psychiatrist. When I thought of this years later, it seemed so appropriate, given the outcome of our lives.

Chapter Thirty-Three

During the early years of Donna's marriage, it was a pleasure to visit them. She and her husband worked hard and built a home next door to my parents. Often, I would drop in and play board games for hours. When my brother-in-law tried to get me to play chess, I discovered I had not the patience nor aptitude for the game. I enjoyed their company, however. While their pleasures were quite simple they had a relationship to be envied.

My sister and her husband seemed to have it all. They had beautiful children, a nice home and steady employment. Donna sewed up adorable Halloween costumes and had the children's photos taken professionally, seemingly on a monthly basis. Donna was dedicated to her family and was always trying out some recipe. Each summer, they took a vacation to Milwaukee to see the zoo and other attractions. Donna worked tirelessly to make dolls for disadvantaged children or collected clothing or purchased some at garage sales to send to orphanages. She donated her sewing projects to the church. Her heart always went out to anyone in need. She was one of the most generous people I knew. I hoped to be as happy as she and her husband.

Donna did worry a great deal. It caused her to be troubled at times. She coped well, however. In her work as a nurse she had developed the skills necessary to greet patients in a friendly manner. Her life seemed charmed. Of course her first two children were born prematurely. Just like for me, our mom had been given DES during her pregnancy for Donna. For her first two pregnancies, she could not carry a child full-term. By the time she had a third child her uterus was capable of stretching enough for a full term pregnancy. The stress of the pregnancies did take a toll on her. She had been hospitalized briefly because she had become psychotic.

At the time of Donna's illness I was in graduate school learning to be a therapist. I worried about Donna and was not sure what to make of it. It was clear to me that I would not mention it to my fellow graduate students. I did confide in one person, though. No one knew for sure what caused schizophrenia and one belief was the mother of the patient was at fault because she related to the child with a bizarre and paradoxical communication style. She would send contradictory signals and the patient would be troubled by the double-bind presentation and became unable to answer. I did not want people thinking of my mother and sister that way and I did not want to be from a family like that. Donna came out of her psychotic condition and for a while it seemed it was going to be a one-time occurrence that she could put behind her. She seemed fine again. She was a very attentive and loving mother. She read every book she could find on parenting and fretted over the nutritional quality of food.

However, during another stressful time Donna again became psychotic and was diagnosed as schizophrenic. It did not seem possible this was happening to my sister. Once again, she pulled out of it, but a depressive quality persisted. She had three children. She had to abandon her career as a nurse. It was so unfair for her to have to have schizophrenia. She had lost so much of the best years of her life. Beyond her employment, Donna would have more losses.

During a gynecological exam, it was determined her uterus had precancerous cells. She had a hysterectomy. The surgery upset her a great deal. She had wanted more children. Because of the schizophrenia, most of us were relieved she would not be having more children. After all, it would be enough for her to care for herself and her existing family. However, Donna grieved the loss of the children she would never have. Despite having a diagnosis, she was a wife and mother. Within her were the same feelings other women had. Unfortunately it was hard for me to acknowledge those feelings because my concern got in the way.

When I saw Donna and her husband after Donna's illness had progressed, I could not believe it was the same couple. Her husband seemed so depressed as they lived year after year with Donna's mood swings and voices speaking to her louder than the family around her. He looked as though she had died. During a visit back home before we moved to Louisiana, he spoke of the situation with such hopelessness. Donna was not compliant with her medicine. She fought the concept of medicine. When one of us would try to persuade her to take her full dose of medicine or try a new kind, she would get quiet and you could see her visibly withdrawing from the conversation.

After repeated hospitalizations, when she came home from the hospital, she was still having symptoms of the disease on a daily basis. At any time she might burst into a sermon about how evil we were and how we needed to change.

Donna said she was a prophet and was suffering for so many days until she completed her suffering time. She visited other realms and had contact with their inhabitants. She watched religious programming for much of the day. Days turned into weeks and months with these ideas.

She would get defensive in most of my attempts to persuade her to try new medicine or treatment. On one visit home I tried to persuade her to go to the day treatment program where there would be classes and activities. I would always end up begging her to take a risk during these conversations. Usually I went away feeling disappointed and even hopeless. I would hang up the phone feeling intensely frustrated. The days of her life went by with her in a state of quiet misery. With the rage episodes and suicidal ideation, life was quietly miserable for her family.

One ordinary morning, while Donna's two oldest children were at school, Donna walked down the street to visit my mother. Her little girl aged two or three was with her. Donna made arrangements with my mother to look after her daughter. Donna's daughter, who usually enjoyed visiting Grandma, was very agitated. She clung to her mother and cried for Donna after she left. The desperation of my niece's behavior had never occurred before. Mom had a feeling something was clearly wrong. She walked to Donna's home as rapidly as possible with her arthritic legs, to discover Donna had a gun. Mom managed to defuse the situation

At times Donna would appear interested in taking her medicine as prescribed but the feeling would pass. On one occasion she listened to my plea enough to ask her psychiatrist about a medicine. He had known Donna a long time and the fact she trusted him was a statement to his patience. He allegedly told her to first try taking the Stelazine she was prescribed at full strength. We never knew how well she could do because outside of the hospital she had never taken her medicine as prescribed. She said she was afraid to take more medicine because when she was in the hospital she had seen patients "flip out" when given new medicines to try. I wanted to say, but did not, "How much worse could it possibly be? You spend half your days in bed or sit smoking on the sofa. You are missing your children's' growing up years as you suffer with depression."

Yet she was still alive. What if she were right and she had a bad reaction to the medicine? My dad had been noncompliant with his heart medicine. After Dad had sat for a while looking at his medication, he would make a judgment call about what he would take at that time. He always said, "If I took all the medicine they gave me I would be dead by now." I later learned when I worked with cardiac patients that one of his medications had indeed been found to be harmful. So what if Donna were right? The medicine she was on had tardive diskinesia as a side effect. If she had taken it as prescribed would she be living with symptoms similar to Parkinson's disease?

But what if she was wrong? Maybe it was time to reevaluate. There were more new medicines coming out every day. What if a medicine could help her to erase the haze which surrounded her? What if she could live without the crippling depression? To have my sister live a satisfying life meant so much to me. She deserved to be happy and so did her family. They had all paid so dearly because of her illness. The rest of us stood by helplessly and not clear about what to do. If it were a matter of coming up with enough money or going somewhere exotic for treatment, we would have done it.

Through the years of Donna's illness I pretty much kept my thoughts and feelings to myself and a few trusted friends. My life would change in a wonderful way when my husband made friends with a man named Donald Duncan. He was president of a local NAMI (National Alliance for the Mentally Ill) chapter. He called one evening to talk with George. As my husband was not home yet, we started talking. My husband had told him about my sister's diagnosis. Throughout the conversation I felt such a relief to talk about my love for my sister and how I agonized over her illness. He gave me up-to-date information on schizophrenia. The power of that conversation to comfort me was compelling. The NAMI organization was a brilliant concept. I felt so grateful and I started to share with others how I felt having mental illness in my family. Having the latest information was reassuring and to know this organization was advocating for the rights of the mentally ill gave me such hope.

My sister lost a lot of irreplaceable moments because of her illness. Now I was faced with an equally challenging illness. I wanted to be compliant. It would be with pleasure I would rise each day and take the medication I felt grateful to have. My doctor's appointments would be kept. Yet I worried if it would be enough. Was I doomed to misery and locked into staying in bed or making a spectacle of myself in a manic state?

How long would I have until sanity retired again? Would taking the lithium be enough? I did not want to spend my life as a crazy, bizarre person whom people would not want to be around. It was of utmost importance to me that my children not be ashamed of me. Perhaps there would be no choice. I was at the mercy of an illness and the medication to treat it. My part would be to take my medicine regularly and make sure the doctor knew if I did not sleep through the night. In the meantime did I dare leave town or make plans for the future? I might get sick again. Could another doctor help me? What if my doctor went on vacation and I got sick? I was full of questions. Suddenly I felt so dependent and I did not like the feeling. It was scary and I felt so alone. There were so many concerns as I prepared for my first official outing as a treated manic-depressive.

Since it was a Sunday morning, I dressed carefully to go to church. Surely it was the place to start. God never gave up on anyone. I would find peace there. They had to take me there. Churches were for the lost as well as the found. My faith was all that remained of my self-esteem. At church I could start to think things through. I would be safe there. Maybe I could start a new life there.

My dress was conservative and seasonal. It was not like me, except while manic, to draw attention to my appearance. I was conservative with my make up. No foundation and a dab of mascara and blush and lipstick. I would go to a church I had not been to before. I did not want to visit any church I had attended while manic, especially the Presbyterian church which had been our family church. I doubted I could ever go there again. There was too much embarrassment.

As I walked to my car, the elderly neighbor who lived next door was outside with her little dog. She smiled at me and said, "You look like a different person."

"I'm glad to know that," I answered. "I feel much better." She did not press me for details and I was into pretending nothing much had happened. The lady was almost eighty and treated me like a daughter. Her friendship over the coming months helped me immeasurably. She had seen me at my worst and had purchased a meal for my children without ever knowing I would pay her back. I did. She was an inspiration to me. She had been widowed and dearly missed her husband. Our conversations gave me confidence. I would act like a normal person. Better yet, I would act like myself.

There was a lot to straighten out in my life. I was starting at the beginning to go on with my life. There would be oodles of phone calls to make, but they could wait. For now I just needed to practice being a person again. It was my own little social experiment to see if people could know I had a mental illness without my saying so. Could I manage a conversation without referring to it? It was so prominent in my life. It felt good to have little conversations about the weather or some program on TV. Such mundane little conversations helped me feel well again.

At the Methodist church I was greeted warmly and brought to the sanctuary. The pastor was getting up towards retirement. He had the kindest face and though I did not want to share my troubles with anyone, he looked like he had probably heard it all before and had given up judging people a long time ago. The parishioners were sweet, mostly elderly, and smiled at me. I listened to the sermon and service. Yet my mind could not help but wander some. It was a safe place to be. What had been had been. I could not change it. I prayed for strength to keep going despite the fact I was alone and afraid. I knew in my heart God would not desert me. If he was on my side it would have to turn out okay. Surely other people had gone through this. Certainly some ended up living good lives. Although I was still somewhat in shock about my illness and all that happened, I found hope to go on. Hope could carry me a long way.

After church, I was led to the Bible study for singles. It was hard to get used to the term. There had been so many changes at once. Now I was soon to be single. The group leaders were a married couple and they were assisted by a singles minister. I told the group leader that I was separated from my husband. He made a point to emphasize I had not said divorced. The distinction of marital status escaped me. I hated being new in a group. It was painful, and I felt shy to get to know people unless I was on the mildly manic side. How could I be sitting in a singles group at a Methodist church when just a couple of months ago I was married with children and attended the Presbyterian church? Despite my feigned enthusiasm, I wanted at that moment to be in my home with my family. I wanted it all to have been a bad dream I could have told George about over pancakes. Instead I was sitting here in a robin's egg blue-colored suit with high heels that pinched if I walked too far, and making small talk with strangers.

The group was welcoming. They were going to have a pizza party social in a week or two. Since childhood I had not experienced such a thrill about a party. The pizza party would be a new beginning for me. It would be something to rub in George's face to hopefully make him envy my new life. Maybe I could make some new friends. My visit at the church went well and I had not mentioned my illness.

The next day I phoned my psychiatrist and spoke with his receptionist. I told her to tell the doctor I was well now and understood how ill I had been, and wanted to know when I could return to work. I also said I appreciated his help. I knew the surest the way to start paying off my bills was to go back to making my regular salary. Being on short-term disability was only sixty percent of my salary. I had been raised with the work ethic. Hard work was no stranger to me. Thinking of money at this point and survival, I had not thought out what I would have to overcome to walk back in the doors of the place where I had insidiously slid into insanity.

Chapter Thirty-Four

The receptionist at my psychiatrist's office phoned back. She said the doctor was glad I felt better but needed to see me before I went back to work. Since I had paperwork, he would need to sign before I went back. I went along with the doctor's plan. I had an appointment scheduled in about ten days. It became clear to me at that moment I was not the one calling the shots any more. Maybe handing over some of the power would be a good thing. I felt I had been battling all alone. With that in the works I relaxed and swam each day and sat by the pool talking to other residents of the apartment complex. One of the residents was especially friendly and since her son had a mental illness, I told her about mine. I watched her face to see the impact of my statement. She was kind and told me I would feel better after I returned to work. It felt good to have taken the little risk.

On Sunday I returned to the Methodist church. I felt offended when the minister for singles gave us a lecture on commitment and implied how divorced people just give up too easily. He may have hit a nerve. He of course had never been married and I doubted he had ever had a long-term relationship. I disliked having so many new labels to describe me.

I doubt he had thought out the repercussions to his words. How dare he say such a naive thing? For a moment, I felt like setting him straight. How dare he walk into a room full of single people and suggest if they were divorced it was because they did not try hard enough? Then I remembered how I might have said something every bit as dumb myself in the past. With two main concerns in my life being mental illness and divorce, divorce had surprised me as so much more painful than I would have thought. Mental illness was also worse than I imagined. Mental illness was not really your fault. The people with education understood it was biology. The others thought you were weak. Most people wanted to change the subject to anything else because it made them so uncomfortable. You could possibly hide it. Divorce left a question mark. Who was at fault? Mental illness was devastating. Divorce just plain hurt.

I started to think maybe George had been a good husband after all. He was so intelligent and interesting and had confidence to spare. He was strong and enjoyed my warped sense of humor. But then I remembered he no longer wanted a relationship with me. I no longer thought he would have poisoned me but I decided there must have been some truth to my anger with him. I was horrified when the pacemaker crisis happened. There had been so many losses, my baby and my father. To fear my husband would die too was incomprehensible. Anything seemed better than facing that. To walk away was better than him leaving me. There had been so much pain in my life. By leaving I could be in control. Maybe I could stop the hurt before it began.

I loved him so much and it took a lot to turn me away, but he had. In the beginning of my illness he had become angry with me. He refused to believe I was actually ill. His response had been anger. He took the part as the wounded husband amazed at my strange behavior. He took an attitude of anger throughout the illness and even when given the truth. He had been put through the mill. It was traumatic when I regained my sanity to realize all the hurt I had caused. The point George never seemed to grasp was I did not do it on purpose. I did not want to be ill. The idea of hurting people was horrible to me. Being publicly humiliated was not a goal I had ever wanted to reach.

George never laid a hand on me. He did not destroy my possessions and he was not cheap when buying gifts. I never worried about him being unfaithful and he seldom drank alcohol. He did support most of my activities and was polite to my company. Yet, as many couples do, we needed to work out a satisfactory conclusion to our control issues.

I went on to consider how he had been with our money. He would tell me he needed things for school so I gave up everything to buy him a fabulous computer instead of furniture I wanted. He had said he needed them. Then I realized one day that George saying, "I need something," was like me saying, "I want something." The possessions were really not necessary, he was just used to having almost anything he desired. His parents could easily afford to give things to him. I could not. I had gone without things I truly did need to give him things he implied were life and death needs.

I often requested George's permission before I made a long-distance phone call. I did this when I was the sole wage earner. Once, he had asked me with complete sincerity if there was something wrong with the phone. I stopped asking permission for the phone, but I still struggled with submissiveness. My dad had been a powerful force to grow up with. His word was the law. He would not have approved of long-distance phone calls and wanted to be in control at all times. In the event we needed to make a long-distance call, Dad would stand in the background looking tortured and disgusted. When George had phoned me person-to-person when we were dating, my dad hung up the phone saying he could not understand what the operator said. I was sure it was George and Dad was afraid he was trying to make a collect call, when that was not the case. Fortunately George called back person- to-person and I was there to receive the call.

There had always been a price for making independent decisions. Once, on a trip with my parents, we had stopped to eat at a burger place. My dad had gone for a walk and Mom and I sat in the car chatting. I looked up at one point and realized we were in a handicapped parking place. The car was a standard so Mom was refreshing my memory as to how to drive it. I started the car and was backing out when my dad appeared around a corner. He started swearing at us quite loudly. I immediately stopped the car and let Dad take over. After he was through fussing, the subject was dropped, not to be talked about again unless we wanted to listen to the lecture again. He did not thank us for trying to move an illegally parked car. The rule was, Dad is to be consulted in all matters.

As a senior in high school I had been driving my girlfriend with me to put a deposit on our class trip to Florida at the local travel agency. I had saved for a long time to take the trip. The roads were slippery so I maintained a low speed level that allowed me to control my dad's car. Before I knew it the car in front of me, which had been traveling too fast for conditions, went into a snow bank. I managed to drive my car gently into a snow bank without hitting the car ahead. Just as I was feeling good about my driving skill, the car behind me, which had been tailgating me, smashed into my dad's car. The man was on his way to the airport so he drove off after giving us his name and number.

I went to a parking lot near where the accident had happened, got out and asked to use the phone at a local store. The shopkeeper was irritable and it seemed hated to let people use her phone. She grimaced through the call to the police. When I called my father to tell him what happened, even the shopkeeper seemed to feel concerned for me. Dad fussed at me seemingly forever. My friend and the shopkeeper could hear him. He did not ask at any point if my friend or I were okay. It did not matter that I was not at fault in the accident because I had upset him. Later, he would calm down and he would be relieved.

The day it finally occurred to me George was my partner and not a substitute father, our marriage began to improve. He was not to blame for my dad's rages. Yet he was responsible for being hurtful. We had to shape our marriage along the way. I had a responsibility to make my needs known while considering George's as well. I had told myself from now on I would obtain things I needed and did not sit back waiting for George to consider if I had done much for myself lately. We discussed this and eventually George would encourage me to spend my money on myself. With reminders he became more considerate. As I reflected on this, I compared my marriage to those of my friends at church. Everyone has at least one kind of problem. My grandmother always said if all the problems in the world were sitting on a hill and you could pick anyone's, you would pick your own.

Talking with the other women in the church singles group was comforting. I missed the status of being married and I had always been proud of my husband's education and accomplishments. Now those accomplishments had nothing to do with me. There was a pervasive sense of loneliness. There was no one with which to share things. I tried hanging out with the girls, but it was not like college, when we had all the time in the world. My life was more complicated now. There was not a partner in facing the day-to-day struggles of life, much less the massive problems life could bring.

It would soon be time to return to work. I tried to make peace with my life. It would be best to avoid talking about my "breakdown." I would minimize it at all times. It was very important to me that people not know I had been psychotic. It was easier to talk about the other areas of my life. I tried having a few phone conversations with some of the people I knew from the hospital to practice. One lady said, "I think you started to go around the bend." I replied, "Well, I never lost touch with my sanity and I am thankful for that." I was sure the way to go was to make people forget how things had actually been. If by subtle suggestion I could continually imply I had been fine but just tired and stressed then I could eventually persuade others to believe it too.

When the day came to see my psychiatrist again, I dressed nicely as I wanted to prove I was completely normal. It was awkward as his receptionist said, "You're Faye Shannon. I remember we used to talk on the phone when you worked in the psyche unit." She was a sweet lady, trying to be friendly, but I wanted to be inconspicuous. When I was called to see the doctor, I walked in trying to look confident. Surely he would question I had ever been sick when I looked so relaxed.

We talked about how much better I was doing. Of course I had shared about the custody dispute and the pending divorce. I told him George had the children and I had given them to George while I was sick. Throughout the conversation I tried to make everything as normal sounding as possible. We were just another divorcing couple experiencing stress. He then blew me away.

He said, "How about that? You were acutely psychotic and still had the motherly instinct to protect your children. At any other time you would have fought tooth and nail not to let George have them." I was stunned. He knew I had been psychotic. I had not told him of my delusions yet he still knew. Another layer of my denial had been chipped away. I guess I was not so good at disguising what had been after the fact. Then I decided he was a doctor so it was probably best he knew. I shared how I had an evaluation by a court psychiatrist coming up for custody. I had realized in this session honesty was the best policy. Do not try to con a psychiatrist. Despite all the movies and comments of people who feel they analyze their psychiatrist, the truth can take you a long way. It will take you further than the little lies you tell yourself.

I asked how I tell someone new about my illness. He told me to get to know them first. Then say, "I have an illness and when it flares up I become irrational. I require medication to keep myself sane."

We agreed I would return to work the following Monday. He tried to persuade me to take off more time to rest. I pushed for the soonest available time. I needed the money and I wanted my life to fall back into some kind of order and routine.

I am not sure who I was trying to convince. I felt if I said many times how I had remained sane, it would make it go away, like it never happened. Maybe even make it true. I did not want to be an object of pity or suspicion. It would not do for people to think I could not do my job. Yet deep inside I wondered if I could pull it all off, but I had to. I needed to support myself. If I lost the job on top of everything else I would be living on disability and could not pay my bills. My lifestyle was so meager in contrast to what it had been. It was difficult living with less money. I still had almost six months on my lease. I did not want to live in a less safe area or give up my car.

    Coming to terms with the divorce action was exhausting. It was next to impossible to put together all that had gone before. There had been much love once. Perhaps even hero worship on my part. Now I felt only a profound sadness. I wondered how so much could have happened in such a short period of time.

Chapter Thirty-Five

    I spoke to my sister Ruth again the night before I returned to work. I called seeking advice. As a big sister she was ready to give some. With bittersweet feelings I recognized some of her advice as the same advice I had once given to her at a difficult time. She told me I would be a one-week wonder. This too shall pass. At first there would be looks and stares but after a while people would grow bored and find a new person to torture. Yes, the first days would be tough. But they must be faced. I could do it. I must dress up in my best outfit including nice underwear and stockings. Dressing well would give me confidence. My hair must be fixed, makeup tasteful. Nail polish should be worn but either a clear coat or pale pink would be suitable. It was not necessary to bring attention to myself in any way other than to be clean and neat looking.

    I took her advice to heart. I may have gone a little overboard with my second-hand store, champagne-colored Laura Ashley dress. It was a little too similar to a prom dress or bridesmaid's dress. But I looked and felt good in it. As I left my car and headed into the hospital, I was terrified. I wanted to run. It reminded me some of the walk I had to make in a high school swimming class before I jumped off the high dive. It was miserable and painful but it must be endured. However, then my swimming teacher climbed up and threw me off. Now I walked the plank alone, remembering the sooner I did it the sooner it would start being over. Mom's words urged me on through the years of attempts to procrastinate, "Get it over with." My feet felt heavier with each step toward the back entrance. Just as I reached the steps into the building, I looked up, when a lady who I had never noticed before told me how pretty my dress was. I thanked her and felt for a minute I might make it after all. I walked down the hall to the social services office, examining every stain on the carpeting or smiling and nodding to a visitor. I wondered if they would want a smile from a manic-depressive person. To hesitate before opening the door would have given me time to back out. I walked on through and felt several pair of eyes on me. For a moment, there was an awkward silence. I was without words so I headed to my desk. People recovered enough to say hello. Then some got overly sweet to me. They were trying hard and I appreciated it. We were all fumbling initially. One of my coworkers, Jamie, kissed my cheek and I wanted to cry a little. Debbie, the transplant social worker, just welcomed me back in her natural tone of voice. I stayed at my desk for a while to catch my breath. It had not been wonderful but I had made it that far and felt a sense of relief. There was no etiquette book for words to say to someone who has just had an acute episode of mental illness. We were all doing the best we could.

I sat at my desk and just looked around as it had been a while since I was there. I breathed a sigh of relief to know I was getting paid again. At least I would be paid for the first five minutes, half expecting my boss or someone from administration to tell me to go home. As much as I tried to act confident and secure, I was scared to death inside. So much in my life had gone wrong. My marriage, my finances, my parenting. I just could not fail at something else. It was about all I had left. To have joint custody, I needed a steady income and maybe more than that I wanted to fit in somewhere and be needed.

I ventured to the cafeteria to get my usual breakfast of skim milk and a bagel. My imagination had me convinced the whole place would stop what they were doing and gape at me. It was not that way. I was not that much of a sensation. I managed a few weak hellos to acquaintances and survived the trip to the cafeteria intact. As I returned to our office, no one stared or stopped talking as I passed through the office. If I could just stay at my desk I might do okay, although at least half the time I needed to be on the floor. The floors I worked had gone on without me. I was not indispensable. Even though I tried to go the extra mile I wondered if anyone would remember. There was a time I received lots of praise. I feared their only remembrance would be the extremely talkative, bouncy, social worker who cried at the drop of a hat, that they had seen of late. The moody one who finished your sentences and rushed to the telephone or chart with dramatic flair after discussing a case. Would they remember how my voice had gotten louder and my words ran together faster than usual?

After I had my breakfast, I thought about heading upstairs to the cardiac floor where I did most of my work. The paperwork had not changed. My confidence was returning. As I got off the elevator, I saw the same woman

I had seen on my way into the hospital. She again complimented me and lifted my spirits. I decided later she must have been a guardian angel as she seemed to appear when I was most afraid. I felt strong enough then to last out the day. The floor had a lot of temporary staff working. I was pleased to notice it. A nurse who worked in a different department sat by me and talked with me some. Our conversation was pleasant until she got ready to leave. She turned and looked at me and said, "Just keep taking your lithium." I found her comment to be condescending. I felt like faking a blank expression and asking her if I was supposed to refill the lithium prescription, just to shock her. Surely her intention was to be helpful, but it felt condescending. What had happened to me was not because I had been noncompliant with medication. I had not known I needed medication. Also, because she was a recovering alcoholic I was tempted to say, "Just don't drink." However, I had always respected her standing up to her addiction. I let it go. As with so many annoying comments in life, she had good intentions.

Most of the people I knew were on vacation or had moved. I stopped to chat with a head nurse from another floor. We talked about life in general. The conversation was typical until another nurse appeared. The two nurses exchanged greetings and one said she was having a bad day and needed her lithium. Their manner was friendly and I was not sure if it had just slipped out. It did not seem intentionally rude. It was more like the inevitable stupid comment one makes when trying desperately not to say the wrong thing while the topic looms in your thoughts. I chose not to take it personally.

Things calmed down again. I was about ready to take a big sigh when out of the blue I saw a doctor and nurse I had acted particularly bizarre towards. I ran to the patients' kitchen and hid for as long as I could. It was difficult to breathe My face was ten shades of red and I needed to cry. A newspaper was on the counter so I grabbed it and desperately held it in front of me. After waiting a considerable amount of time, I peeked out of the room and did not see either of them.

Since I had work to do I rushed to the nurses' station, hoping I could get my most pressing tasks out of the way so I could go back downstairs to the office. I had just started relaxing when a doctor I had scolded and lectured about his morals appeared in the nurse's station. Part of me wanted to stand up and beg his forgiveness and explain I had been ill. Besides the fact I was terrified, I decided any apology needed to be private lest I embarrass him again unintentionally. Not sure what to do I stared at a chart like I needed to memorize it. He appeared not to notice me or decided to ignore my existence. It was a terrible moment which seemed more like an hour.

Ultimately I grabbed my notebook and headed to the bathroom where I tried to recover and to cry just a little. How could I have been so foolish to insult people? He had never complained about me, but I had shared with my boss what I had done. Why would anyone even want me back at work? I closed my eyes and prayed for courage and endurance to keep facing the players in this wide-awake nightmare. This was a scene I would repeat numerous times in the days to come. There were a hundred reasons to quit or give up. I tried not to feel sorry for myself but I still did just a little. Somehow the day passed and the next and the next.

Overall it had not been so bad returning to work. But the moments that hit hard all but overwhelmed me. It was difficult to sit in the office and notice someone else had taken over a task which had previously been mine. Losing a responsibility I had earned rising through the ranks was especially tough. No explanation was given and I was left to appear as though I did not mind. It was unclear how many changes would be made to my job description. Some tasks were on a wait-and-see basis, it seemed. I really did understand they needed someone they could count on for some tasks, like scheduling work and vacation time. It still hurt, especially because I was unsure how long I could pull my return to sanity off. I tried to maintain a positive attitude and I truly felt grateful to still have my job. The hospital policies were supportive and Kim expressed confidence in me. As a clinical social worker she understood bipolar illness was a medical illness and could be treated. She knew I would be compliant with my medication. It was not a pity offering and she would hold me to the standard of excellence expected in our department.

Chapter Thirty-Six

From time to time I would hear through the grapevine issues about my illness. One person had told Kim she did not want to be alone with me. She was afraid of what I might say or do. My whole life, people had trusted me; it was the foundation of social work. It was unthinkable someone could be afraid of me. Yet I had pulled this person aside and said bizarre things when I was ill. I felt so rejected. Her response was probably logical. It seemed the illness was the gift that keeps on giving. Every time I felt I had moved ahead in my attempts to recover I was pulled back. Some aspect of the illness would be there tapping me on the shoulder. I had changed in one way. I no longer felt compelled to strike up a conversation with everyone I passed by. It did not seem necessary to update so many people about my weekend or what stunt the boys pulled. The pun on the tip of my tongue did not need to be told. Before I approached people I stopped to consider if they were busy and deep in thought. This was because of the lithium I believe. It occurred to me that some people could care less what was going on in my life. They simply wanted to do their job. If someone else started up a conversation with me I felt welcome in sharing my comments. If someone laughed at a comment I made or commented how I was funny, I felt safe talking. I was trying to figure out how much talking is too much. Memories of Dad talking people's ears off loomed in my mind.

On more than one occasion I had been told how I talked too much or changed the subject so much it was rude. One person I worked with only a short time criticized me for talking on and on. She asked me why I did that. I truly did not know and I know she did not really care. I told her maybe it was anxiety. It left me feeling put down and without a clue to change it. She may as well have suggested I grow an inch taller.

A supervisor who I had much admiration for told me I changed the subject too frequently. She brought it up as a problem area to work on. She genuinely wanted me to improve myself. I did not want to hear it and told her I guess I changed the subject if I was bored. It seemed like talking too much had always gotten me in trouble. While attending elementary school and junior and senior high I would frequently receive good grades with a conduct a tad above unsatisfactory, because I could not keep my mouth shut. Often I was asked to slow down my speech, usually by some condescending male. Women could usually keep up with me. When I would get such feedback, it hurt. Despite my many shortcomings I still strove for perfection.

I would beat up on myself because I was imperfect. The fear of being like my dad was just below the surface. Being overly talkative was like a crime to me. I hated myself for not having a better handle on it. When I was nervous, I babbled. I tried to wait out the other person's remarks before jumping in. It was frustrating at times because it took them so long to make their point. Usually I knew what they were going to say. I did not understand why others needed so much time to think out every thing they said. With my lengthy comments I used half the time because I said things so fast. Surely this was considerate. I was making each second count for more. My mind was like a radio channel scanner stopping here, then there and so on. My mind just worked differently. Now it made sense. The excessive talking was a symptom of my illness. It was not necessary to be mad at myself any more. It was not my fault. The medicine reduced the behavior. I also tried to steer myself in directions where the skill was useful. Public speaking was a perfect place for me.

People do not sit around thinking about you twenty-four hours a day. Life goes on and new things happen to capture their interest. Yet some of the events of my manic episode were so bizarre and horrifying I doubted my relationships with those involved would ever be normal again. In general things were going well but in particular I felt humiliated with every contact or glimpse of certain people. No matter how good a day I was having, seeing certain folks made me want to cry. Yet I learned to tolerate them too. Sometimes I would see someone I had been on positive terms with and tried to wave hello or signal for them to come over and chat. Our eyes would not meet no matter how long I tried. It seemed by the law of averages they would look my way eventually. I did not want to be paranoid but when it happened more than once I had to let it go. Hurt as I felt, the ball was in their court. Most eventually came around and acted as if nothing had happened.

I eventually ended up alone on the elevator with the doctor to whom I had been the rudest. I apologized to him, sobbing in the midst of it. He was very sweet, obviously affected by my tears. He said something like we all have bad days, it was okay. I told him I had not just had a bad day, I had been legally insane at the time. I stopped myself from rambling on so that I did not create yet another event to be ashamed of. I was grateful for the chance to apologize. I sensed though that his life had not stopped because of my episode. Clearly it was much less distressing to him than it had been to me.

After work, I would swim a mile each afternoon in the pool of the apartment complex. Then I would walk. It was strange to live alone again. So many parts of my life were altered quite radically. I spent time with the boys but still had more free time than I was used to having. Thinking up ways to entertain myself was a challenge. One of the nurses I knew who worked with Beverly invited me to go out to dinner with her. Bobbie was a very considerate person and it felt so nice to have somewhere to go. I had been so lonely and she had listened to my stories. Her sense of humor was like my own and she was good company. It was great to have an invitation as I felt most people wanted to run from me. The shock was wearing off and my life was returning to a routine. I realized I could live with the illness and was determined to lead as normal a life as was possible.

I thought my mental health was a topic too serious to discuss unless I brought it up. I had forgotten I worked with a group of social workers. At lunch one day we discussed a new policy about overtime. We had misgivings about the policy but had felt pressured to sign our consent. I mentioned I was not in my right mind when I signed it so mine should be invalid. A male coworker said, "No, Faye, you are thinking of your commitment papers." I laughed more than I had since it had all began. Someone was brave enough to tease me.

It was going to be all right. Everyone knew a manic episode was a serious medical situation. Medical social workers often develop a gallows humor to survive what can be extremely intense days. We were the problem solvers and crisis experts. When bad news has been delivered, the social worker stays behind and gets the family member through the crisis which is just beginning, true unsung heroes there to see it through. It was clear to me if I needed help they would be there. Eventually I did an in-service for my department about bipolar illness and the use of lithium, and with every newsletter from either NAMI or NDMDA they received the latest updates. I was also given information when one of them came across something. They understood it was a brain disorder. The affection shown by my coworkers was a great support to me as I rebuilt my life.

Chapter Thirty-Seven

Each night I returned to my empty apartment. It was lonely but I managed to get interested in some TV shows and books. Without fail George would call me and no matter how pleasant the call might begin, one of us either hung up or started griping. Even though we were planning to divorce I used to be able to talk things over with him. We would always be the parents of our sons and we needed to establish a rapport which would help the boys.

The upcoming evaluation we would each have with a court-appointed psychiatrist would be paid for by George. His motivation was to get ammo to use against me in the custody fight. He would call me and I would hang up from these phone calls and cry my eyes out. It was so difficult to recover from the manic episode with George so angry at me and constantly demanding an apology. I had apologized, but apparently I did not sound sorry enough. If he had ever backed off I might have let myself feel sorry for him. Life had been hard on me too. I know I turned his world upside down and broke his heart. I did not cause him pain on purpose. He did not accept the fact that I had an illness. He was in denial.

His intentional behavior was very hurtful to me. It was hard to try to restore your self-esteem while waging a battle at the same time. Except George was hurting me in any way he could. He was trying to punish me. He searched out acquaintances to testify against me. I played it straight and was going to stick to honesty. It was my understanding we would share joint custody. George was planning to rip me apart while pretending to go for joint custody. I was not going to fight dirty. He would show me letters from his family members or share comments from friends with suggestions and accusations about me which were patently incorrect.

George received plenty of well meant advice from family and friends. It was implied I had secret motives and George should not trust me. One person advised George not to be too generous with me because this whole mental illness thing might be a trick. I was appalled to have someone accuse me of faking the wretched existence I had been leading of late. I had no plan to take advantage of George. I hadn't the strength to plot and scheme. I was trying to stay sane. People should recognize their limitations when giving advice. The comments made me angry and led me to think less of those who suggested them. George could have kept the comments to himself.

I knew my behavior had brought pain to George and my sons. I did not want anyone to suffer because of me. However, I did not have a choice in becoming ill. My behavior was beyond my control. I was insane. The illness did not send me a letter of intent to take over my mind. It just appeared. Now I know it's there so I can make decisions accordingly. I can work with my doctor to stay sane. I have fair warning.

Looking back I could see samples of my illness. George purchased a radio because there was a hurricane headed our way. He spent about four times what we had agreed we would spend. He could be impulsive with purchases. We could not afford for him to be impulsive. He felt justified with what he thought was the best choice. I did not agree and proceeded to drop kick his radio across our back yard.

There had been other arguments, usually because his desire to fall asleep watching TV kept me awake. When I am tired, my patience all but disappears. Sometimes his dog would bark endlessly unless we left him in the house. If he was in the house he wanted to sleep under our bed and lick himself. I had patience for many things but not for being kept awake. Our worst arguments were at these times. In one situation the dog barking caused a neighbor child to be punished. He was tired from not sleeping and did poorly in school that day. Our dog had woken him many times. When this news got back to me, I relented and let the dog in at night.

I tried so many times to get George to be considerate about my need to sleep. My complaints fell on deaf ears. The only thing that would get his attention was when I threatened to throw or give one of his books away. He was very possessive about his books. He had a multitude of them, and they were precious in his mind. On a rainy night I would stand at the front or back door after one of these fights and wave a few of his books around. He usually complied with my request then. However, I really never disposed of any books but I felt sadistic glee watching him squirm.

In the quiet moments of my day I would wonder about the fights. I resented George for being so immature. I secretly worried about the lack of control when I was tired. My father had thrown tantrums while I was growing up when he was tired. He had broken Mom's things. I felt my behavior was more similar than I would have liked. Now I wondered if my manic-depressive personality had reared its ugly head in those circumstances. I had to take responsibility for my outbursts.

I also experienced difficulty with my moods if I were hungry. I try to keep up a routine time to eat lunch. The amount of light I was exposed to, the temperature or the level of sound affected my moods also. While traveling in a car with George we continuously debated over the hot and cold temperature controls. I preferred natural light and it upset me to have music or TV on too loud. My sensitivity to my environment seemed greater than others. So I just had to plan accordingly. Now my life needed more structure.

While I was psychotic my impressions of George were grossly distorted. Yet there had been a thread of truth about the dissatisfaction in our marriage. At the same time I knew real couples argued and disappointed each other. The issue of George's behavior must be addressed. If I were oversensitive about my environment, George was insensitive to my needs. Even if we continued with the divorce we needed to make peace with these issues.

The court-ordered evaluation came and went. Since I had a psychiatrist and was being treated for my illness, it did not seem necessary for me to have another evaluation. However, I went as George had, since we had agreed to do so. I was honest and I think the psychiatrist could tell. When I saw a copy of the letter he wrote, I was pleased. He said I had knowledge of the illness, a good response to lithium, and a positive attitude about being compliant with my medication. He said I had a good prognosis. It was reassuring to read the letter. Someone believed in me. Now I could believe in me too.

While at work one day I worked on paperwork and listened to a radio in the background. The song "I Don't Wanna Fight (No More), sang by Tina Turner came on. George called me right after the song was finished. I did not ask if he heard the song, but he was nicer then. I was nicer then too. We began to have normal conversations.

Chapter Thirty-Eight

To pull it all together, and to help others, I started working on a story about my illness. George agreed to type it up. It is hard to understand in retrospect why I gave this task to George. Perhaps I wanted him to understand what I had been through. We could never quite get there in a conversation. There was not anyone else locally I trusted. Since the odds were against a magazine being interested, it would be less embarrassing when the article was snubbed. He did type it for me and without my knowledge he sent a copy to his parents. After reading the article, his mother told him we should get back together. She said I had been sick. I was surprised that I felt a tug at my heart upon hearing those words.

During one of our better phone calls, George said he wished we could go away somewhere and start over. But he knew things had gone too far and there were so many others involved in our situation it would be impossible to start over. He told me he was going to a workshop on parenting for single parents. I was glad he was opening himself up to new information. We were starting to be friends again.

George had become less abrasive and was helpful to me by toting things for me in his truck. He would bring the boys by on Sunday, I would cook a meal and we would take the boys swimming. George would say, "Faye, this is ridiculous, we should be together as a family." Our Sunday visits went well and I began to envision us as a family again. I was cautiously optimistic.

George had signed up to take a course sponsored by the National Alliance for the Mentally Ill, entitled, "*Journey of Hope*". He said he would learn about my illness and also have a chance to talk to other family members of mentally ill individuals. Besides general information the class had pointers on handling difficult behaviors and how to handle your own feelings. Even if we were getting divorced, I was glad George wanted to know more. It could only be a good thing. He would stop by after the class and show me the material they received. My quest for knowledge was never-ending. I was thrilled to read the wonderful materials.

The class helped him come to terms with the illness and my behaviors over the years, just as all the sharing I had done about the painful parts of my marriage had done for me. I was not covering up my anger for George. The secret was out. I felt a sense of freedom. The worst thoughts I had about George had been said out loud. If you can talk about it you can fix it. He learned how to evaluate his own behavior and the way he interacted and how to determine if it was helpful or not. There was no longer a sense of uncertainty.

George had so many good points and most of the time we got along well. I wanted to salvage our relationship. My eyes were open. I believed he would work on our relationship now. He had been making changes and questioning himself. The "*Journey of Hope*" began the healing in our marriage. After a period of more pleasant contacts, I invited George to come to my psychiatrist's office so we could talk about our relationship and the illness. The doctor told us that neither of us were to blame for the bipolar illness. Hearing that more than anything gave us a clean slate to start over.

We talked about many things. Out of the blue I told the doctor that George and I were thinking of reconciling. George was stunned when I did that. The doctor said we needed to make a decision jointly that we wanted to make our marriage work. He said we each had to make a commitment to try to the best of our ability. It would not work if only one of us tried. Our doctor suggested perhaps George became frustrated with me because I was acting in a manic or hypomanic way at the time. However, maybe I became so frustrated and acted out because he was inconsiderate. It was a "What came first, the chicken or the egg?" type dilemma. Either way we both had to improve our problem solving and conflict resolution. For the sake of our children, whom we both loved, and for the love we once knew, we made a commitment to be a family again. A happy and healthy family.

My doctor encouraged us to date again and start anew. We each had limits of behavior we would not tolerate. George would voice his concerns or questions in an assertive manner. My need to get adequate rest must be respected and I was not to be engaged in a power struggle for peace and quiet. I was to take my medication and get the appropriate amount of rest. I was to voice my complaints in an assertive manner. Throwing and breaking things was not acceptable. We had been so much in love once, surely we could get there again.

When we started dating, it was almost secretive behavior. Having both been so public about how horrible the other had been made it difficult to get back into a routine. We were both nervous about being seen together. Out-of-the-way restaurants helped us to get to know each other again without the pressure of explanations or people staring in amazement. While we knew there were many other people having traumas in their lives and the world did not revolve around us, we were so vulnerable. Any comments made by others about us were carefully considered. It was as though we needed the approval of others for us to be a family again.

Even worse was telling our families. My sister Ruth was so angry at me. She had listened to my tearful concerns and worried I was making a mistake. We had analyzed George and relived every selfish or insensitive thing he ever did. Ruth was so troubled and disgusted with me our conversation was short. At least I had brought her up to speed. She would get over it.

I spoke with my mother and she wanted to know about my being with George. She wanted me to be happy and if I could do that with George it was great. She did not want me to put up with selfish and cruel behavior for the rest of my life. People did not expect you to stay married it you were miserable anymore. I assured her I would not. Since she was on an antidepressant, her thinking seemed so much clearer. It was like my mother had been released from a haze of exhaustion and was completely alert for the first time in a very long time. In undergraduate school I had done a paper on my mom as an anonymous case study. My instructor had commented that my case study sounded clinically depressed and might seek help from a doctor for this. At the time it was unthinkable to get help for depression as it was just so embarrassing.

Mom had arrived after seeming absent for so long. I told her I had given the situation thought and distance. I shared with my mom my new philosophy derived from a conversation with a woman I met on an airplane coming back from my dad's funeral. She had told me when deciding whether or not to stay married, "You must decide if you are happier with or without him." I felt happier with him.

Chapter Thirty-Nine

To hear my mother so clear and strong-sounding was music to my ears. I was reminded of the days in my childhood where "the girls" in the family would pile in the car and go to the Airport Drive-in theater. On the way we stopped at a nearby cemetery to wash the car by driving through all the sprinklers they had going. This was an early form of recycling. The water our car was washed with would have just landed on the pavement. As we sat waiting for the next spray, we would giggle about how cheap we were but loving every minute. When going to the drive-in, there was an unspoken rule that someone must be smuggled in. It was like a variation of the WW II shows where the hero had to be sneaked through the enemy line.

The origin of this behavior was my mother herself. As a child she found a way to get into a carnival for free by climbing over the fence. She ran to the gate where her sisters were standing in line and gloated over her brilliance. Little did she know until it was too late the ticket man heard her bragging and proceeded to throw her out. For the drive-in usually Teresa or myself would scrunch up on the floor of the back seat with pillows or a coat over us and the feet of our older siblings digging in our backs. One time Donna and I thought of a new plan. We would be dropped off in a wooded area behind the drive-in and wait until it was dark; then we would sneak to the car. Nothing is more boring than sitting around staring at your family's car and having to sit around slapping mosquitoes and wait for over an hour to join your family. We scratched that idea.

The drive-in was a wonderful place to me because it is where I would hear my mother laugh over the movies. For those few hours, she was absolutely content with the world. She escaped into the screen with the heroine being her. Her face would glow from the happiness she felt. Next to laughing, hearing Mom sing was second best. On a lovely spring day she would be working around the house and belt out, "Bill Bailey(Won't You Please Come Home)". Her other set of favorite songs were, "Three Coins In a Fountain" and "He's Got The Whole World in His Hands."

When Mom was happy, all was well with the world. She became beautiful when she had light in her eyes and a relaxed expression. She was so much fun at those times. I wish they had not been so seldom. Once the word got out how George and I were reuniting, there was a quiet that occurred whenever the subject was brought up. My family was trying to catch up with the latest twist in our lives. Shifting gears had thrown them. I had gone from one extreme to another in typical manic flare. A few weeks later, George spoke with my mother on the phone. George declared when he got off the phone how she had never seemed as logical or relaxed in all the years he had known her. He was stunned by the difference. I told him she was taking medicine. He said it was definitely working.

Chapter Forty

Reconciling meant moving into the pitiful excuse for a residence George had. He felt in six months of living rent-free we could save enough money to use as a down payment on a new house. Six months was a lot of time to be somewhere you did not want to be. I had to really feel determined to make things work to agree to live there. At the same time it upset me to no end what had happened to our family because of this illness. The dreams we had for the children were laying by the wayside. All of the energy now went to preserving our family as a unit. There were new priorities. We were back to basics: providing a secure and loving home. Fancy homes and circle driveways could wait indefinitely if necessary. When push comes to shove, family is everything.

Some of the people at work were stunned when George dropped by the office to pick something up for me. I thought the secretary's jaw would hit the floor the way it dropped when I told her George would be coming by for my check so he could deposit it for me. My boss had always left that door open and said she had seen people reconcile again even when it looked hopeless at first. Her permission helped me when we started to work things out. But just as I learned to face people about the path of my mental illness I learned to face them with the latest facet of our situation. They were our lives to live, we at last decided; people would just have to get used to it.

The person who had initially said she did not want to be alone with me told me a few weeks later how I seemed happier with George than I had alone. I felt that way also. When I saw my psychiatrist, he told me to continue to work to keep my family together as he thought it was the right thing for me. As we went along, life began to fall in place again.

One evening, George's parents called. After he spoke with them a while, he told me his parents wanted to talk with me. They always had in the past. I had missed them terribly. George's mom was one of my best friends. Now I felt uncomfortable as George handed me the receiver. There had been so much pain for everyone. I was their only daughter-in-law and had recently been their worst nightmare. We had all been through the wringer. Surely they would not fuss at me? They would be too polite to do something like that. Indeed, they were pleasant and asked me about the boys. It was just like all the phone calls in the past. I felt they had accepted us as a family again. I appreciated their ability to let us mend our fences amidst some very turbulent events.

When I began having conversations with George's parents, it became clear how much I had missed them. George's parents were such a comfort to me in so many ways. While I reveled in the relaxed feeling I felt once again with my in-laws, I had to forgive too. It was necessary for me to let go of any ill feelings towards them in their supporting George.

It was no different with my sisters. Lots of angry things had been said about George. Ruth later told me, after George and I had been reunited for a while, how she had been so against George so she could be on my side. I was her little sister after all. She then said George was a good guy and she was glad it had worked out. The more a family will let bad feelings heal the better the outcome of the central characters, in this case, George and me. We were lucky both families were willing to move forward with us. I appreciated George's sisters helping George when I was ill. His sister Sandra sent a box of children's video tapes for the boys and his sister Carol had sent a box of clothing her son had outgrown. They and the others offered George moral support at such a confusing and difficult time. I needed my family too and I needed to see them in person.

In October of 1995 I flew to Seattle to visit Teresa. It had been stressful to take the trip. I was nervous about being away from my doctor. In the days before the trip I was prescribed sleeping pills because I was so anxious about the trip. My sister met me at the airport with flowers and I could see in her beautiful blue eyes her joy because of my visit. We had a lot of time to talk, go sightseeing and just hang out in her apartment. One morning Teresa, her friend and I were getting ready to drive to Vancouver to shop. Teresa had a two-door car. I proceeded to climb in the back seat. Suddenly I was overcome with nervousness and could not stand to be in such a confined space. When I got out of the car, Teresa said she would sit back there. On the road trip I relaxed as Teresa's friend was a fine driver. When we got to Vancouver in heavy traffic, I had to hold on to the dashboard if the car speed was up over 50 miles per hour.

Teresa took one look at my pale face and horrified expression. She said, "So you drove 100 miles per hour when you were manic, huh?" Her words were a logical interpretation. The images while manic were memories and my rational mind had to make peace with them. Being an extremely cautious driver was in my character. It was hard to reconcile to the fact I had ever been anything but that. I was again so grateful for what must have been nothing short of a miracle, that no one was harmed. For the rest of the trip I was fine. I did not get in the back of her car again. My visit was over before I knew it. I left feeling pleased I had not fallen apart being away from my doctor. I felt more independent. George and the boys picked me up from the airport. My life was coming together finally. It seemed like we would make it as a family.

Chapter Forty-One

When I went for my Pap test and exam by my gynecologist, we talked of my illness and how I was doing. In the course of the conversation I asked about my having another child. She had always been straight with me and had brought me through two high-risk pregnancies. Her opinion commanded my attention and ultimate respect. She advised I not have more children. She said lithium caused some serious heart defects. When I asked about Tegretol, she said it was not any better. Also, I did not need to be pregnant and not taking the medicine I now needed. In addition to all my other problems carrying children, it was not the way to go. She told me to be very careful not to get pregnant. I asked about a tubal ligation and she responded it might be best if my husband had a procedure done instead. She was concerned surgery to eliminate my fertility might traumatize me and send me into a depression. Now I was able to fully comprehend Donna's loss about not being able to have another child.

Not long after George and I moved in together and were surviving our residence, our lives got shaken again. This time it was of a positive nature but still a little stressful. An editor from *Good Housekeeping* magazine phoned and wanted to feature my story in their "My Problem and How I Solved It" column. This was initiated by my sending them a manuscript about the episode and its aftermath. It would require me to use my real name and be photographed. I wanted to help people by providing something to read at a time you are desperate to learn about mental illness. George was supportive and it mattered because he would also be a major focus of the story. We agreed to go ahead with the story. George stood behind me as I faced this illness. He shared his personal fears yet refused to be intimidated in any way about being public. He was as interested as I was in breaking the silence around issues of mental illness. We wanted to give others hope and information about manic depression.

The editor wanted to speak with my psychiatrist to verify my story. I was reluctant to call and tell my doctor I was giving consent for him to talk to an editor from *Good Housekeeping* magazine. I was afraid he would increase the dosage of my medication thinking I was getting grandiose. The editor laughed when I told her my concern but expressed her own by saying if she called without my calling first he would think she was selling magazines. Somehow it worked out fine and he was very cooperative.

The story allowed us to explore the events and our feelings more thoroughly than we had. The magazine had high standards for accuracy. Every fact had to be checked and rechecked. Discussing the situation at length helped me to put it together in my mind. It was exciting that we would be in a magazine. Somehow there was no reason to hide it anymore. To be in a magazine gave credibility to my illness and my attempt to live as normally as possible. Quite frankly I was honored by the opportunity. I had never known anyone who was featured in a national magazine.

It was awkward when the art editor was trying to arrange to have my picture taken at my home. It was unthinkable to me she would want a picture of me at home. The words escaped me as I struggled to put into words how embarrassed I would be to have a photographer come to our current residence, much less share it with the world. Mentally I tried to select which friends would let me pretend I lived at their house. I feared I was making the lady angry with my stalling. I shared with her how I was not trying to be difficult it was simply too uncomfortable being photographed at home. Not sure of how many people were in the office at the time I was trying to be discreet.

I was not ready for them to know of my situation. It was hard enough to have self-esteem in front of them. She asked for an alternative and I suggested we take a picture at work. Debbie was listening at a desk near me, and aware of my discomfort, suggested a pleasant lobby area of the hospital. This was workable. The crisis was over. Considering the content of the story it might seem odd to worry about a picture. Yet my childhood feelings of pain were deep regarding issues of poverty. That was one leap I could not make. It might have been intriguing to show where we lived before the episode and were we ended up. The pictures might have told the story in a way I could not. But I could not do it.

We held on tight and proceeded to take things a day at a time. We would spend a long hard winter and hopefully blossom in the spring. Depression was giving me a run for my money due to the day-to-day existence of living in a tiny place. There was nowhere to hang clothes without jamming them together. Baths could be taken in about two inches of water if you wanted warm water. In the middle of winter the plumbing was messed up. The toilet quit working. We had to go outside to potty temporarily. We went to a hotel for a while as we were getting the plumbing fixed. Despite the bleach and other cleaning agents, the tub never seemed clean to me. I would sponge bathe most of the time. We went out to eat often because it was so difficult to cook. With the lithium I had an increased appetite. Unfortunately the menu choices were high in fat and I gained weight. We did not socialize much with others. In part we were still getting comfortable with our friends again. We would have been embarrassed to have company because of the place. So much of the time I tried to think of reasons to be away from the house.

    I tried to make things right for the children. It was difficult, though. At Christmas we could not fit a tree in the house so we decorated one with lights on the porch. We did not go the our usual church as I was too embarrassed to return there. On Christmas, Santa had come and left presents in an armchair. My sons were still thrilled. I heard my son George singing "Silver Bells" and saying it was the best Christmas ever. We tried to go to a buffet for Christmas dinner only to discover from the incredibly long line that many others had the same idea. We left and drove around looking for somewhere to eat. We finally spied a Waffle House. It was not the meal I intended for the children on Christmas Day. Yet I was thankful for the food and that we had the money to buy it. I had become thankful for all the simple blessings of life. We ate waffles and drank orange juice and milk as we studied the out-of-towners who had come to town for the upcoming bowl game. George left a Christmas Day-sized tip for our waitress. We returned home with thoughts of how next Christmas had to be better. We had a goal to work toward.

    The New Year brought hope but also a sense of sadness. Our living conditions made me miserable. The short-term future looked bleak. Surely it could not be good for my illness to live like this. So many things were boxed up I could never find clothes or dishes I needed. I hated living out of a box. Intellectually, I knew that I was not being punished to have my life present me with a constant struggle to keep going. On a personal level it seemed quite likely I deserved the isolation and shame my current living situation brought to me. Yet I kept going, getting myself ready for work and the children ready for school. As bills were paid off and we made progress in saving money, I began to see there would be a new home. There was a light at the end of the tunnel.

Chapter Forty-Two

A few months later, George performed a museum consultation at Ormond Beach, Florida. It was a one-time thing and the best part was it was near Disney World. We planned a vacation and agreed to meet my in-laws there. My life was one of extremes. I left a dive of a home and headed with my family to stay in a condo at Disney World. We had received an unexpected windfall. We were in a position to buy a house now. Other than the birth of my children and my wedding day, there was no time more anticipated than the upcoming vacation at Disney. We had all been through so much.

Every moment I spent in our condo or touring the compound was treasured by me. I especially enjoyed the tributes to foreign countries at Epcot Center and the rides at Disney. My boys seemed to have the most fun at the pools near our hotel and the character breakfast where they could be visited by Mickey Mouse and Goofy and others during the meal. Since George had never been to Disney World before, it was fun seeing it all through his eyes. My in-laws loved Epcot and the fascinating exhibits. They had been there before and enjoyed the rest of us seeing Epcot for the first time.

I was not sure how it would feel to see George's parents. We had not seen each other since George's surgery. Conversations were created and practiced in my mind. I decided it would be better to say less than usual. Perhaps less would be more. When we met each other at a hotel, we had no awkward moments. It was like any other visit. My mother-in-law had a honey baked ham sandwich in my hands in less than five minutes. The ham was her trademark. I reflected back on it and I realized I had not been nervous to see them again. We were all so excited about the vacation.

It was at Disney that I realized how much weight I had gained. Looking at the instant Polaroid pictures Mrs. Shannon took were unbelievable to me. My appetite had increased after I started taking medication. There had been no full-length mirror in our humble abode. It was horrible to realize how much weight I had put on. I thought back to one of the first times George and I had been out to eat after my episode. George and I were talking and I mentioned my appetite had increased and he said he noticed I had eaten much more than I had in the past. Even though I was eating more, it did not occur to me I would probably gain weight.

Being overweight was almost worse than the manic-depressive illness. Medicine could make the symptoms go away. The weight gain destroyed my confidence. It had been a struggle to face my life only to now have another opponent. When I put on my swimsuit, I was appalled.

I had not seen all the pictures my mother-in-law took. I feared she would show every one in the family the pictures of the vacation. She was a visual person and she had photographed every significant moment since long before I met her. I persuaded her to give me as many of the pictures as possible. When I lived alone, I swam each day at the apartment complex so my weight stayed in check. I was not exercising much with our current situation. I was miserable. It made me feel less confident. I obsessed about it. Did these issues plague everyone? It was bad enough everyone heard what I had been through. Like my houses, a before and after picture of me probably would show the turmoil and agony I had endured.

Still, I managed to enjoy the trip. While my in-laws watched the boys in the evenings, George and I walked around Disney World. We also went to an improv comedy club. I was joyful until the day came to pack. I did not want to go back home. I did not want to leave paradise. Bad thoughts started to fill my mind even as we waved goodbye to our in-laws. It had been a nice visit, the first I had seen of them since my illness. I had always had a tough time with the blues at the end of a fine experience or vacation. It was over. Now what? There had been some tragic news story and I obsessed about it. My mood was dark as we headed home.

By the time we were nearing our residence and there were only a couple of hours to go, I began to feel better. Using a black, low-heeled shoe as a puppet, I proceeded to give the boys a song and dance routine featuring the character I developed named Shoe. When Shoe did not sing or dance, he conversed with the children. He asked them all kinds of questions and they were delighted by his attention. When I tired of this, the children begged for Shoe to reappear and visit with them. As the long drive was winding down, I began to feel pleased the journey was behind us.

Yet my dark mood returned upon arrival at the cabin. Reality had a way of slapping me in the face. Even if we were in a position to buy a house now I still had to come home to this dump in the meantime. With the warmer weather there were more creepy crawly bugs hanging around. A stinging millipede stung George in the middle of the night. It took a while after we turned on the lights to find him and destroy him. It was bad when you were afraid to sleep for fear of being harmed. There was a red wasp's nest built into the wall of the cabin. A can of bug spray sat on my knee as I watched TV lest a wasp should appear. When one did, I would spring into a defense mode and track down the wasp and spray it. Amazingly, the children were never stung.

After a few days of being home, I was still depressed. Wrapped up in a blanket of guilty thoughts and perceived imperfections, my self-worth plummeted. Surely I was the worst person ever born. How could people stand me? I debated whether or not to talk to the doctor. Since I was already on an antidepressant, I didn't figure much would be helped by complaining. I just did not feel like myself. When I went for a drive, I started to freeze on the exit ramp. I felt terrified and slowed the car down to twenty-five and less. You would have thought I was driving the car across a tightrope on two wheels. My body seem to freeze. My muscles went limp. It was with great effort I got the car out of traffic into a parking lot as soon as I could. This was not the first time it happened. It had happened a few months before when I had visited Teresa, but I convinced myself it was just a freak event. I also remembered at Disney World I became frightened on a children's ride. My son and I were on the Dumbo ride. The ride was thrilling to my 4-year-old child, and apparently to the other children as well.

I accidentally pulled a lever and our elephant-shaped car went further up into the air. I scolded my child if he even got his hand close to the lever lest we go higher again. My skin felt clammy and I suffered until the ride was over. I was grateful to climb out of the car and onto the platform. I was relieved and felt foolish at the same time. Though I talked little about my depression, thinking there was nothing my doctor could do, I told my doctor about the extreme anxiety while driving, especially with high-speed driving. I told him about my driving while manic and he asked if I had ever done that before. I quite sincerely told him no, I never drove that fast before. He told me I was having panic attacks. He switched my medication to Tofranil and as I left his office I studied the prescription. He said it would help me relax while driving. I already knew classical music was a calming influence on me. However, I did not fill the prescription. I held on to it too afraid to make a change. I knew I could make it through being anxious and depressed. To feel different was the unknown. I was afraid.

Chapter Forty-Three

We became interested in buying a new home. Each night we would drive around the area where we wanted to live. The homes we looked at were more modest than the one we had given up but in contrast to where we lived at the time every home was a palace. We found a home we loved but hesitated on the price. We also did not know what our credit status was like. In the past our credit had been excellent. With the manic episode and all there had been late payments. We decided we had nothing to lose for trying. When we were finally convinced, we made a bid but it was too late. Once again, I was depressed. Surely it was impossible to miss out on the house. Someone else's offer was more appealing than ours. It had been the perfect house for us, we were certain.

My in-laws told us there would be another home for us. We had been crying to them on the phone. They could not understand, there would never be another home for us. We had just plain lost out. Needless to say the next day we took a drive past the house to remind us of how disappointed we were so we could continue sulking. We drove around the neighborhood. Not far from the house was a house being built and the slab had recently been poured. There was a wooden frame, enough so we could make out the plan. The lot was much nicer as it was on the thirteenth hole of a golf course. We told ourselves a hundred reasons why we could not have the house. Later, I called the builder and we agreed to meet with him the next day. He had lowered the price he initially quoted us. We were a pretty easy sell as we were on the rebound from the other house.

The house was more than a house. The house represented to us an opportunity to rebuild our lives, which we were doing day by day. With sincerity we approached the finance company and without going into every detail persuaded them to give us a try. We were then in the process of watching our home be built. Each day after work we would drive by the house to see what had been done.

At times it seemed like forever. There were a few setbacks. Our cabinets were delayed or had not been ordered. Then the bricklayers did not want to work in the heat. The builder got another house to build and put his people on building that house for a while instead, pushing the day we moved in back by a couple of weeks. Despite the setbacks the house finally got built. Just as we endured setbacks of our own.

One extremely difficult moment came just days before we were to sign the papers for a new home. I was called into my boss' office. She noticed I was not prepared for a meeting and I appeared to have trouble concentrating. My energy was sparse. I was not my usual self and appeared depressed. Since I had a prescription for Tofranil, it was time to try it. I had been afraid the change in medications might throw me into a manic episode. She told me the other medicine I was on was not working and was depressing me. She needed to document that I had not met all the expectations. I was written up and if all went well it would be forgotten in three months.

Certainly I had been depressed, but after all the years I had in would my boss get rid of me? Basically I was on probation. It had been such an effort to walk into a meeting with my peers who had seen me behave in an obnoxious and pitiful manner. Yet I had learned to dredge up my skills and hold my own. I could not rest on my laurels, I had to continue to deal with this illness. I did not want to be anything other than an excellent social worker. I felt sick to my stomach. Here we were about to get a new home and now my job was uncertain. Maybe I could not cut it as a social worker any more? George and I had brought the boys to Burger King. As the meal was ending, I told George I needed to talk with him later without the children. He said he wanted to know now what was wrong. After a couple of guesses, we landed on the topic of work. The boys had wandered off to play on the recreation area toy. George asked me if I had done something bad. I told him no, but that it upset me a great deal anyway. I had felt glazed at times with the former antidepressant. Choking back tears, I told George I would try my best to make it come out okay. George said, "I can't believe we are days away from moving into our new house and you may not have a job." He did not say it in a mean way but more of a matter-of-fact way. I did not want to disappoint George. We had been through so much to lose it all now.

That night I went straight to bed and the next day all I wanted to do was sleep. Around noon George made me get out of bed and said, "Faye, don't let this defeat you." I vowed I would not. I told him I might try the new medicine my doctor had prescribed. He agreed absolutely. I had been afraid to take it as I knew the side effects included the ability to trigger a manic episode. Somehow amidst the misery I survived the weekend. All day I looked forward to going to sleep that night. It did not hurt when I was sleeping, unless I had a bad dream. Sleeping was an escape from reality and I definitely wanted to escape from mine. The new medication was taken as prescribed. We bought a kitten for the boys on impulse. When I held the tiny black kitten, I could relate to her fears of being in a new home and uncertain of the future. My son George named her Fig, short for Figaro. She seemed especially close to me those first days. I am not sure who needed the other most. There were many issues I could not control in my life. However, I could keep the little fuzzy kitten safe and warm.

On Monday, despite the inner fatigue and fear, I bounced into the office as pleasantly and as competently as I could muster. I forced myself to have a cheerful countenance. It was difficult to drag myself to every meeting as prepared as possible. At first I felt pitiful and desperate. I needed the job. Losing was not a familiar theme to me, even with all my illness had served up. I took my medicine religiously. One unexpected result on the new antidepressant was after about three weeks I felt good again. My other medicine had not done that. I did not know enough to complain, as I thought having manic depression meant I would never feel good again. Suddenly I did not worry about the sad times in my life. I could think of them and consider them logically. My heart felt lighter and content. Not in a manic way but in a casual, relaxing way. Sex was better. Sex was another reason I wished I had tried an antidepressant sooner.

Maybe most amazingly I was willing to forget the slights of an average day. It seemed clear to me I had at times overreacted and taken conversations out of context and brooded about them. My marriage seemed much better than when I picked apart each conversation looking for a latent content. There were real issues but it was easier to find a solution. Giving out positive energy brings it in return.

Chapter Forty-Four

As time went on, I felt more secure at work. I took it one day at a time and tried not to worry. One day, I caught myself smiling. It had been a long time. Much too long. My confidence was returning. Now I was ready to make things the way they needed to be. Long before the three months were over I knew it would be okay. I had been depressed and it was treated and there was a difference in my work performance. The house deal was in full swing. I decided not to think about it so much and pursued the house on faith. Somehow all the pieces fit together and it was time to move into our new home.

The first night, we brought sleeping bags, clothes and some toiletries. Looking forward to a relaxing soak in our whirlpool bath, I filled the tub to the correct level so the whirlpool could be used. The tub was large and sparkled with its newness. Sinking into the warm water I held my bar of Lever 2000 and a new celery and cream colored checkered washcloth. It was part of the bath towel sets I had purchased for the home. Taking a bath in our whirlpool tub had been a goal over the summer. A fine bath at last. Plenty of water and lots of room.

I reached over to the button which started the whirlpool and waited. Nothing happened. Thinking I had pressed the wrong button I searched the tub and pressed anything resembling a button. Still nothing happened. I pressed the initial button again several times varying the amount of pressure. Still nothing. Finally, calling George to the room, I let him try, being certain it would work for him and he would rib me about not being mechanical. It did not work for him either. George did an inspection and determined it had never been hooked up. So much for my luxurious bath.

But I told myself not to pout as I knew we would get it fixed. The thing about goals is they may not always occur exactly at the moment you expect them. But with persistence they probably will appear. I did get my bath in the whirlpool tub. It was as wonderful as I knew it would be. The master bathroom was my favorite room. It had beautiful pink and blue floral wallpaper and glossy white trim. It lifted my spirits just to walk in there.

It was with the greatest joy that we endeavored to begin our lives again. Our neighbors were delightful people. We could not have chosen anyone finer. John was a builder and Kate was also a social worker. From the very first they welcomed us. She was very athletic and encouraged her children to be. I was thankful she included my children in the activities. I never knew what I would see when I peered across the street in their yard. Kate might have organized a soccer, baseball or basketball game. Occasionally my son George would come home frantically searching for his swimming trunks so he could go with the neighbors to the pool.

Their beautiful children, Brady and Jordan, seemed like my own. My son George adored Brady. He taught George how to ride a bike. They spent many afternoons bike riding and exploring the area. Jordan was so precocious when I heard her speak I thought she was several years older. She could have done commercials with her sweet face and winning smile. One sunny afternoon Hunter and Jordan pushed around her doll stroller which held baby dinosaurs and were the cutest little couple. I tried to counter her physical conditioning with intellectual interests. We played games with the children with musical chairs being the hit. Also, the kids played on the computer with the many CD-ROM's we collected. We tried to choose ones with an educational format. I read to the children. We alternated taking the children fishing. The time we spent near them is a pleasant memory. It was a calm and peaceful time. They are on my list of all-time favorite people.

At first I was afraid to let Kate and her family know about my manic-depressive illness. She seemed to have the most perfect life and I was afraid I would worry her. My deeper fear was she might reject not just me but the children. When the *Good Housekeeping* article came out, I told her about it. I was so nervous I babbled about it and confused her the first time I mentioned it. One evening while chatting she asked about the article. We gave her a copy. She took it home to read it. After she left with the article, I wondered what she would say. I prepared myself for the rejection I knew was coming. I suspected she would be polite but would tell me she would prefer I not have my children play with hers or maybe she would never respond verbally but we would just observe the changes. After a while, I received a phone call from Kate. I tried to relax as I took another breath. My mouth felt dry because of my medication, which gave me a slight speech impediment until I drank water.

Kate was friendly as ever and told me she enjoyed the article. I told her I was afraid she wouldn't want to know me. She said I should never be afraid to talk about my illness. Her mother had manic-depressive illness and had been active on many boards in the community. She had done well since she was put on lithium. I don't know when I had guessed more incorrectly. Not only was Kate's life not perfect, but her childhood had been difficult because of this illness. There were many occasions when her mother was hospitalized which left other caretakers to care for the family. She did not think less of me for speaking out. As Kate was saying I should never feel I have to apologize for the illness, I knew I never would again.

I was fortunate I had the opportunity to meet Kate's mother, Olive. We had the chance to speak at a birthday party for one of the children. She had been taking lithium for about twenty years and managed to rear her children in a stable household and not be hospitalized. She was such an inspiration to me. All of my research did not comfort me the way listening to her did. I had desperately needed to know that with medication and taking care of myself I might go twenty years without a manic episode myself. It could happen. On top of that with new medications coming out there might even be a cure for this illness in my lifetime.

Chapter Forty-Five

Once the article came out, I received lots of attention. People at the hospital went out of their way to give me their support. One lady saw me and ran across the parking lot in high heels to tell me how highly she thought of me. At times it was awkward because people I did not know felt they knew me because the article had been very personal. I tried to politely catch up with them as to whether or not they worked with me at the hospital. The last thing I would ever want was for someone to see me as stuck up. There was no hesitation now when I walked in the door of the hospital. There were a couple instances of awkwardness along the lines of "What do you say?" I was proud of the contribution I made in telling what it is truly like to be so ill and how you can return to sanity.

Every time someone spoke up about mental illness, it was easier for the rest of us. There was more correct information floating around. I rejoiced every time I came across a book, movie or article dealing with serious mental illness. It is more difficult to discriminate against or fear people with mental illness when you realize it is a medical illness. Though I would never receive any of the letters sent to *Good Housekeeping* as they do not forward them, I hoped somewhere my disclosure had made a positive difference. I remembered when the editor of the "My Problem" column said if I helped one person it would be worth it. I responded it was pretty difficult sharing some of it and I sure hoped it helped more than one person. In my heart I hoped it would find its way to a desperate soul who needed to hear they could make it and not to give up. There is so much hope now with medications and counseling. If you are lucky to have someone who cares about you, whether it be family, friend, prayer group, therapist or doctor, your outlook is even better.

After the article had come and gone, George and I continued our efforts to educate people. We appeared in the newspaper and on television. We went with a panel to the state conference of the National Association of Social Workers and had the highest number of registrants come to see our program.

George and I also spoke at the local chapter meeting and received wonderful feedback. We dedicated our time to educating people about these issues. An especially precious moment came when I discovered I had won an award for advocacy from the Louisiana Chapter of the National Alliance for the Mentally Ill. In August of 1998 I received the Client Award for having done the most to improve the lives of others with a mental illness. They gave me a beautiful Wedgwood clock which was engraved on the back. To stand in front of a conference room full of clapping people was a beautiful reminder of how far I had come from the frightened woman praying to find the courage to keep going after a diagnosis with a brain disorder.

In an NAMI newsletter we learned of three women who were creating a photo-text exhibit focusing on people whose lives have been affected by mental illness. The photos and text in the exhibit would help to dispel harmful stereotypes, myths and misconceptions about mental illness. The exhibit would travel the nation and could be displayed in schools, colleges, libraries, mental health centers, hospitals, corporate offices, etc. They were also preparing a book featuring the families in the exhibit. Their book, *Nothing To Hide: Mental Illness in the Family*, by Peggy Gillespie, Jean Beard and Gigi Kaiser, is scheduled to be published in 2001 by New Press. George and I were so impressed. Our first thought was to determine how we could bring their exhibit to our area. After hearing more information, we also decided we would love to participate if there were any vacancies. It turned out there were. The ladies traveled to our area and interviewed us and some other families who were also interested. The book covered many aspects of mental illness besides bipolar illness such as schizophrenia, obsessive-compulsive disorder, major depression, and anxiety disorders. The director of the local mental health center pledged his assistance and along with the local mental health coalition bent over backwards to make the exhibit a reality. It was so clear this was a valuable contribution and opportunity to educate. The exhibit was eventually scheduled at a local art exhibit. Much to my dismay I would not get to be present when the exhibit came to town. However, since it was an ongoing exhibit, I knew there would be other opportunities.

We found out in the fall of 1998 we would be leaving Louisiana to move to North Carolina. After a national search, George was offered a wonderful position to be the director of a museum there on the coast. There had been

150 other highly qualified applicants so George was flattered to be offered the position. He had just completed his task of improving the museum he worked for in Louisiana. The move was also an opportunity to be near family. I had mixed feelings. I had many friends there and finally knew my way around. There were many memories there. Yet it was time to begin anew. Life is ever changing. Someone once told me all you can be sure of is that things will change. It has certainly been true for my life.

My work situation had changed. My boss needed to take an extended leave for a family medical emergency. I was left to fill in as acting director and oversee approximately twenty social workers in different hospitals settings. I had routinely filled in before but this was the longest she had ever been gone. The time I spent in that role was very rewarding. The department ran beautifully and I received much positive feedback. Staff members were cooperative and respectful. Given all that had been, it was a nice going away gift to know I not only won my job back, but would leave in a blaze of glory.

Lifecare Hospital is a physical rehabilitation facility in Louisiana with which I worked on many of my cases. Our working relationship had always been positive, as they provided excellent care. I was stunned to hear they were hosting a farewell party on my behalf. Marty Milner and Lindora Baker, from their marketing department, outdid the wonderful events they always planned. I was thrilled to see the beautiful cake, refreshments and decorations. To everyone's surprise they presented me with a plaque to honor me for my compassion and dedication as a social worker, and to thank me for my work as an advocate on behalf of the mentally ill. I was flattered and overcome by their kind award. I could not find the words to express how deeply their effort touched me.

At another going-away party I was led to a room with a sign on the door proclaiming "FBI Talent Search." My colleagues had a wonderful luncheon, lovely gifts and endless banter for me. I was pretty wound up due to the move and all. I remember pausing for a moment to look at all the faces and thought how much I cared for these people. We had been through so much together. Often we laughed, sometimes we complained and occasionally we cried. So many times they had rallied by my side. I would miss them.

Moving meant I had to find a new doctor. Finding a new doctor proved difficult. When you are new to an area, you haven't been around to have heard about the psychiatrists. Even at my new job the subject had not come up. Since I was not ready to share about my illness yet, I did not broach the subject. I made an appointment with a physician who saw patients on Saturday. Upon my first visit, I registered with the woman in the reception area and proceeded to look through an assortment of magazines. My named was called and a pretty little girl of about eight greeted me and led me to her father's office. I could not help smiling because she was so very sincere and acting so grown-up. I remembered as a child my dad would let me push buttons on the cash register for him as he rang up a purchase at his shoe repair shop. I felt so important. I figured any doctor who inspired such confidence in his child and included her in his work must have the right values.

My new doctor was kind and did not seem judgmental. He was very thorough in his questions. For every question I had he had an intelligent answer and would build upon his statement by quoting a recent study. Since I read a lot, I recognized the material he spoke of and felt he had a clue about psychiatry. It was easy to tell him about the ruminating I did or my sleep habits which gave an indication if my medicine dosage needed to be adjusted.

I did miss the familiarity of my former doctor who knew my husband and me long before I was his patient. Yet it was easier to share my troubled thoughts that I was too embarrassed to tell my other doctor about. With either doctor I knew they could help me to the extent I did my part as a patient. It was important I ask questions and tell about scary thoughts or bad feelings. Also, they needed to know when I felt well and when my medicine was working just fine.

Being near family had been a motivation to make the move, especially to assist George's parents as they were getting up in years. It is also delightful to be able to visit them relatively easily. When we visit his parents, George's sister Karen often comes to get me and we go shopping. It is great to have a shopping buddy. It is also nice not to miss baby showers and other events

Life with manic depression has been difficult. There are side effects: the weight gain, acne, dry mouth and constipation caused by the medicines which keep me sane. It is exciting that some of the newer medications offer fewer side effects. It is understandable with side effects why many people try to make it without medicine. I am afraid a manic episode could come again and tear my life apart. Surely there are ways to be humiliated I have not yet thought about. I have great respect for the illness. It is powerful and ruthless. Yet I go about my business with the confidence I get from taking my medicine and being honest with my physician and family about how I feel.

There are times when maintaining an appropriate and civil mood are most difficult. When I feel pressure and not even a lot of pressure, I start to churn inside. For a while, I can hold it off but then I have to slip away and compose myself because either I will burst into tears, ramble incoherently or become aggressive. Perhaps worst of all is I will ruminate about the problem and stare into space as my thoughts resolve nothing. It is at these times I fear I appear mentally ill. While I try to make peace with my nature I still like to present a stable exterior. Being honest does have its drawbacks. When confronting someone I supervised, I had my illness thrown in my face. Unfortunately when this first happened it really took me aback. I backed down and the other person got out of their responsibility. Now I hold my ground but assess myself and take time out to think it over if I have any hesitation. I have also had events from the past brought up with the idea suggested that any disagreement was my fault.

Living with manic depression is about balance. I try not to get too up or too down. It is tricky, though, because getting too down can just seem like I am tired and need to rest. It is only after I have wasted half a day sleeping that it occurs to me something else is going on. Yet I then consider I am on two medications which can cause drowsiness or lethargy. In addition I run slightly anemic. At times I clarify with my husband if I am acting troubled or legitimately weary. He has been a tremendous help for bouncing off ideas and for a sounding board. But worse than being tired is the burst of energy state which feels delightful but at times leads me to make offers of generosity I would have been better to have not made. Whether it means volunteering to work at the school fair or buying gifts for someone I know only casually it is a step further than I need to go. I like to do nice things for people and usually enjoy it if I have. But at times I feel regretful and do not want to tell George my spurt of generosity.

Sometimes with my expansive mood I am extremely lenient with my children. In contrast, on a bad day I may expect too much. It is difficult for me to accept these mood changes but I realize it is the best I can do. I take my medicine seriously and regularly so along with that I forgive myself for my imperfections. I can feel the forgiveness most when I pray. I hope the day will come when mood disorders treatments can be even more finely tuned than now. My goal to maintain my sanity remains a constant one. It inspires me when I hear of someone who has done well.

    I consider my illness to be fascinating and one that will be cured one day. My children are fine but I worry they may get this illness or others. It is my belief that medicine will be so advanced at any time they could need help, it would be much easier to reach a positive outcome. If I had doubts about my strength to endure difficulty I am reassured. The manic episode I experienced made many changes in my life. Because of it I was able to consider my loved ones and forgive them their faults and made my expectations for them more reasonable. My own faults I have forgiven too. I know I am a survivor and am less intimidated or surprised by life. I feel I am a finer person for having survived it. I pray it is always so.

Chapter Forty-Six

    Growing up in the midst of untreated mental illness, it took a while to realize troubling behavior could be treated successfully. I wonder how my life might have been if my parents had been able to take medication for their respective illnesses. Mom would have lived her life more fully no doubt and Dad would have had more inner peace. My sister Donna and her family could have avoided years of misery. I wish I had taken an antidepressant about ten years before I ultimately took one. So much unnecessary suffering.

    After noticing an advertisement for family member participants in a genetic study of bipolar illness, I called to find out the particulars. The study was being conducted by the National Institute of Mental Health and needed siblings and parents in a family where two or more members had a major mental illness like bipolar illness. Once I consulted with the social worker coordinating the family interviews it became a wish that I could persuade my family to participate. The study required participants to donate blood for genetic testing and respond to a very intimate interview conducted by a professional social worker. I needn't have worried. Each family member, including my sister Donna, was willing to participate. Even Mom, in her poor health and living with Ruth, had her home health nurse draw her blood. To a person there was the desire to help the next generation and hopefully take away some of the power from this illness. It gave me goose bumps to know they would support me in a study that meant the world to me. It's the way I feel when I hear the national anthem. My dad fought for our flag. There are so many ways a person can help. A clinical study or questionnaire is a way to impact the lives of people you will probably never know. Joining an organization such as the National Alliance of the Mentally Ill or the National Depressive and Manic Depressive Association gives support to advancing the lives of the mentally ill and people who love them. Within the newsletters from these organizations are opportunities to help and be educated.

    My family has always been much more honest than most. I share their stories from my perspective with my admiration of them. Just because I focus on how mental illness may have affected their life in negative ways does not mean they have not done well with what they have. Also, just because they happen to have a mental illness does not mean they deserve any less respect than anyone else. As a whole my family are the finest people I have ever known. They are at once funny, creative, good, determined, generous and sensitive although also irritable, stubborn and frustrated. I would choose no other, but would choose treatment when needed.

I keep in perspective how my family members were affected by their illnesses. Sometimes I find myself losing my temper by a real or perceived slight. At times my frustration escalates my mood and I fight for control. It happens most when I am on the phone being held hostage by the modern-day phone communication. After a couple of "press 1 for information about your checking account, press 2 for savings account," etc., I begin feeling frustrated and resent the lack of a live human voice to greet me. Driving annoys me as people tailgate and don't use blinkers. My children annoy me when they continue to repeat behavior I have asked them to stop. Such are modern times. With practice I have learned ways to cope with these situations.

When I have to make phone calls, and as a social worker phone calls are endless, I try to wait until I am fairly calm. I wait until my mind is clear and prepare to listen to the details of the call. Sometimes I call the first time for the sole purpose of listening to the options. Sometimes I have to hang up and call back when I am less annoyed. If I am the recipient of many phone calls and I am too overwhelmed I ask that a message be taken. There was a time I would have tried to juggle three lines at once.

When I drive, I have found classical music comforts me and soothes me in tense situations. At other times I might pull over at a gas station and compose myself. Paramount in my mind is not to make a mountain out of a molehill. So what if someone cuts me off or does not indicate they are turning. It is rude but there is no reason to give the frustration more attention than the few moments it took for the offensive driver to move on.

When my source of frustration is my children, I have learned to say less and leave the room if possible. At times I have gone into another room and leaned against the door until I am calm enough to respond. Instead of me fussing at them I ask them to suggest an appropriate response to their behavior. Most of the time I do well but there have been times I started crying or yelling. Since I adore my children, I do my best to behave in an intelligent manner. I double check that I have taken my medicine on days my coping skills seem low. Also going for a walk helps me regain perspective. I remember how my father would leave after a fight and now see there were some positives from the behavior, as opposed to staying and fighting longer or harder. I am not perfect with these methods but they work most of the time. Inside I remind myself I have a disorder of my moods so I must be vigilant to mood swings.

Music consoles me and energizes me. It adds to my day and is like another dose of calming medication. A walk along the ocean shore helps me face up to and cope with any problem. Something about the natural setting puts my life and feelings in perspective. Problems seem so insignificant when I watch the waves roll. Also, I get outside myself when I see my children frolicking on the beach. I try to add to my life that which is comforting and I find it helps me to overcome trivial grievances.

Reading books and magazines and watching movies lift my spirits. I make a point to watch upbeat movies or ones that require concentration. I avoid sad and scary movies and books as my life has had more than its share of misery. I try to keep positive thoughts around me. I do enjoy autobiographies and biographies. I particularly enjoy memoirs especially if related to manic depression I usually find some bit of wisdom or comfort in how others have stood up to the illness and dealt with a work situation or their families. I am amazed at how people from many different walks of life have had quite similar delusions. Even if the same part of the brain is affected there are so many different possibilities.

I hear of situations so similar to mine. Even the jokes and observations other bipolar patients make about their illness are so similar, the choice of words to describe the illness and resultant behavior. It is often described as some aberration of weather such as a tornado, cyclone, hurricane, tidal wave, white water rafting over rapids of incredible strength. As people recover, they are sweeping up, soaking up, wiping up and mopping up the debris.

Sometimes I see a theme of bipolar patients being angry with one person in particular, in my case my husband. Or I hear of a theme of adoration of one person and belief in a special relationship although this is contrary to common sense, especially if you hardly know the person. I have read of other people who gave away possessions or money and some who made poor business decisions. Often the person has humiliated themselves. Of course there are the usual symptoms of rapid speech, flight of ideas, delusions of grandeur. But people do keep going and survive the bad feelings.

The lack of sleep is always my red flag that there is a problem. If I do not sleep through the night and have fitful sleep I make an effort the next day to remedy this. I will watch my diet closely and eliminate stimulants like caffeine. I will take a soothing bath before bedtime and if I am truly revved up I will take a sleeping pill. The following night I attempt to sleep on my own again and usually can go to sleep. If life is really hectic I will take the sleeping pills a couple of nights. I have respect for sleeping pills and find them comforting just to know they are there if I cannot sleep. Yet I make considerable effort not to take them continuously. If I can't sleep for many nights I feel it is time to consult my physician to see if my medication needs to be adjusted.

Chapter Forty-Seven

It is my responsibility to stay healthy and while my doctor can help with suggestions and good prescription judgment, I must ultimately decide to work for a good life. I have gotten carried away with good intentions. After reading a book on kindness, I got the idea to call up one of my favorite teachers and tell her how wonderful she had been. The book had suggested writing a letter, but I thought a phone call would be more personal and I felt like making the call right then. I found the number and dialed. My teacher was in bed and her sister whom she lived with refused to wake her. I felt thwarted in my efforts. Then it dawned on me I knew this woman in elementary school and she might well be in her seventies or eighties. Also, I had dialed a different time zone and it was not a reasonable time to call her. I politely got off the phone but asked her sister to tell her how much she had meant to me. Afterwards I felt foolish for troubling them. My spirit was so genuine but timing is everything. Impulsivity, thy name is Faye.

Once, I found myself ordering ten magazine subscriptions in one week. It seemed like a good thing to broaden our horizons. You could never read too much. They were not all for me, but it still seemed excessive. While I did not feel emotionally that I had acted impulsively, intellectually I knew it was not a good thing for me to overdo purchases of any kind. I shared this behavior with my doctor and he agreed it was excessive.

Having a good relationship with your physician is crucial to maintaining a healthy lifestyle. If there has been an unpleasant experience between the physician and patient a good place to start is by having a meeting with the doctor to discuss concerns and clear up confusion. Having the same physician is usually in your best interest as he or she will be most aware of how you handle stress, what you have had to overcome and your response to medicines.

At least half the time a meeting with patient and family members can clear the air. However, if after meeting with a doctor and unsuccessfully trying to resolve a conflict it may be time to have a consultation with another physician. It may be after talking with another doctor you can better understand the action your doctor choose. If so go back and pick up the pieces. If you cannot or if there has been a compromise of ethics, you would probably be better off with a new doctor.

How different my childhood family life could have been with these choices. To receive help for a mental illness without being treated like a leper. In past years it was next to impossible to endure the humiliation of being labeled as abnormal. Even if risking the label there was little to chose from in terms of treatment. This is no longer the case. Virtually every year new medications are available. Support groups exist where respect for the illness is commonplace. People are less afraid to share their affliction or those of family members. New laws protect people from discrimination.

The doctor who initially diagnosed me treated me until I moved out of state. I was glad he had seen me psychotic in the sense he had an idea of how bad off I could get and could plan accordingly. After working with him, I was more inclined to share some of my more awkward questions and darker secrets. I learned to feel safe talking about my obsessive-compulsive impulses for the disabling behavior it could be. It was a conversation I had waited twenty-five years to have. The antidepressant eliminated most of my obsessive thoughts and compulsive behavior. The ability to talk about it freely was also quite therapeutic. My doctor did not faint or look dismayed when I talked about this anxiety disorder. It was safe to talk about it now.

To make peace with myself I had to learn to see myself beyond the role of psychiatric patient. Even with my illness, I was a mother, wife, social worker, friend, sister and so forth. Many people who meet me will never know of my illness. These other parts of my life are equally significant. As the mother of an elementary-aged child I helped chaperon the class field trip to the local roller skating rink. I stood in the middle of the rink and did the Hokey Pokey with a band of first graders. It was fun and as I helped untie skate laces I was just George's mother. When I pack a bag full of plastic Easter eggs, each bearing a special candy treat, and present them to Hunter's preschool teacher for the Easter egg hunt, I am simply Hunter's mother. George does not introduce me as his manic-depressive wife as we chat with others casually at a Rotary Club function or museum party. However, if the subject is relevant and I feel up to it, I will share how I have this illness and what it has taken to have a good life.

My children know that their family has intelligent and good people and they are emotionally stronger than many people. They are honest about having these medical problems because they might save a life or at least help make bad feelings go away for someone else. They also know their family is not alone because millions of other people have been affected by some form of mental illness. If all else fails I tell them they will understand when they grow up.

Life is a challenge and provides so many opportunities to give up as well as persevere. Never give up. Wishing on a star or saying a prayer, my dreams had come true. Love, regard, support were all around me. When I was depressed, no one could convince me of the good in my life. When my mood lifted, I saw so many possibilities I perhaps expected too much. I had to do some work learning to accept others for the way they are and give people the benefit of the doubt. My husband and the father of our children is the true love of my life, not a delusion of an ideal man with no faults. I do believe I was not alone though through those difficult hours. I believe the Lord was with me and comforted and protected me. Strangers comforted me at times, gave me food, money and assistance. Their kindness did not go unnoticed even if I did not thank them properly at the time. I think the next best thing is to pass kindness on.

Thinking back to Aunt Betty's prediction, she was right, "the lovers came out on top." George and I went on to build upon our relationship. We learned to feel happy again and walk along the beach and hold hands watching our boys splashing in the waves and being carefree. We talk over our day and share dreams and slowly we forget about those days when there was so much hurt and confusion. We are dedicated to maintaining my mental health. There are days when I get worked up about one problem or another, usually because someone hurt my feelings or was uncooperative with me. We talk it over and I'll pray about the problem and we move on. It may have been easier to have walked away from George but I am glad I found the strength and the patience to work out our differences. We have a family life just as I always wanted one to be. If we could do it, despite how far apart we had grown, there is hope for just about any one.

The acceptance and support of our families of origin helped us cement our bond. Too often families hold grudges out of a lack of understanding. I am so glad our families moved forward with us. While everyone was welcoming, two incidents stand out.

During the first time we got together after my manic episode, George's sister Karen chauffeured me around to the best shopping places, as though nothing had ever happened.

I received a letter from George's sister Sandra after we moved to North Carolina and spent Thanksgiving at her home. It conveys the positive spirit our relatives have shown us. Sandra's letter said, "Dear Faye, I found your "My Problem" article. I read it again and felt so proud of you! The first time I read it was so fast that I really didn't understand all you went through. I talked and wrote to George during the time you were ill and he told me what was going on; but it was nice to read for myself what you went through. I think it is wonderful that your medicine has helped you get back to where you were... Just want to let you know I was thinking about how well you've done. The family is very proud of you. Merry Christmas! Sandra." George has some great sisters.

My sisters mean the world to me. Certainly we fall short of the mark at one time or another. We all have, but if I hurt or get good news, the first people I run to are my sisters. With them I find a comfort which is irreplaceable. I have burned up many a phone line crying my heart out or dreaming about the ideal vacation. Having the link of knowing someone my whole life is sacred to me. We have comforted each other and encouraged each other through all kinds of storms. There is nothing I could not tell my sisters and I hope they feel the same. From them I have learned to never give up and keep reaching out in darkness or sunshine.

Never could I have guessed my sister Ruth along with two of her sons would have to jump off the roof of a burning house with only minutes existing between life and death. The day Ruth called me I could not identify her voice but could understand there was familiarity. She sounded raspy and weak, like a very old woman. The carbon monoxide poisoning and smoke inhalation had them sick for days after they left the hospital. Ruth awoke, smelling a horrible smell and thinking her neighbors were burning something as she looked out the window to see, she was horrified to see flames coming out of her home.

She managed to get her sons to crawl through the upstairs bathroom on to the roof. She did not realize at the time that the bathroom floor was on fire from underneath and flames had started to lap through. Her son burnt his foot. As they waited for the fire trucks, Ruth was horrified that one of their dogs was still inside. My nephew was particularly disturbed. Due to the efforts of a brave fireman, the dog was saved. At moments like that, your values become very clear.

After days of nightmares and an exaggerated startled response, they began to heal emotionally as well as physically. Even after the "worst headache you can imagine", my sister and her sons went on. With the perspective of someone who came very close to death, it made other problems less pressing. My nephew, who had been so upset about my dad dying, now having been near death himself, said, "You know when something bad happens it is okay to feel upset, but there comes a point when you have to let it go." My nephew has since been diagnosed with early onset bipolar disorder. His medication was changed and he is reponding quite well.

Mental illness has added complexity to our lives. It is only part of us, though. Like everyone else we have the same day-to-day struggles to earn a living and are as vulnerable as all humans to the elements like a fire. We are all more alike than different. Heredity is no one's fault. The mistakes of family members who were untreated are accepted for what they are, mistakes. No one wanted to become enraged easily any more than they wanted to lie in bed for hours on end in the dark and hopeless world that is depression. However, we have choices now with all the new medicine and a world that is beginning to get a clue about these medical illnesses. We are not the only ones who have had these hardships. We talk about ours in hopes of removing the veil of shame that is draped over those with mental illness.

As I came to terms with my genetic inheritance, I became intrigued who my ancestors were. I sent away for copies of birth and death certificates. Elderly relatives were phoned and interviewed. I searched the web for information. Eventually I traveled to England to further understand my heritage. I wanted to know how my relatives lived and coped, the food they ate, their religion, education and pastimes. Of all my discoveries, afternoon tea was the one I most enjoyed. Little sandwiches with the crusts cut off, cream tea, sweets, scones and cream and jam. Another thing I enjoyed about England was the climate. It felt right to me. It was also beautiful, especially the Cotswald area. I could so easily envision myself living in one of the cottages and strolling through a meadow. The simplicity was charming and peaceful. My parents would have liked it.

My parents will forever be in my heart. Right, wrong or in between, they did the best they knew. Although there are so many people I love, no one else could ever replace my parents. There is no need to. There is enough love for everyone. Mom was still oriented enough to read my magazine article and show it to everyone in the nursing home. She told me she was proud of me and what I had done would help people. She also told me she loved me as I left the nursing home to fly back home. It was the last time I saw her cognizant of the world around her. I had flown up for her 75th birthday party.

When she heard I was coming, she asked if I wanted to sleep on the floor next to her bed, like a slumber party, so she could have lots of time with me. Of course I did not sleep on the floor, but sometimes I wished I had. After all, there really is so little time we have with each other. The next time I flew home to visit she had been heavily sedated because of a skin graft to repair a decubitus ulcer on her thigh. My sisters and I stood around her bed. After a while of not feeling a connection, I said, "Mom, it's me, your smart daughter."

Much to my enjoyment and my sisters' surprise, she said, "Faye?" While I knew she was responding to my voice and not what I said, I still teased my sisters about it. I see a part of Mom in me when I squirrel away a special treat or salivate walking by a dessert bar. Food reminds me of Mom, not just the bingeing, but the warmth of a family in their home anticipating the blueberry pie or cinnamon rolls in the oven. I have memories of me as a little girl cutting out shapes of doughnuts with the lid from a pickle jar, helping my mom and feeling so important with the finished product. Mom enjoyed food immensely. Sadly, as she lay slowly wasting away from dementia and a constellation of other maladies, she was unable to swallow at the end. One of her only pleasures had been taken away from her. She lost sixty-five pounds in one year. Knowing this helped me let go. Mom would not want to live if she could not eat food.

She was buried next to my dad in the same cemetery where we used to drive through the sprinklers to wash our car. In the innocence of childhood I never imagined we would be burying our parents there. I never imagined burying my parents at all. Time was forever and my sisters and I would always live together, along with our parents. There were still conversations to have and pictures to take. I always dreamed of giving my mom a beautiful house to live in with lots of pretty clothes. She would not have to cringe and make excuses when someone asked about coming to our home. Her car would be brand new and there would be plenty of money for restaurants and bouquets of spring flowers. Except for the new car, she never had those other things.

My ability to understand my mother came full circle when I was diagnosed with diabetes a couple of weeks after she died. My symptoms of thirst, hunger, exhaustion and confusion had been blamed on lithium and my antidepressant. To care for myself with diabetes I had to face up to my overeating behavior. Perhaps the medicine stimulated my appetite as my weight had increased after taking it. It could be the diabetes fed upon itself. Diabetes sent signals to my brain for me to drink for the thirst and eat to appease the hunger which never seemed to go away.

For a long while, my weight was an unmentionable topic. In my mind I was still a size 7 or 9 and reasonably well toned. However, my denial would occasionally be pierced by someone asking me if I was pregnant. My confidence would then be leveled. A comment about my weight would throw me into a tailspin of self-loathing. Or at times it was what was not said. Like the comments about how nice the color I was wearing was. I then could not pass a mirror or reflection in a window without a covert glance to observe my figure and secretly hope my stomach had shrunk. I did manage to lose some weight as evidenced by a acquaintance asking me how old my baby was. I said he was nearly five. She said, "Weren't you pregnant last year?" I mumbled something about medication side effects and sighed with relief when the elevator door opened and she disappeared along with her sincere but painful question.

Coming to terms with having diabetes helped me smooth out the part of my life which was not in balance. Besides the increased energy was a sense of well-being I had been missing for a long while. I felt better, did see my belly shrink and my thinking was more clear. Despite its horrid reputation diabetes made me do what dozens of hurt feelings could not. It made me take pride in my body again.

When Mom died, at first it did not seem to trouble me, but as the days continued, I realized I was in the grasp of a major depression. At times I had no energy and wanted to sleep. There were days I had no appetite and even though my calories had been reduced to 1500 a day I had little desire to eat that much. As a child, I remember sobbing on our front porch because Mom was going to a meeting with other women. It was almost her only outlet. One evening in particular I was especially distressed. I cried and carried on for a longer amount of time than usual. Suffering from separation anxiety, it hurt so much to be without her. I hardly got to see her because she worked all day. I felt if I cried enough she would turn around and return to me. After her death, it was much the same. I felt cheated that there had not been enough time before she moved on. I was glad I had sent her plants in the nursing home on a regular basis. I know she especially enjoyed her favorite, African violets, in three colors.

    I tell the children they had another grandmother who loved them too. She spent the part of her life when they were little being sick, old and weak. She held George once and bounced him on her knee and made clicking sounds with her mouth. She radiated joy as she held him. That was about the amount of time they had together. I know she loved the boys, though. I want them to know she existed and knew about them in her lifetime. I always regretted that my mom's mother died before any of us were born.

    Since Mom died, I can only remember good things about her. There were so many good things. Although I had previously found ways to silently object to some aspect of my mother's appearance, now I realize it would take a miracle for her to stand before me again looking good, bad or indifferent. How fabulous it would be to see her again. I thought about all the inconsequential moments in her life, like her walking down a dusty road, washing dishes or playing with her sisters.

    I wondered what her memories of me were, before dementia ruled the day. Once, I had called her on the phone. I told her I had been thinking of her. She said she had been thinking of me too. She had remembered me shouting to the deer to run when my dad had stopped the car to point them out and threatened to shoot at them. She thought that was cute. I remembered her love for a good cup of coffee. She would be so excited to open any package. She loved to watch *Nightline* and probably did not miss a day of the Iranian hostage crisis coverage.

    I always remember her advice to face problems and get it over with. I feel I have done just that. My ability to walk back into the hospital where I had been so humiliated came from Mom. When I have a presentation, I think of her telling me to "have luck" as I walk out the door. I enjoy expressions as Mom did, my favorites being "Don't put all your eggs in one basket," "A bird in the hand is worth two in the bush", and, most relevant, "Time heals all wounds."

When I was little, I had an autograph book. I asked Mom to write in it, as I had asked anyone who walked in the door. She wrote a little poem. Perhaps it was in vogue when she was a school girl.

"Down in the valley, written on a rock, three little words, forget me not."

I think of the poem sometimes and become tearful. I can think of no other moment in my life better than the feeling I would get looking out the living room window and seeing that "Ma" was home. The equivalent feeling for me is to open the door to our home and see my children running to me and hear them squeal with delight. Mom was so important in my life. She gave birth to me and almost hemorrhaged to death doing so. She gave me her middle name. Although as I got older she did not handle hearing my problems as well as when I was child, I could and did tell her everything. She got up at five in the morning to go to work to earn money to feed me. She called me her pride and joy, which I now call my children. We had golden moments and I wonder if she ever looked at my sisters and I and thought this time is so precious, but they are too young to understand. I think I remember her best sitting in our living room with the family and eating butter pecan ice cream that one of the kids had run to the local grocery to get. We were a loving family and I cherish those memories.

Dad is also in my thoughts so much of the time. I remember the everyday moments and the time we shared. I did not understand it would really end some day. I believed in my heart of hearts he would always be there. In some ways he still is. I find myself using some of his phrases or I meet someone who reminds me of Dad. When I see his temper in me, I put a cap on it. I stop to think about whether or not I have taken my medicine or if I am overtired. But I also get the same smile from what my children say as he did from my sisters and me. Hopefully I have his ability to forgive. This generation has an advantage and I hope I work hard enough so my children will have more of the good part of me and less of the bad part.

The song "The Lion Sleeps Tonight" comes into my mind sometimes when I think of living with this illness. In my mind the lion represents my illness, especially the mania, but also the depression. Because I take my medicine I feel relief and feel like I can enjoy my life. Yet I know it is always out there waiting to pounce on me should I doubt its strength or pretend it's not a problem any more. When I hear the song on the radio, I feel especially connected to the part, "Hush my darling, don't fear my darling, the lion sleeps tonight." I am so grateful for the medicine which helps me live a normal life. The drug companies I once resented because they made DES now give me and my family the ability to have a peaceful and joyous life.

Chapter Forty-Eight

My children are a constant source of wonder to me as I am sure we were to my parents. Even when I step on a Lego piece on my way to the bathroom in the middle of the night or find my child has used the sharpener for my eye liner pencil to sharpen his crayons, I know I am blessed. Holding their school art project of the Amazon Rain Forest in my hands and telling them which tree is my favorite or reading one of what seems like several hundred dinosaur stories which line their bookshelf, is pure delight. While trick or treating with a mini Darth Vader and a pumpkinette, I stand in the background prompting them to say thank you. While watching them I want to say thank you too, not just to the greeter wearing the witch's outfit who sends a candy bar for me, but for the opportunity to be there with my children, sharing the moment.

I chuckle when I think of my son George saying he wanted mistletoast for breakfast on Christmas morning. When he asks me if there are werewolves and vampires in Pennsylvania, I gently suggest he might be thinking of Transylvania. Or when his younger brother comments during a conversation about tornadoes that tomatoes can wreck houses, I just have to smile. Having them is a privilege I try to never forget.

I remember our first son and could probably tell at any given time how old he would have been if he lived. But he is safe in heaven. I like to think he watches over his brothers and sends his love to them in secret ways like when the gentle rain of a sun shower washes over them or when we stop for ice cream and they unexpectedly get a bigger scoop than the other children in line. The pain is much less and certainly bearable. I still wonder what it would have been like to have three boys in line at the movies or posing for a picture at a unique vacation spot. I wonder what his favorite cookie might have been. Yet I am pleased with my life and feel grateful for the goodness I allowed myself to find.

George and I did some soul-searching to be more supportive. We both contributed an incredible amount of effort to improve our marriage.

MANIC BY MIDNIGHT

Unfortunately we do not get it right sometimes. But if we are making mistakes the other one will point it out briefly along with the behavior we want to see. We have done pretty well that way. We also have made our family the center of our world and try to be the best parents we can. I am sure we will still fail in some ways, being human. God oversees us and listens to our prayers. We have seen some hard times but we have persevered.

When Hunter graduated from preschool, my in-laws, my husband and his older brother and I went to the graduation ceremony. He was adorable wearing dark sunglasses with his white shirt and indigo shorts for a song and dance routine. The show stopper, however, was him and his classmates doing the macarena. I cried happy tears to see him so confident. I looked around at my older son, my husband and his mom and dad. We were all so clearly touched. Probably none of the adults could have done it. I felt so much joy that we could all be together to share the moment. Even sitting on preschool size chairs we were delighted. It had been a long, bumpy road for us. Yet we got through it with mutual love and respect.

As we rode home that night, I wanted to freeze the moment in my mind because we were laughing and happy. We marveled over Hunter being a little bit of a ham and stealing the show. Some of the other parents said how adorable he was and how he was clearly the star. I had come a long way from the lady sobbing into unneeded baby clothes or desperately smashing heirloom teapots into a dumpster. There seemed to be so many happy times now. The medicine gives me a peace of mind I had always longed for. My children are the light of my life and time as a family is where I find fulfillment. George and I have gained a new respect for each other despite our negative qualities. The good outweighs the bad by far. Mom used to ask us if we wanted the world with a fence around it when we were unrealistic in our wants. Yet I believe I have just that. While I once feared life, I now embrace it.

I often find comfort in reading the words of a great man who also struggled with depression. The man is Abraham Lincoln and my favorite of his works is the letter he wrote to Fanny McCullough on December 23, 1862 regarding her adjustment to the death of her father. I believe he was suggesting that sorrow comes to everyone, and while it may take time, relief will come and you will surely be happy again.

* * *

Resource List

The National Alliance for the Mentally Ill (NAMI)
Colonial Place Three 2107 Wilson Blvd., Suite 30
Arlington, VA. 22201-3042
Phone (703) 524-7600
NAMI HelpLine (800) 950-NAMI (6264)
Web site: www.NAMI.org

NAMI is a grassroots family and consumer self-help organization dedicated to improving the lives of people with severe mental illness. Mental illnesses are biologically based brain disorders that can disrupt a person's ability to think, feel and relate to others. A network of local and state affiliates offer educational meetings, advocacy activities, and information about treatment and community resources. They provide up-to-date, scientific information through publications. They have a toll free help line and a web site. The NAMI *Advocate,* a bimonthly newsletter, provides timely and practical information; legal, policy and legislative updates; research findings and book reviews. NAMI advocates for greater access to treatment, housing, employment and better health insurance. They actively support research for causes and treatments of serious brain disorders.

The National Depressive and Manic-Depressive Association.
730 N. Franklin Street, Suite 501
Chicago, Illinois 60610-3526
Phone (800) 826-3632 or (312) 642-0049
Fax(312) 642-7243
Web site: www.ndmda.org.

The National Depressive and Manic-Depressive Association (National DMDA) is the nation's largest patient-run, illness-specific organization. It is guided by a 65-member Scientific Advisory Board composed of the leading researchers and clinicians in the field of depressive illnesses.

National DMDA's mission is to educate patients, families, professionals and the public concerning the nature of depressive and manic-depressive illnesses as treatable medical diseases; to foster self-help for patients and families; to eliminate discrimination and stigma; to improve access to care; and to advocate for research toward the elimination of these illnesses. National DMDA publishes written materials and videos about depressive disorders and distributes a bookstore catalog with materials discounted for members.

National Mental Health Association
1021 Prince Street Alexandria, VA. 22314-2971
Telephone (703) 684-7722
Toll free (800) 969-NMHA TTY(800) 433-5959
Stigma Watch (800) 969-NMHA Fax (703) 684-5968
Web site: www.nmha.org

The National Mental Health Association is dedicated to promoting mental health, preventing mental disorders and achieving victory through advocacy, education, research and service. Established in 1909 by former psychiatric patient Clifford W. Beers, the National Mental Health Association is the only organization dedicated to addressing all aspects of mental health and mental illnesses. Beers, a Yale graduate, created NMHA to correct the injustices he observed and experienced during his hospitalizations for bipolar disorder.

Nothing to Hide:
Mental Illness In The Family- Photo Text Exhibit
Family Diversity Projects. Inc.
PO Box 1209
Amherst, MA 01004-1209
Phone (413) 256-0502 email: info@family div.org
Web site: www.familydiv.org/nothingtohide

Nothing to Hide: Mental Illness In The Family- (Photo Text Exhibit) is a traveling exhibit that focuses on people whose lives have been affected by schizophrenia, bipolar disorder, obsessive-compulsive disorder, major depression, anxiety disorders, and other mental illness. The exhibit can be displayed in schools, colleges, libraries, mental health centers, hospitals, corporate offices, workplaces, social work or medical schools, etc. The book *Nothing To Hide* by Peggy Gillespie, Jean Beard and Gigi Kaiser will be published in 2001 by New Press.

* * *

Printed in the United States
3284